QUEEN ANNE FOUR POSTER IN THE BEDROOM.

2 STARS IN MICHELIN.

HEATHROW IN EASY REACH.

MASTERCARD IN YOUR CORNER.

MasterCard

The Future of Money

INTRODUCTION

From Balgonie Country House, Ballater, Aberdeenshire
Winner of the 1997 Johansens Most Excellent Country House Award

Like our immediate predecessors, we are pleased and proud to bring Johansens Most Excellent Country House Award to our country for the first time. Scotland is often regarded as "too far" by many potential visitors. If only they knew what we have to offer: matchless scenery and a dramatically contrasting coastline, with a variety of activities to suit all ages and abilities.

Having run a successful enterprise in Ballater for several years, we had long fostered the dream of a small country house hotel of a very special kind. When Balgonie House in its quiet and secluded setting came onto the market in 1990, our dream became a possibility and then a reality.

With minimal conversion, to preserve the family atmosphere and yet to ensure the most modern of comforts, Priscilla took the furnishing in hand. We set out to create an atmosphere whereby we share our home with our guests whilst giving the freedom to think it their home too. Total attention to detail is our aim, but there is always time for a chat with the passing visitor.

Nothing is too much trouble to ensure the comfort of our guests and the welcome at our door is always specific for every guest, wherever they may come from. And thanks to Johansens and the reliability of their beautifully presented guides, they do come. Again and again.

John Finnie

Arlington Court* –
overall winner of the NPI National Heritage Awards in 1996

Guess who will help you find the perfect place for your pension?

At NPI, we've been helping people find the right place for their pensions for over 160 years now. Helping them find the right balance between growth and security to give them peace of mind about their financial future.

And we've been rather good at it. We are now looking after over £10 billion in assets on behalf of our 500,000 plus policyholders.

Being a retirement specialist, we're confident that we can tailor the right retirement scheme for your individual needs. And the same goes for group schemes.

For more information about retirement planning advice from NPI, contact your Financial Adviser or NPI Membership Services on 0800 174192. Any advice given, or recommendations made by NPI Membership Services relates only to the products sold by the NPI Marketing Group.

NPI

PROVIDING PENSIONS SINCE 1835
Regulated by the Personal Investment Authority.

AS TIME GOES BY YOU'LL BE GLAD YOU CHOSE NPI

National Provident House, 55 Calverley Road, Tunbridge Wells, Kent TN1 2UE. Telephone: 01892 515151, Facsimile: 01892 705611

*Arlington Court photograph supplied by the National Trust Photographic Library/Nadia MacKenzie.

Moët & Chandon – **JOHANSENS** *exclusive champagne partner.*

The White Horse of Kilburn,
Yorkshire

Johansens Recommended Country Houses in
England

Castles, cathedrals, museums, great country houses and the opportunity to stay in areas of historical importance, England has much to offer. Whatever your leisure interests, there's a network of more than 560 Tourist Information Centres throughout England offering friendly, free advice on places to visit, entertainment, local facilities and travel information.

ENGLISH HERITAGE
Keysign House
429 Oxford Street
London W1R 2HD
Tel: 0171 973 3396
Offers an unrivalled choice of properties to visit.

HISTORIC HOUSES ASSOCIATION
2 Chester Street
London SW1X 7BB
Tel: 0171 259 5688
Ensures the survival of historic houses and gardens in private ownership in Great Britain.

THE NATIONAL TRUST
36 Queen Anne's Gate
London SW1H 9AS
Tel: 0171 222 9251
Cares for more than 590,000 acres of countryside and over 400 historic buildings.

REGIONAL TOURIST BOARDS

CUMBRIA TOURIST BOARD
Ashleigh
Holly Road
Windermere
Cumbria LA23 2AQ
Tel: 015394 44444
England's most beautiful lakes and tallest mountains reach out from the Lake District National Park to a landscape of spectacular coasts, hills and dales.

EAST OF ENGLAND TOURIST BOARD
Toppesfield Hall
Hadleigh
Suffolk IP7 5DN
Tel: 01473 822922

Cambridgeshire, Essex, Hertfordshire, Bedfordshire, Norfolk, Suffolk and Lincolnshire.

HEART OF ENGLAND TOURIST BOARD
Woodside
Larkhill Road
Worcester
Worcestershire WR5 2EZ
Tel: 01905 763436
Gloucestershire, Hereford & Worcester, Shropshire, Staffordshire, Warwickshire and West Midlands. Represents the districts of Cherwell and West Oxfordshire in the county of Oxfordshire.

Premier House
15 Wheeler Gate
Nottingham NG1 2NA
Tel: 0115 988 1778
Derbyshire, Leicestershire, Northamptonshire, Nottinghamshire and Rutland

LONDON TOURIST BOARD
26 Grosvenor Gardens
London SW1W ODU
Tel: 0171 730 3450
The Greater London area
(see page 15)

NORTHUMBRIA TOURIST BOARD
Aykley Heads
Durham DH1 5UX
Tel: 0191 375 3000
The Tees Valley, Durham, Northumberland and Tyne & Wear

NORTH WEST TOURIST BOARD
Swan House
Swan Meadow Road
Wigan Pier, Wigan
Lancashire WN3 5BB
Tel: 01942 821222
Cheshire, Greater Manchester, Lancashire, Merseyside and the High Peak District of Derbyshire

SOUTH EAST ENGLAND TOURIST BOARD
The Old Brew House
Warwick Park
Tunbridge Wells
Kent TN2 5TU
Tel: 01892 540766
East and West Sussex, Kent and Surrey

SOUTHERN TOURIST BOARD
40 Chamberlayne Road
Eastleigh
Hampshire SO5 5JH
Tel: 01703 620006
Eastern and Northern Dorset, Hampshire, Isle of Wight, Berkshire, Buckinghamshire and Oxfordshire

WEST COUNTRY TOURIST BOARD
60, St David's Hill
Exeter
Devon EX4 4SY
Tel: 01392 425426
Bath, Bristol, Cornwall and the Isles of Scilly, Devon, Dorset, Somerset and Wiltshire

YORKSHIRE TOURIST BOARD
312 Tadcaster Road
York YO2 2HF
Tel: 01904 707961
Yorkshire and Northern Lincolnshire

ARROW MILL HOTEL AND RESTAURANT

ARROW, NEAR ALCESTER, WARWICKSHIRE B49 5NL
TEL: 01789 762419 FAX: 01789 765170

OWNERS: The Woodhams Family

| 22 rms | 22 ens | SMALL HOTEL |

S: £56
D: £76

Once a working flour mill, Arrow Mill is proud of its listing in the Domesday Book, when it was valued at three shillings and sixpence. Since Norman times standards and inflation have risen. Today it remains a historic and charming building, although it offers its guests the most modern and comfortable accommodation.

Its rustic charm, enhanced by log fires and exposed beams, is complemented by a spectacular yet secluded riverside setting. Creature comforts are plentiful in the individually furnished bedrooms and panoramic views take in the mill pond, River Arrow and surrounding countryside.

A highly trained team of chefs uses only market-fresh ingredients in maintaining their uncompromising standards. The Millstream Restaurant incorporates the original working floor of the mill, with its wheel still driven by the flowing stream. It offers an à la carte menu and carefully selected wine list to satisfy the most discriminating palate. Similarly high standards are assured by the luncheons from the Miller's Table.

Residential conferences, business meetings, hospitality days and product launches can all be accommodated. **Places of interest nearby:** Stratford-upon-Avon, Warwick Castle and the Cotswolds are all nearby. Arrow Mill is closed from 26 December for two weeks. **Directions: Set back from the A435 1 mile south of Alcester.**

JOHANSENS AWARDS FOR EXCELLENCE

The names of the winners of the 1998 Awards will be published in the 1999 editions of Johansens guides. The winners of the 1997 Awards are listed below. They were presented with their certificates at the Johansens Annual Awards dinner, held at The Dorchester on 4th November 1996, by Jean Rozwadowski, Senior Vice-President and General Manager Europe, of MasterCard International.

Johansens Country Hotel Award for Excellence
Marlfield House, Co. Wicklow, Ireland

Johansens City Hotel Award for Excellence
The Castle at Taunton, Somerset

Johansens Country House Award for Excellence
Balgonie Country House, Royal Deeside, Scotland

Johansens Inn Award for Excellence
The Manor Hotel, West Bexington, Dorset

Johansens London Hotel Award for Excellence
The Leonard, London W1

Johansens Most Excellent Value for Money Award
Appleton Hall, Appleton le Moors, N. Yorkshire

Johansens Most Excellent Service Award
Alexander House, Turner's Hill, W. Sussex

Johansens Most Excellent Restaurant Award
Freshmans Restaurant, Belbroughton, Worcestershire

Candidates for awards derive from two main sources: from the thousands of Johansens guide users who send us Guest Survey Reports commending hotels, inns and country houses in which they have stayed and from our team of twelve regional inspectors who regularly visit all properties in our guides. Guest Survey Report forms can be found on pages 509–512. They are a vital part of our continuous process of assessment and they are the decisive factor in choosing the Value for Money and the Most Excellent Service Awards.

Published by
Johansens, 175-179 St John Street, London EC1V 4RP
Tel: 0171-490 3090 Fax: 0171-490 2538
Find Johansens on the Internet at: http://www.johansen.com
E-Mail: admin@johansen.u–net.com

Editor:	Rodney Exton
Group Publisher:	Peter Hancock
P.A. to Group Publisher:	Carol Sweeney
Regional Inspectors:	Christopher Bond
	Geraldine Bromley
	Robert Bromley
	Julie Dunkley
	Susan Harangozo
	Joan Henderson
	Marie Iversen
	Pauline Mason
	John O'Neill
	Mary O'Neill
	Fiona Patrick
	Brian Sandell
Production Manager:	Daniel Barnett
Production Controller:	Kevin Bradbrook
Designer:	Michael Tompsett
Copywriters:	Sally Sutton,
	Jill Wyatt
	Norman Flack
Sales and Marketing Manager:	Laurent Martinez
Marketing Executive:	Samantha Lhoas
Sales Executive:	Babita Sareen
P.A. to Managing Director & regional editorial research:	Angela Franks
Managing Director:	Andrew Warren

Copyright © 1997 Johansens

Johansens is a member company of Harmsworth Publishing Ltd, a subsidiary of the Daily Mail & General Trust plc

ISBN 1 86017 5023

Printed in England by St Ives plc
Colour origination by Catalyst Creative Imaging

Distributed in the UK and Europe by Johnsons International Media Services Ltd, London (direct sales) & Biblios PDS Ltd, West Sussex (bookstores). In North America by general sales agent: ETL Group, New York, NY (direct sales) and The Cimino Publishing Group, INC. New York (bookstores). In Australia and New Zealand by Bookwise International, Findon, South Australia.

HOW TO USE THIS GUIDE

If you want to identify an Country House or Small Hotel whose name you already know, look for it in the Regional Indexes on pages 274–278.

If you want to find an Inn or Restaurant in a particular area you can

• Turn to the Maps on pages 266–272

• Search the Indexes on pages 274–278

• Look for the Town or Village where you wish to stay in the main body of the Guide. This is divided into Countries. Place names in each Country appear at the head of the pages in alphabetical order.

The Indexes list the Country Houses and Small Hotels by Countries and by Counties, they also show those with amenities such as fishing, conference facilities, swimming, golf, etc. (Please note some recent Local Government Boundary changes).

The Maps cover all regions. Each Country House and Small Hotel symbol (a green square) relates to a Country House or Small Hotel in this guide situated in or near the location shown.

Red Triangles show the location of Johansens Recommended Inns with Restaurants. If you cannot find a suitable Country House or Small Hotel near where you wish to stay, you may decide to choose one of these establishments as an alternative. They are all listed by place names on page 265.

The prices, in most cases, refer to the cost of one night's accommodation, with breakfast, for two people. Prices are also shown for single occupancy. These rates are correct at the time of going to press but always should be checked when you make your reservation.

All guides are obtainable from bookshops or by Johansens Freephone 0800 269397 or by using the order coupons on pages 281–288.

In association
with MasterCard

CONTENTS

Cover Picture: Pen-Y-Dyffryn Country Hotel, Rhydycroesau, Shropshire (page 137)

FOREWORD BY THE EDITOR

*P*eople who use Johansens guides often ask why we never say anything critical about a hotel, an inn, a country house or a business meetings venue which we recommend. The answer is easy. If we knew anything bad to say about one of our selections we would not recommend it

We visit all establishments regularly and irregularly, overtly and covertly – our professional inspectors non-stop, the rest of us ad hoc; but the many thousands of you who use our guides are really the best guardians of quality. Our recommendations must be reliable, so keep sending us those freepost Guest Surveys which you find among the back-pages of our guides. They provide our inspectors with the first hint of any fall in standards, though, as you will be glad to read, the majority of Guest Surveys are entirely complimentary. In 'The Caterer & Hotelkeeper' a regular columnist recently wrote that a characteristic of Johansens guests is that "they come to enjoy themselves". Keep helping us to help you do just that – to have a good time!

Rodney Exton, Editor

1

KEY TO SYMBOLS

	English	French	German
12 rms	Total number of rooms	Nombre de chambres	Anzahl der Zimmer
MasterCard	MasterCard accepted	MasterCard accepté	MasterCard akzeptiert
VISA	Visa accepted	Visa accepté	Visa akzeptiert
AMERICAN EXPRESS	American Express accepted	American Express accepté	American Express akzeptiert
Diners Club	Diners Club accepted	Diners Club accepté	Diners Club akzeptiert
	Quiet location	Un lieu tranquille	Ruhige Lage
	Access for wheelchairs to at least one bedroom and public rooms	Accès handicapé	Zugang für Behinderte

(The 'Access for wheelchairs' symbol (♿) does not necessarily indicate that the property fulfils National Accessible Scheme grading)

	English	French	German
	Chef-patron	Chef-patron	Chef-patronn
	Licensed	Avec Licence	Schankerlanbnis
en famille	Guest and Hosts usually dine together	Table d'Hôte	Mit der Familie essen
M 20	Meeting/conference facilities with maximum number of delegates	Salle de conférences – capacité maximale	Konferenzraum-Höchstkapazität
8	Children welcome, with minimum age where applicable	Enfants bienvenus	Kinder willkommen
	Dogs accommodated in rooms or kennels	Chiens autorisés	Hunde erlaubt
	At least one room has a four-poster bed	Lit à baldaquin	Himmelbett
	Cable/satellite TV in all bedrooms	TV câblée/satellite dans les chambres	Satellit-und Kabelfernsehen in allen Zimmern
	Direct-dial telephone in all bedrooms	Téléphone dans les chambres	Telefon in allen Zimmern
	No-smoking rooms (at least one no-smoking bedroom)	Chambres non-fumeurs	Zimmer für Nichtraucher
	Lift available for guests' use	Ascenseur	Fahrstuhl
	Indoor swimming pool	Piscine couverte	Hallenbad
	Outdoor swimming pool	Piscine de plein air	Freibad
	Tennis court at hotel	Tennis à l'hôtel	Hoteleigener Tennisplatz
	Croquet lawn at hotel	Croquet à l'hôtel	Krocketrasen
	Fishing can be arranged	Pêche	Angeln
	Golf course on site or nearby, which has an arrangement with the hotel allowing guests to play	Golf	Golfplatz
	Shooting can be arranged	Chasse	Jagd
	Riding can be arranged	Équitation	Reitpferd
H	Hotel has a helicopter landing pad	Piste pour hélicoptère	Hubschrauberlandplatz
	Licensed for wedding ceremonies	Cérémonies de noces	Konzession für Eheschliessungen

In association with MasterCard

LOVELADY SHIELD COUNTRY HOUSE HOTEL

NENTHEAD ROAD, ALSTON, CUMBRIA CA9 3LF
TEL: 01434 381203 FAX: 01434 381515

OWNERS: Kenneth and Margaret Lyons
CHEF: Barrie Garton

S: £75.50–£85.50
D: £151–£171
(including 5 course dinner)

12 rms | 12 ens | SMALL HOTEL

Two-and-a-half miles from Alston, England's highest market town, Lovelady Shield, an AA 2 red star hotel, nestles in three acres of secluded riverside gardens. Bright log fires in the library and drawing room enhance the hotel's welcoming atmosphere. Owners Kenneth and Margaret Lyons take great care to create a peaceful and tranquil haven where guests can relax.

The five-course dinners created by chef Barrie Garton, rounded off by home-made puddings and a selection of English farmhouse cheeses, have won the hotel 2 AA rosettes for food.

Many guests first discover Lovelady Shield en route for Scotland. They then return to explore this beautiful and unspoiled part of England and experience the comforts of the hotel. Golf, fishing, shooting, pony-trekking and riding can be arranged locally.

Places of interest nearby: The Pennine Way, Hadrian's Wall and the Lake District are within easy reach. Facilities for small conferences and boardroom meetings are available. Closed 3rd January to 4th February. Special Christmas, New Year, winter and spring breaks are offered and special 3 day and weekly terms. **Directions: The hotel's driveway is by the junction of the B6294 and the A689, 2^1/$_4$ miles east of Alston.**

In association with MasterCard

APPLETON HALL

APPLETON-LE-MOORS, NORTH YORKSHIRE YO6 6TF
TEL: 01751 417227 FAX: 01751 417540

OWNERS: Norma and Graham Davies

| 9 rms | 9 ens | SMALL HOTEL |

S: £58–£66
D: £116–£132
(including 5 course dinner)

Appleton Hall is in the centre of the pretty Yorkshire village of Appleton-le-Moors – which is on the southern side of the North Yorkshire Moors National Park. The hotel is surrounded by beautiful landscaped gardens where guests can sit and relax or wander at their leisure. The elegant refurbished rooms assure visitors they have come to a peaceful and comfortable country house where Graham and Norma Davies and their staff guarantee a high standard of service and hospitality.

The nine en suite bedrooms are all fully equipped to provide the modern necessities – two have their own lounges. One of the rooms has a four-poster bed.

There is a small well-stocked cocktail bar to pass the time before dinner. The delectable five-course table d'hôte menu changes daily and is accompanied by a comprehensive selection of wines.

Places of interest nearby: The moors are a walkers' and bird-watchers' paradise, or visit Harrogate and York, returning to inviting log fires on chilly afternoons.
Directions: Leave A1 at Thirsk turning, taking the A170, signposted Scarborough. After passing through Kirkbymoorside the village is on the left.

In association
with MasterCard

ARUNDEL (Burpham)

BURPHAM COUNTRY HOUSE HOTEL

OLD DOWN, BURPHAM, NR ARUNDEL, WEST SUSSEX BN18 9RJ
TEL: 01903 882160 FAX: 01903 884627

OWNERS: George and Marianne Walker

| 10 rms | 10 ens | SMALL HOTEL |

MasterCard VISA AMERICAN EXPRESS

S: from £37
D: £78–£95

This charming Country House Hotel set in the heart of walking country nestles in a fold of the Sussex South Downs – just perfect for a 'Stress Remedy Break'.

The ten en suite bedrooms have all been tastefully refurbished with direct-dial telephone, colour TV, hair dryer, radio/alarm clock and tea/coffee making tray. A lovely old world garden with a croquet lawn surrounds the hotel.

Drinks before dinner can be enjoyed by the open fire in the comfortable Cocktail Lounge. A good wine list is available with most countries represented. The Hotel has a full residential and restaurant licence. Swiss born Marianne Walker has won a well-deserved rosette from the

AA for her culinary skills and a constantly changing menu using only the finest ingredients is presented in the Rösti room. The Hotel has recently been awarded a Highly Commended Certificate by the English Tourist Board.

Special breaks are offered throughout the year. Golf riding, fishing and sailing are all readily available in the locality. Racing at Goodwood and Fontwell.

Places of interest nearby: Burpham has a beautiful and historic Norman church, while Arundel, with its Wildfowl Sanctuary and renowned Castle, is three miles away. The coast lies within six miles. **Directions: The Hotel is signposted on the A27 east of Arundel railway bridge. Turn off here and follow this road for 2½ miles.**

In association
with MasterCard **MasterCard**

THE BEECHES FARMHOUSE

WALDLEY, DOVERIDGE, NR ASHBOURNE, DERBYSHIRE DE6 5LR
TEL: 01889 590288 FAX: 01889 590559

OWNERS: Barbara and Paul Tunnicliffe
CHEF: Barbara Tunnicliffe

S: £39.50
D: £50

The Beeches Farmhouse Hotel and Restaurant was opened in 1986 by Barbara and Paul Tunnicliffe. It is situated on the dairy farm which Paul's family has worked for 50 years. Located in the Derbyshire Dales, The Beeches is surrounded by lots of things to see and do, whatever your age or interests. Families are most welcome: children love staying on the working farm, where they can, they watch the cows being milked and feed the many pet animals. For executives there are spacious en suite rooms with direct-dial telephones and access to the fax.

At the heart of The Beeches' popularity is Barbara's splendid cooking. Like the dishes she demonstrates at the BBC Good Food Show, Barbara's menus feature bold country recipes. Specialities include local boneless beef rib with port, Guinness and pickled walnuts and casserole of spiced lamb with apricots and miniature herb dumplings. Vegetarian and fresh fish dishes are also offered. Everything is freshly prepared with seasonal ingredients.
Places of interest nearby: Sudbury Hall, Calke Abbey, Tutbury Castle, the Potteries museums and Alton Towers.
Directions: Heading east to west on the A50 Derby –Stoke road, turn right at Doveridge down Marston Lane, signposted to Waldley. At Waldley take first right turn, then first left to The Beeches

In association
with MasterCard

PORCH FARMHOUSE

GRINDON, STAFFORDSHIRE MOORLANDS ST13 7TP
TEL: 01538 304545 FAX: 01538 304545 E-MAIL: PorchFarmhouse@msn.com

OWNERS: Sally and Ron Hulme

3 rms 3 ens

S: £48
D: £86
(including dinner)

With beautiful views over the hills and dales of the Peak District National Park and surrounded by National Trust estates and historic market towns, Porch Farmhouse is a peaceful and secluded establishment. It is a traditional 17th century Staffordshire stone farmhouse, mellowed by the passage of time, offering a calm retreat.

Porch Farmhouse has been sympathetically renovated and restored, ensuring that none of its character has been lost and at the same time bringing it up to the highest level of comfort. Individuality and tradition are evident in the bedrooms which all have full facilities, including television and electric trouser presses. Period furniture and well filled bookcases abound. There is a sunny conservatory where visitors can enjoy breakfast. The delightful beamed dining room serves traditional English dishes at a polished table with fine china, elegant glassware and family silver. Log fires add to the warmth and comfort in winter. The hotel is not licensed, but guests may bring their own wine. They are invited to join owners Sally and Ron Hulme for a glass of sherry before dinner. Closed Christmas-New Year.

Places of interest nearby: Chatsworth, Haddon Hall.
Directions: From M1, exit at junction 25 onto A52 towards Derby, Ashbourne and Leek. Grindon is signposted on the right approximately six miles after Ashbourne.

In association
with MasterCard

Blagdon Manor Country Hotel

ASHWATER, DEVON EX21 5DF
TEL: 01409 211224 FAX: 01409 211634 E-MAIL: Blagdon_Manor@compuserve.com

OWNERS: Tim and Gill Casey

7 rms	7 ens		SMALL HOTEL

S: £60–£70
D: £95–£110

Blagdon Manor lies off the beaten track and nestles in twenty acres with superb views of rolling countryside. Blagdon is a Grade II listed building dating back to the Doomsday Book but the present building is mostly 17th Century.

Inside the manor, heavy oak beams, worn slate flagstones and handstitched soft furnishings create a relaxing and welcoming atmosphere. The beautifully appointed en suite guest rooms have tea and coffee facilities with home made shortbread, luxurious crisp bed linen and fluffy towels. Log fires and fresh flowers add to the enjoyment of a perfect break from the hustle and bustle.

Guests dine in a country house party style and enjoy the very best of English cuisine

Places of interest nearby: An ideal base for golfing, fishing or walking holidays, for visiting the stately homes and wonderful gardens of Devon and Cornwall, Blagdon lies close to the River Tamar, the border with Devon and Cornwall, and is a convenient centre from which to visit the delightful attractions of both counties. **Directions: From Launceston join A388 towards Holsworthy. Pass both Chapman's Well and first sign to Ashwater, turn right at second sign to Ashwater, then first right. Hotel driveway is second on the right.**

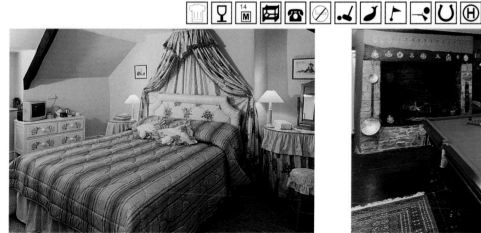

CHAPEL HOUSE

FRIARS' GATE, ATHERSTONE, WARWICKSHIRE CV9 1EY
TEL: 01827 718949 FAX: 01827 717702

OWNERS: Chapel House (Atherstone) Ltd
MANAGING DIRECTOR: David Arnold

10 rms	10 ens	SMALL HOTEL

S: £45–£59.50
D: £59.50–£69.50

Chapel House was the dower house of the now demolished Atherstone Hall, home of the Bracebridge family since the early 18th century. The oldest part of the house dates from about 1720 and subsequent additions were made until 1879. Many original features have been retained and others carefully restored so that the house now furnished in traditional style retains the elegance of an earlier age. Chapel House is discreetly tucked away in the corner of Atherstone's market square within a well-tended, walled garden that still is a particularly attractive feature of the property.

Awarded its second AA Rosette 1996, Chapel House has acquired an enviable reputation for high quality,

imaginative food and an excellent selection of wines. Chefs Adam Bennett and Gary Thompson use only the very best ingredients and their particular specialities are fish and game. Special dietary needs can be catered for by prior arrangement. Closed on Christmas Day and Boxing Day. Chapel House is just 25 minutes from the centre of Birmingham and is convenient for the NEC.

Places of interest nearby: Bosworth Battlefield, Tamworth Castle, Arbury Hall, Lichfield and Coventry Cathedrals and the many industrial museums of the Midlands. Also close is the Belfry Golf Centre. **Directions: On A5 about 8 miles south-east of M42 junction 10. Chapel House is in the market square beside the church.**

BAKEWELL (Rowsley)

EAST LODGE COUNTRY HOUSE HOTEL

ROWSLEY, NR MATLOCK, DERBYSHIRE DE4 2EF
TEL: 01629 734474 FAX: 01629 733949

OWNERS: Sue and Peter Mills
CHEF: Simon Hollings

| 15 rms | 15 ens | | | SMALL HOTEL |

S: £68
D: from £90

This graceful 17th century lodge on the edge of the Peak District was originally built as the East Lodge to Haddon Hall, the Derbyshire seat of the Duke of Rutland. Converted to a hotel in the 1980's, East Lodge is now owned and run by Sue and Peter Mills and their attentive staff. It is AA 3 star and ETB 4 Crowns Highly Commended.

The attractive lounge with log fire, charming restaurant and spacious hall offers high levels of comfort combined with a warm and relaxed atmosphere. The 15 en suite bedrooms are tastefully furnished, each having its own distinctive character. Imaginative lunches and dinners are served daily in the excellent AA Rosetted restaurant with lighter meals available in the lounge. A wide selection of fine wines is on offer.

Set in 10 acres of attractive gardens and surrounded by rolling Derbyshire countryside, East Lodge provides a tranquil setting for relaxing breaks, conferences and corporate activity/team building events.

Places of interest nearby: Peak district National Park, which boasts some of the country's most spectacular walks. The famous stately homes, Chatsworth House and Haddon Hall, are within two miles. Bakewell, Buxton, Matlock and Crich are a short drive away. **Directions: Set back from the A6 in Rowsley village, three miles from Bakewell. The hotel entrance is adjacent to the B6012 junction to Sheffield/Chatsworth.**

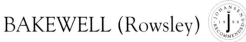

THE PEACOCK HOTEL AT ROWSLEY

ROWSLEY, NR MATLOCK, DERBYSHIRE DE4 2EB
TEL: 01629 733518 FAX: 01629 732671

OWNERS: Jarvis Hotels plc
MANAGER: Pat Gillson
CHEF: Raymond Cherry

| 14 rms | 14 ens | SMALL HOTEL |

S: £85–£95
D: £136–£146
(including dinner)

Once the Dower House to Haddon Hall, this superb 17th century country house is now a marvellous hotel with gardens leading down to the River Derwent.

When first a hotel in 1820 it attracted bathers who plunged into the nearby River Wye! Fishermen are spoilt here. There are 12 rods on the River Wye and two on the Derwent. Tickets are available, and the Head Keeper offers advice and tuition. Fish caught will be cooked by the hotel or put in the freezer. The dedicated can enjoy the Angler's Picnic, brought to the riverside. Walkers get a delicious picnic in a thermally insulated knapsack.

The hotel is beautifully furnished throughout, with antiques and flowers in abundance. The bedrooms are extremely comfortable and thoughtfully equipped.

Resident and non-resident diners can enjoy an aperitif in the delightful bar or lounge before dining in one of the three rooms, two of which feature furniture by "Mousey" Thompson. Both lunch and dinner are served in traditional style and smoking during food service is discouraged. A special diet can be catered for with prior notice. Special rates may be available on weekdays at certain times of the year. There are excellent facilities for small meetings in a delightfully furnished room.

Places of interest nearby: Haddon Hall, Chatsworth , Crich Tram Museum. **Directions: M1/exit 28, head for A6. Rowsley is midway between Matlock and Bakewell.**

In association
with MasterCard **MasterCard**

WAREN HOUSE HOTEL

WAREN MILL, BAMBURGH, NORTHUMBERLAND NE70 7EE
TEL: 01668 214581 FAX: 01668 214484

OWNERS: Peter and Anita Laverack
CHEFS: Leo Emery and Lee Irving

10 rms	10 ens		SMALL HOTEL

S: £80–£100
D: £110–£140
Suite: £145–£180

"To visit the North East and not to stay here, would be foolish indeed". So says one entry in a visitors book that is filled with generous and justified praise for this delightful traditional country house which lives up to all its promises and expectations and beyond. The hotel is set in six acres of gardens and woodland on the edge of Budle Bay Bird Sanctuary overlooking Holy Island and two miles from the majestic Bamburgh Castle.

The owners, Anita and Peter, do not cater for for children under 14, so they are able to offer a rare commodity of peace and tranquility even during the busy summer months. Throughout the hotel the antique furnishings and the immaculate and well-chosen decor evoke a warm, friendly and charming ambience.

Seated in the candle-lit dining room, surrounded by family pictures and portraits, guests can select dishes from the daily changing menu and wines from over 250 bins. There is a boardroom for executive meetings. Dogs by prior arrangement. Special short breaks available all year.

Places of interest nearby: The Farne Islands are just a boat trip away, while Bamburgh, Alnwick and Dunstanburgh Castles along with Holy Island are nearby. Waren House is open all year. **Directions: There are advance warning signs on the A1 both north and south. Take B1342 to Waren Mill. Hotel (floodlit at night) is on south-west corner of Budle Bay just two miles from Bamburgh.**

LITTLE BARWICK HOUSE

BARWICK VILLAGE, NR YEOVIL, SOMERSET BA22 9TD
TEL: 01935 423902 FAX: 01935 420908

OWNERS: Christopher and Veronica Colley

S: £75
D: £130
(including dinner)

This listed Georgian dower house, set in 3½ acres of lovely grounds, stands on the edge of the village of Barwick. It is an ideal resting place for visitors seeking to explore the beautiful counties of Somerset and Dorset.

The bedrooms are enchanting, with most overlooking the gardens or offering delightful rural views. All feature a full range of modern comforts and amenities, including colour TV, telephone and tea and coffee-making facilities.

Afternoon tea or pre-dinner drinks are served in the secluded garden, bar or comfortable lounge depending on the weather.

Dinner is a fixed priced two or four course menu making extensive use of fish, game and other local produce. Sample Veronica's mouth-watering Sussex pie, created from tender steak cooked in stout, port and mushrooms; Thai roast guinea fowl with lime and ginger sauce; or brochettes of pork fillet char grilled with aubergines, mushrooms, pepper and courgettes. Interesting and realistically-priced wines are available to complement any meal.

Places of interest nearby: The historic towns of Bath, Sherborne and Wells are all within easy reach. Also many National Trust properties and gardens, including Thomas Hardy's cottage, Montacute, Stourhead and Tintinhull.
Directions: From A30 approaching Yeovil take A37 Yeovil to Dorchester road. Turn left at first roundabout (1 mile) and Barwick House is on the left.

APSLEY HOUSE

141 NEWBRIDGE HILL, SOMERSET BA1 3PT
TEL: 01225 336966 FAX: 01225 425462 E-MAIL: apsleyhouse@easynet.co.uk

OWNERS: David and Annie Lanz

 S: £45
D: £60–£95

One mile from the centre of Bath, this elegant Georgian house was reputedly built for the Duke of Wellington in 1830, and is set in a delightful garden.

The hosts, David and Annie Lanz, greet guests with a warm welcome into their home, with its magnificently proportioned reception rooms which have been refurbished in great style and comfort including the addition of 2 new rooms opening onto the garden. A quite delicious breakfast is the only meal served, although drinks are available. David and Annie will recommend local restaurants and inns which visitors will enjoy.

The bedrooms are invitingly romantic with lovely drapery and delightful en suite bathrooms. Televisons almost seem to intrude in this timeless décor.

Places of interest nearby: There is so much to see and do in Bath, the centre of which is just a 25 minutes stroll from Apsley House. The magnificent architecture includes the Assembly Rooms, mentioned so often in Jane Austen's and in Georgette Heyer's historical novels, the Royal Crescent and the Roman Baths. Fascinating museums, the thriving theatre and excellent shopping all add to ones enjoyment of this lovely city. The Cotswolds, Mendip Hills, Stourhead, Stonehenge, Avebery and Longleat are within driving distance. Internet: www.gratton.co.uk/apsley **Directions: The hotel lies one mile west of the centre of Bath, on the A431 which branches off A4, the Upper Bristol Road.**

In association with MasterCard

BATH LODGE HOTEL

NORTON ST PHILIP, BATH, SOMERSET BA3 6NH
TEL: 01225 723040 FAX: 01225 723737

OWNERS: Graham and Nicola Walker

5 rms | 5 ens

S: from £45
D: £55–£95

The Bath Lodge Hotel, originally called Castle Lodge, was built between 1806 and 1813 as one of six lodges added to a former gentleman's residence known as Farleigh House. This splendid building, with its towers, battlements, portcullis and heraldic shields, is redolent of Arthurian romance and offers guests a delightful setting in which to escape the stresses and strains of modern life.

The rooms, which are superbly decorated and furnished, are beautifully located and have many castellated features within them. Three rooms overlook the magnificent natural gardens with their cascading stream and the adjacent deer forest. The main entrance hall, lounge and conservatory all contain oak beamed ceilings, natural masonry and large log burning fireplaces. All the rooms are furnished in keeping with this unique building.

An excellent breakfast is served at the hotel. A five course dinner is available Friday and Saturday evenings. Alternatively there are many restaurants locally and in Bath. The hotel has a no-smoking policy, but guests may smoke in the conservatory area.

Places of interest nearby: Stonehenge and Longleat. Bath Lodge is an ideal location for enjoying the tourist attractions of the World Heritage City of Bath itself. Wells and Bristol are also both within easy reach. **Directions: From Bath take the A36 Warminster road. Bath Lodge is on your left after approximately seven miles.**

BLOOMFIELD HOUSE

146 BLOOMFIELD ROAD, BATH, SOMERSET BA2 2AS
TEL: 01225 420105 FAX: 01225 481958

OWNERS: Bridget and Malcolm Cox

8 rms	5 ens			MasterCard VISA	S: £40–£55
					D: £60–£100

This elegant country house, Grade II listed, was commissioned in 1800 by a notable Mr Henshaw, later to become Lord Mayor of Bath. It nestles in a tranquil location in grounds that afford magnificent views over the city.

Bloomfield House is one of the most comfortable and relaxing country houses in the area and is furnished with handsome antiques, hand-woven silk curtains and French chandeliers.

The main bedrooms feature canopied or four-poster beds, including "The principal bedroom of the Mayor and Mayoress of Bath (1902/3)". Remote control colour TV, direct-dial telephone and tea/coffee making facilities are available in all bedrooms. There is ample parking.

A comprehensive list of restaurants and menus is available at Bloomfield House from which guests may choose their evening meals. Bloomfield House is a strictly non-smoking house.

Riding, golf, swimming, sauna and leisure facilities are available by arrangement.

Places of interest nearby: The Cotswolds, Castle Combe, Stourhead, Stonehenge and Longleat. **Directions: From the centre of Bath take the A367 Wells road for ¼ mile towards Exeter. Fork right after The Bear Pub; Bloomfield House is on the right before the third road junction.**

EAGLE HOUSE

CHURCH STREET, BATHFORD, BATH, SOMERSET BA1 7RS
TEL: 01225 859946 FAX: 01225 859946 E-MAIL: JONAP@PSIONWORLD.NET

OWNERS: John and Rosamund Napier

| 8 rms | 8 ens | |

MasterCard VISA
S: £36–£44
D: £46–£74

Three miles from Bath lies the charming conservation village of Bathford. Behind a high stone wall, wrought-iron gates and elegant façade, this Georgian home, designed by John Wood, stands in 1½ acres of grounds, giving far-reaching views of the surrounding countryside.

The eight bedrooms, including some large family rooms, all have private facilities, colour television, hairdryers and tea and coffee-making facilities. Cots and extra beds can be provided upon request. There is a spacious drawing room, where meetings for up to 12 people can be held, and a second, smaller lounge. Although dinner is not served at Eagle House, the owners, John and Rosamund Napier are always glad to help with reservations for tables in one of Bath's many good restaurants. For exercise there is a new lawn tennis court.

Set in a walled garden adjacent to the main house is a cottage with two bedrooms, two bathrooms, sitting room and kitchen, which can be occupied for stays of two nights or more. It offers complete privacy with views across the valley.

Places of interest nearby: The beautiful city of Bath, Castle Combe, the National Trust village of Lacock, the Cotswolds, Longleat House, Avebury and Stonehenge.
Directions: From the A4 take the A363 towards Bradford-on-Avon. Go 150 yards, then fork left up Bathford Hill. Take first right into Church Street; Eagle House is 200 yards on the right.

OLDFIELDS

102 WELLS ROAD, BATH, SOMERSET BA2 3AL
TEL: 01225 317984 FAX: 01225 444471

OWNERS: Berkeley and Moira Gaunt

S: £48–£55
D: £60–£78

Oldfields is a large, elegant Victorian house built of the honey-coloured stone for which the city of Bath is famous. Superbly positioned just 10 minutes walk from the city centre, it has a private car park for the use of guests.

Although the house is equipped with every modern feature to ensure that visitors experience maximum comfort and convenience, it retains many of the elaborate cornices and artistry of its original character.

The bedrooms are beautifully furnished with rich fabrics and antiques and offer a full range of amenities.Ideal for the less mobile, two rooms are situated on the ground floor with level entry.

Guests can choose between a traditional English breakfast or the lighter continental alternative offered by an extensive buffet. Unlimited supplies of tea and coffee are available and newspapers are provided for those with time to linger. Bath is full of excellent restaurants, many within a fifteen minute walk of Oldfields.

Places of interest nearby: Within Bath itself are the famous Roman baths and pump room, the Book Museum and No 1 Royal Crescent. The city is also the perfect centre from which to explore the Cotswolds, Glastonbury and Wells Cathedral, east to Stonehenge and Salisbury, west to Bristol and South Wales. **Directions: From the M4 Junction 18 follow the signs to Bath city centre then take the A367 Wells Road.**

PARADISE HOUSE

HOLLOWAY, BATH, SOMERSET BA2 4PX
TEL: 01225 317723 FAX: 01225 482005

OWNERS: Charles and Linda Dunlap

8 rms | 8 ens

S: £55
D: £70–£100

In the peaceful grounds of this early 18th century mansion house, guests are only seven minutes' walk from the Roman Baths, Pump Room and Abbey in the centre of the beautiful and fashionable Georgian city of Bath.

Paradise House has been modernised and restored to a high standard to enhance its classical elegance. Ornate plaster ceilings and a fine marble fireplace can be seen in the public rooms, decorated with lovely antique furniture in keeping with its early Georgian architecture. The large walled garden, with its fish pond and rose covered pergola, is a delightful sun-trap where guests can enjoy the views.

New owners (from Sept. '97) Charles and Linda will assist guests with advice on what to see in Bath. In the Kitchen Garden they intend to grow their own organic herbs and produce. A speciality of the hotel will be a menu which includes tasty organic foodstuffs and also caters to special diets, vegetarian, kosher & halal. Light meals will be available all day and evening and in fine weather guests will enjoy alfresco dining in the magnificent gardens. Arrangements have been made with a local health clinic to provide alternative health therapies for guests.

Places of interest nearby: Wells, Glastonbury and Stonehenge. **Directions: Enter Bath on A4 London Road. Later, turn left onto A36. Take first left after viaduct onto A367 Exeter Road. Go left at Day and Pierce and down hill into Holloway cul-de-sac.**

WIDBROOK GRANGE

TROWBRIDGE ROAD, BRADFORD-ON-AVON, WILTSHIRE BA15 1UH
TEL: 01225 864750/863173 FAX: 01225 862890

OWNERS: John and Pauline Price

S: £59–£85
D: £95–£105

According to the ancient rent books, Widbrook Grange was built as a model farm in the 18th century amid eleven acres of idyllic grounds, traversed by a stream. No longer a farm, Widbrook still reflects its agricultural heritage. Together resident owners John and Pauline Price have converted the Grange with skill and care to combine contemporary comforts with a traditional ambience.

All of the bedrooms, whether a spacious four-poster room or one that is petite and cosy, are well appointed with facilities and antique furnishings. Some of the bedrooms are in the recently converted 200-year old stone barn which forms the courtyard. Evening dinner is available Monday to Thursday in the spacious antique furnished dining room,

and there are also many excellent restaurants locally about which your hosts can advise you. The Manvers suite, with its oak table and carver chairs has been designed for board meetings, seminars and private functions.

Widbrook boasts a superb indoor heated swimming-pool and gymnasium. There is an arrangement with nearby Kingsdown Golf Club. Riding and fishing can also be arranged.

Places of interest nearby: Longleat House and Safari Park, Bath, Avebury and Stonehenge. **Directions: From Bradford-on-Avon take the A363 Trowbridge Road, the Grange is on the right after the canal bridge.**

In association with MasterCard

WOOLVERTON HOUSE

WOOLVERTON, NR BATH, SOMERSET BA3 6QS
TEL: 01373 830415 FAX: 01373 831243

OWNERS: Noel and Marina Terry

12 rms 12 ens

S: £45
D: £55–£70

This early 19th century house, built originally as a rectory for the 'United Parishes of Woolverton & Rode', has been sympathetically converted and restored to become an elegant English country house. It is set in over 2¹/₂ acres of grounds and commands scenic views over the 'glebe lands' on which the parson traditionally had grazing rights.

Today Woolverton House has been developed by its present-day hospitable owners into a retreat where the emphasis is on heritage, history and nature. The gardens are full of colour and also include a narrow gauge steam railway.

All the bedrooms are pleasantly decorated and furnished with private bathrooms en suite. They are fully equipped with colour TV, direct dial telephone, hospitality tray, trouser press, hairdryer and minibar. Both the dining-room and drawing room have log fires in the cooler months and the conservatory bar is pleasant all year.

The restaurant is beautifully furnished in excellent taste with food and wines to match.

Places of interest nearby: There is plenty to explore in the historical and agricultural history of this area – most within a 20 mile radius. Major attractions include Bath, Longleat, East Somerset steam railway, Cheddar Caves, Wookey Hole and Rode Tropical Bird Gardens. **Directions: From M4 exit 17 take A350 and then A361 for Woolverton – or on A36 halfway betwen Bath and Warminster.**

DANNAH FARM COUNTRY GUEST HOUSE

BOWMAN'S LANE, SHOTTLE, NR BELPER, DERBYSHIRE DE56 2DR
TEL: 01773 550273/630 FAX: 01773 550590

OWNERS: Joan and Martin Slack
CHEF: Joan Slack

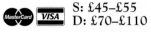

S: £45–£55
D: £70–£110

Set amid undulating countryside high above the Ecclesbourne Valley, Dannah Farm is part of the Chatsworth Estates on the edge of the Peak District. This is an exceptional farmhouse conversion so it is not surprising that in addition to being Highly Commended by the ETB (3 Crowns) and AA Premier Selected, the hotel won the 1993 National Awards for Excellence and Innovation and the 1994 Best of Tourism Award for the East Midlands. As the Georgian farmhouse is still part of a 128-acre working farm, guests and their children will discover plenty of activity within the grounds.

Four-poster, twin-bedded, double and single rooms are offered, all overlooking rolling pastures. There are two residents' lounges and large, safe gardens.

The restaurant has rapidly earned a fine reputation. Aromas of freshly baked bread, home-made soups and piquant sauces escaping from the kitchen whet the appetite for dinner, which is served with good wines in relaxed surroundings and is by arrangement. **Places of interest nearby:** The countryside is criss-crossed with footpaths with walks in all directions. Dannah Farm is optimally placed to enjoy the many attractions of the area – Chatsworth, Haddon Hall, Dovedale and water-sports at Carsington. **Directions: From Derby take the A6 Matlock road. At Duffield turn left onto the B5023 towards Wirksworth. At the traffic lights at Cowers Lane turn right onto the A517 towards Belper, then take the first left to Shottle. Bowman's Lane is 100 yards past the crossroads.**

BIBURY COURT

BIBURY COURT, BIBURY, GLOUCESTERSHIRE GL7 5NT
TEL: 01285 740337 FAX: 01285 740660

OWNERS: Jane Collier, Andrew and Anne Johnston
MANAGER: Simon Gould

S: from £60
D: from £82
Suite: £115

Past visitors to Bibury Court are reputed to have included Charles II and during the reign of George III, the Prince Regent. This gracious mansion dates from Tudor times, but the main part was built in 1633 by Sir Thomas Sackville, an illegitimate son of the 1st Earl of Dorset. After generations of illustrious owners, it became a hotel in 1968.

The great house is set on the outskirts of Bibury, which William Morris called "the most beautiful village in England". As a hotel, it is run on country house lines with one of the main objectives being the provision of good food and wine in informal and pleasurable surroundings. Log fires during the cooler months add to the comfort of guests.

There are some lovely panelled rooms in the house, many containing antique furniture. Many of the bedrooms have four posters, all have private bathrooms, and for those who like greater privacy there is the Sackville suite.

Trout fishing is available in the Coln, which forms the southern boundary of the hotel's six acres of grounds, and there are golf courses at Burford and Cirencester. Watersports and riding are available nearby. The hotel is closed at Christmas.

Places of interest nearby: Bibury Court is ideally placed for touring the Cotswolds, while Stratford, Oxford, Cheltenham and Bath are all within easy reach. **Directions: Bibury is on the B4425, seven miles from Burford and seven miles from Cirencester.**

YEOLDON HOUSE HOTEL

DURRANT LANE, NORTHAM, NR BIDEFORD, DEVON EX39 2RL
TEL: 01237 474400; FAX: 01237 476618

OWNERS: Kevin and Sue Jelley
CHEF: Kevin Jelley

| 10 rms | 10 ens | SMALL HOTEL |

S: £40–£54
D: £75–£95

Kevin and Sue Jelley have achieved a special quality at Yeoldon, a distinguished and attractive country house standing in beautiful grounds in the village of Northam birthplace of J.H.Taylor, England's only winner of 5 Opens. Visitors are charmed by the hotel's refreshingly casual atmosphere and its blend of Victorian grandeur with today's comforts.

A rich green and terracota colour theme enhances the Yeoldon's relaxing ambience. Deep, soft sofas and armchairs in the inviting lounge are so comfortable that guests may find it difficult to leave them for pursuit of the hotel's surrounding charms. The bedrooms are beautifully decorated in country style and have panoramic views over the expansive lawned gardens which slope gently down to the River Torridge and the estuary beyond.

A wide choice of cuisine is served in the elegant restaurant where chef Kevin Jelley takes pride in his à la carte dinner menus. He uses local produce whenever possible and bakes his own bread and biscuits daily.

Places of interest nearby: Bideford, Arlington Court, Rosemoor Gardens, Tapeley Park, Lundy Island and the picturesque village of Clovelly. **Directions: From the M5, exit at junction 27 and follow the A361 to Barnstaple and then the A39 to Bideford. At Torridge Bridge roundabout turn right onto the A386 towards Northam and then take the third turning on the right.**

In association with MasterCard

BIGGIN HALL

BIGGIN-BY-HARTINGTON, BUXTON, DERBYSHIRE SK17 0DH
TEL: 01298 84451 FAX: 01298 84681 E-MAIL: 100610.1573@Compuserve.com

OWNER: James Moffett

18 rms   18 ens

S: £30–£45
D: £45–£70

Centrally situated in the Peak district National Park, Biggin Hall is a 17th century, Grade II listed property set in eight acres of grounds. Situated 1,000 feet above sea level, the air may particularly benefit insomnia and asthma sufferers. Visitors come here for the peace and quiet and to enjoy the landscape with its dry-stone walling, deep wooded valleys, heather-clad moorlands and historic market towns and villages. Walkers will appreciate the many uncrowded footpaths nearby.

The rooms of this house feature massive oak timbers and antiques, with one containing a superb four-poster bed. One of the sitting rooms has an open log fire where guests can enjoy a convivial atmosphere. A recently converted 18th century stone building, comprising four self-contained studio apartments and two-roomed suites, each with a private bathroom, is situated 30 yards from the main house. The traditional farmhouse cooking puts emphasis on free-range produce, wholefoods and natural flavours. Dogs are accommodated in the apartments only.

Places of interest nearby: Chatsworth, Bolsover Castle, Kedleston Hall, Alton Towers, American Adventure Theme Park, Buxton, Ashbourne and Bakewell.

Directions: This country house is situated at the end of Biggin Village, which is off the A515, nine miles from Ashbourne and ten miles from Buxton.

MAINS HALL HOTEL & BRASSERIE

MAINS LANE, LITTLE SINGLETON, NR BLACKPOOL, LANCASHIRE FY6 7LE
TEL: 01253 885130 FAX: 01253 894132
INTERNET: http://www.blackpool.net/mains_hall E-MAIL: mains.hall@blackpool.net

OWNER: Roger Yeomans

10 rms   10 ens

S: £50-£70
D: £60-£110

Built in 1536, Mains Hall is a Grade II listed Historic Country House of classical style and elegance in a beautiful setting overlooking the River Wyre. The hotel's present owner has established the Hall as a select Country House retreat, with a gourmet reputation for fine cuisine.

The Hall was once the home of the Prince Regent before he became George IV and it was here he sometimes shared seclusion with the notorious Mrs Fitzherbert. Each room is individually created to complement the period of the house. Some bedrooms have unique four poster or half tester beds, all the rooms are en suite or have private facilities.

The imaginative Brasserie menu offers a wide choice of the freshest foods and of wines from around the world.

Mains Hall, with its comprehensive facilities and idyllic location, is now regarded as one of the most perfect settings in Lancashire for wedding ceremonies, or conferences. It offers a perfect overnight stop for anyone travelling north or south on the motorway.

Places of interest nearby: The Hall is within easy reach of the Lake District, Royal Lytham golf course and the bright lights of Blackpool. **Directions: Leave the M55 at Junction 3 and follow the signs for Fleetwood (A585) for 5 miles (ignore signs for Singleton). Mains Hall is a half mile past the second set of traffic lights on the right hand side.**

LOWER BROOK HOUSE

BLOCKLEY, NR MORETON-IN-MARSH, GLOUCESTERSHIRE GL56 9DS
TEL/FAX: 01386 700286

OWNERS: Sybil and Ann Porter-Miles

3 rms | 3 ens

S: £30–£35
D: £45–£50

Lower Brook House has been skilfully created from a well-built detached property dating back to the 17th century and it epitomises the traditional Cotswold stone house of its period. It is quietly situated in the village of Blockley, famous in the 1700s for its silk trade. Standing within attractive gardens Lower Brook House offers a warm welcome to those in search of good hospitality and comfortable accommodation.

The hostesses take great care to ensure that guests' requirements are swiftly attended to. The three en suite bedrooms have antique furnishings and plenty of interesting bric-à-brac. One of the rooms has a four-poster bed and all have tea and coffee facilities, a colour TV and hairdryer.

Memorable breakfasts are enjoyed along with unlimited amounts of fresh and cooked fruits, but evening meals are not provided. However, there are a number of places that serve good food in the local area.

Places of interest nearby: Blockley is a short drive from Cheltenham, Oxford and Stratford-upon-Avon. It is also a good point of departure for day trips around the picturesque local villages – perhaps to hunt for antiques.

Directions: As you enter the village from Moreton-in-Marsh, Lower Brook House can be found on your right.

QUARLTON MANOR FARM

PLANTATION ROAD, EDGWORTH, TURTON, BOLTON, LANCASHIRE BL7 0DD
TEL: 01204 852277 FAX: 01204 852286

OWNERS: Pauline and Philip Davies
CHEF: Pauline Davies

S: £39–£65
D: £59–£84

Standing in its own 20 acres at the heart of rural Lancashire's hill country this sprawling 17th century stone-built farmhouse is the essence of peace and tranquillity. It is ideally suited to those seeking the friendliness and warmth of homely, family accommodation. It has built up an excellent local reputation for its food. Huge open fireplaces, heavy oak beams, antique furnishings and wholesome farmhouse cooking add to the hotel's charm. Guests enjoy sumptuous five course set dinners around a large table in the galleried dining hall or in the conservatory with its panoramic views over the countryside and hills. Business meetings are welcome. Two double-bedded rooms and a twin share the same bathroom. The main bedroom is en suite and has a huge four-poster bed. There is another four-poster in the en suite ground floor family flat which also has bunk beds. All bedrooms are non-smoking Pauline and Phil have horses and there are stables and grazing for guests who wish to bring their own. **Places of interest nearby:** Manchester, The East Lancashire Railway, Jumbles Country Park and Turton Tower. **Directions: From Bolton take A676 (A56) towards Burnley. After two miles turn left at traffic lights into Bradshaw Road and after one-and-a-half miles turn left at crossroads. Turn right at the Edgworth crossroads into Broadhead Road, then turn right again into Plantation Road and then 1 mile to the end.**

PEACOCK VANE HOTEL

BONCHURCH, ISLE OF WIGHT PO38 1RJ
TEL: 01983 852019 FAX: 01983 854796

OWNERS: Peacock Vane Hotel Ltd
MANAGING DIRECTOR: Lawrence Allen

 D: £70–£98

The Peacock Vane, recently given 3 A.A. stars dates back to 1836 when it was one of the largest dwellings in the the village of Bonchurch. Today, Bonchurch maintains its old world charm with cottages and a pond ringed by lush green willow and beech trees.

Sheltered by St Boniface Down and surrounded by landscaped gardens, Peacock Vane has been restored with sumptuous furnishings chosen to reflect the Victorian era when poets and authors such as Dickens, Thackeray and Macaulay are said to have walked the hallways.

The atmosphere is informal and relaxed. Restful nights are assured in any one of the individually designed bedrooms with their period paintings and antique furnishings. All have every facility. Chef Phillip Baldry prepares the best of English and French cuisine for diners in the elegant Ivory Room and for special occasions, formal dinners and private meetings the imposing Directors Dining Room is an ideal venue.

L.A.'s Bar and Bistro caters for visitors who wish for a more informal atmosphere and for those who like to relax over a drink to the sounds of a soothing piano there are musical evenings in the heavily curtained Piano Bar.

Places of interest nearby: Carisbrook Castle, Osborne House, fine beaches, coastal walks and all the attractions of the Isle of Wight. **Directions: Bonchurch is just north of Ventnor on the A3055 road to Ryde.**

LANGTRY MANOR

DERBY ROAD, EAST CLIFF, BOURNEMOUTH, DORSET BH1 3QB
TEL: 01202 553887 FAX: 01202 290115

OWNERS: Pamela Hamilton Howard
CHEF: Stuart Glanville

| 18 rms | 18 ens | SMALL HOTEL |

S: from £69.75
D: £99.50–£239.50

Originally called the 'Red House', this fine hotel was built by King Edward VII (then Prince of Wales) as a love nest for his mistress, Lillie Langtry.

The bedrooms and suites are exquisite. The Edward VII Suite is furnished as it was when this magnificently spacious room was first built, although today's occupants have the advantage of an en suite bathroom! The Lillie Langtry Suite has a pretty four-poster bed, heart shaped corner bath and Romeo and Juliet balcony. Ideal for anniversaries, birthdays and honeymoons.

While the Manor was being constructed, Edward and Lillie stayed in Langtry Lodge just a few yards away. Today it offers accommodation furnished to the same high standards as the main hotel and guests are invited to use the Manor's dining room, lounge and bar.

Special rates are set for luxury week-end breaks. Celebrations, anniversaries and birthday parties can be arranged at not extra coast. Sumptuous dinners are served in the magnificent dining hall with minstrels gallery. Saturday night guests are invited to take part in a splendid six-course Edwardian Banquet.

Places of interest nearby: Sandy beaches, Hardy country, the New Forest, art galleries, theatres and gardens.
Directions: Take A338 Wessex Way to the station. First exit at roundabout, over next roundabout, first left into Knyveton Rd, second right into Derby Rd.

JOHANSENS
1998
RECOMMENDED

DIAL HOUSE HOTEL

THE CHESTNUTS, HIGH STREET, BOURTON-ON-THE-WATER, GLOUCESTERSHIRE GL54 2AN
TEL: 01451 822244 FAX: 01451 810126

OWNERS: Lynn and Peter Boxall

12 rms   11 ens

MasterCard   VISA   AMERICAN EXPRESS

S: from £45
D: from £90

In the heart of the Cotswolds lies Dial House Hotel, a small 17th Century country house which combines the charm and elegance of a bygone era with all the facilities of a modern hotel. Proprietors Lynn and Peter Boxall have 26 years experience in the hotel industry and extend a warm welcome to their guests.

The hotel is open throughout the year and roaring log fires burn throughout the winter months. In the summer, lunches are served in the delightful and secluded walled garden. Chef Kevin Chatfield creates delicious, freshly cooked food for the à la carte restaurant, which creates an aura of old England with its inglenook fireplace and oak beams. Dial House has received an 2 AA rosettes for its cuisine and every care is taken by friendly staff to provide guests with an interesting choice of dishes and good quality wines. An open fire in the comfortable lounge creates an ideal setting to finish off an evening with coffee and liqueurs. The décor of the bedrooms is light and cheery and some overlook the garden. All are en suite, centrally heated and equipped with tea and coffee making facilities. Bargain breaks available.

Places of interest nearby: Stratford-Upon-Avon, Bath and Cirencester, Warwick Castle, Blenheim Palace, Cheltenham, Slimbridge Wildfowl Trust and Oxford.
Directions: Bourton-on-the-Water is four miles south west of Stow-on-the-Wold off the A429.

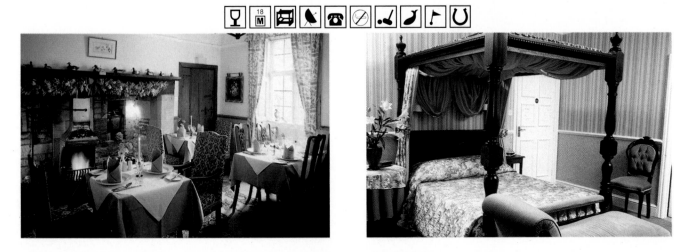

CROSS LANE HOUSE HOTEL

CROSS LANE HEAD, BRIDGNORTH, SHROPSHIRE WV16 4SJ
TEL: 01746 764887 FAX: 01746 768667

OWNERS: Ann and Mike Hobbs
CHEF: Ann Hobbs

| 8 rms | 8 ens | |

S: £40.50
D: £55

Situated just a mile from the heart of the historic town of Bridgnorth this delightful 17th century house, under the hospitable ownership of Ann and Mike Hobbs, is a haven of peace, quiet and comfort amidst the beauty of Shropshire's open countryside.

The hotel is surrounded by two acres of mature gardens from these and from the windows of the house there are stunning views over the Severn Valley.

Although ancient in origin, with an ornate William IV tiled entrance hall, impressive inglenook fireplace and exposed beams throughout, Cross Lane House offers every modern comfort for the discerning guest.

All bedrooms are en suite and most have roll topped Victorian cast iron baths with overhead showers. The restaurant is small and intimate with Ann serving up excellent wholesome traditional dishes complemented by a carefully chosen wine list. Diets can be catered for. Golf, riding, fishing and shooting facilities are a short drive away.

Places of interest nearby: Ironbridge, the birthplace of the industrial revolution, Shrewsbury, the Coalport China Museum, the Severn Valley Railway, the Midland Motor Museum and the Aerospace Museum at Cosford.
Directions: Cross Lane House is on the B4373 Bridgnorth-Broseley road, one mile north of Bridgnorth.

CHELWOOD HOUSE

CHELWOOD, NR BRISTOL, AVON BS18 4NH
TEL: 01761 490730 FAX: 01761 490730

OWNERS: Sue and Jean-Jacques Fontaine

11 rms | 11 ens | SMALL HOTEL

S: £47.50
D: £65–£88

Surrounded by rich foliage and a garden full of colourful shrubs and plants, Chelwood House provides discerning visitors with magnificent, far-reaching bedroom views over lush meadows and the rolling Mendip Hills.

This triple-peaked, sparklingly white-walled former dower house dates from 1681 and is enviably located between the historic and cultural cities of Bristol, Bath and Wells, only minutes from Chew Valley.

Chelwood House offers the utmost comfort and hospitality. A large, impressive staircase leads to eleven well proportioned, en suite bedrooms, two of which have four-poster beds. Antique furniture, ornaments, paintings and beautiful flower arrangements furnish the two restful lounges.

The conservatory dining room, with draped ceiling, large potted plants and a fountain, makes a delightful setting for enjoying appetising French cuisine prepared by chef and co-proprietor Jean-Jacques who makes the maximum use of local and seasonal produce.

Places of interest nearby: Bristol, Wells Cathedral and the Roman Baths at Bath. For active guests there is golf, fishing and excellent walking. **Directions: Chelwood is on the A37, eight miles south of Bristol, between Pensford and Clutton. From Bath, keep on the A368, travel through Chelwood village and then turn left at the roundabout.**

THE OLD RECTORY

CHURCH STREET, WILLERSEY, BROADWAY, GLOUCESTERSHIRE WR12 7PN
TEL: 01386 853729 FAX: 01386 858061 E-MAIL: beauvoisin@btinternet.com

OWNERS: Liz and Chris Beauvoisin

8 rms | 6 ens

S: £50–£85
D: £60–£95

Built of mellow Cotswold stone the 17th century Old Rectory at Willersey is at the end of a lane, opposite the 11th century church. With a back-drop of the Cotswold hills and a dry stone wall surrounding the delightful garden, this is truly an idyllic spot. A mulberry tree, reputed to have been planted in the reign of Elizabeth I, is laden with fruit each year.

A superb breakfast is served in the elegant dining room, with log fires in winter. The immaculate bedrooms, all quite different from each other, have had new bathrooms installed – each one beautifully stencilled and colour washed. Each room has a colour TV, tea and coffee making facilities, radio alarms, hairdryers and Crabtree and Evelyn toiletries. The combination of four poster beds and tranquillity make this an ideal place for honeymooners. Non smoking throughout!

A minute away The Bell Inn serves excellent lunch and dinner. The Rectory is an ideal base from which to tour the Cotswolds – maps and picnics provided. Riding and bicycle hire nearby. Broadway golf course 1 mile away.

Places of interest nearby: Cheltenham, Stratford, Warwick Castle. Blenheim Palace, Snowshill Manor, Hidcote Gardens. **Directions: From Broadway take B4632 (Stratford Road) for 1½ miles. At Willersey turn right (opposite the duck pond) into Church Street, the Rectory is at the end of the road with private car park.**

JOHANSENS 1998 RECOMMENDED

THATCHED COTTAGE HOTEL & RESTAURANT

16 BROOKLEY ROAD, BROCKENHURST, HAMPSHIRE SO42 7RR
TEL: 01590 623090 FAX: 01590 623479

OWNERS: The Matysik Family

5 rms | 5 ens | SMALL HOTEL

MasterCard VISA
S: £70–£90
D: £90–£125

This enchanting thatched cottage was built in 1627 and only became a hotel in 1991. The Matysik family have over 111 years of hotel experience between them, and this is reflected in the careful transformation that has taken place.

Set in one of the prettiest villages in the heart of the New Forest, modernisation for the comfort of guests has not detracted from its original charm. The beamed lounge is an intimate little area for pre-dinner drinks. The tea garden has canaries, lace table cloths and parasols to create the correct ambience. The bedrooms are all en suite, some with a Turkish steam-shower, another with a four-poster.

An amazing breakfast is available until 11.00 am. The restaurant has light snacks or a full à la carte lunch menu.

In the evening exquisite culinary delights are freshly prepared with chefs on show in their open kitchen. A gourmet table d'hôte menu complemented by a selection of fine wines and beverages is set in a unique and casual atmosphere by romantic candlelight. Authentic Japanese celebration menu available by arrangement.

Places of interest nearby: The New Forest is on the doorstep and Beaulieu to visit close by. Other local activities include mushroom hunting, riding, fishing, sailing and golf. **Directions: M27, junction 1, drive south on A337 through Lyndhurst to Brockenhurst, turning right just before the level crossing.**

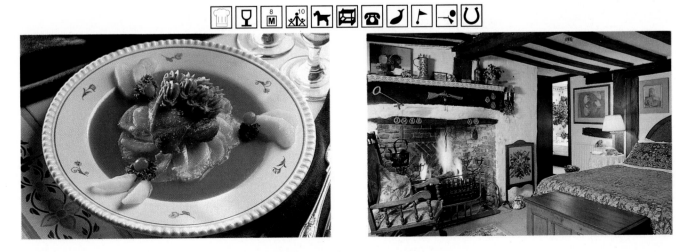

WHITLEY RIDGE COUNTRY HOUSE HOTEL

BEAULIEU ROAD, BROCKENHURST, NEW FOREST, HAMPSHIRE SO42 7QL
TEL: 01590 622354 FAX: 01590 622856

OWNERS: Rennie and Sue Law

S: £56–£60
D: £88–£130

Whitley Ridge, once a royal hunting lodge, was built in Georgian style in the late 18th century. In more recent years the house has undergone extensive refurbishment, enhancing the appeal of its original Georgian features.

The bedrooms are individually decorated, and most have lovely views over open Forest. The public rooms are elegantly furnished with and log fires burning on cooler evenings.

The Restaurant has two AA Rosettes for good food, offering a table d'hôte menu, which changes daily, together with a high standard of à la carte choices, plus a well balanced and imaginative vegetarian menu. The wine selection includes those wines from traditional areas and also interesting choices from further afield.

You are invited to relax in the grounds or enjoy a game of tennis. In addition, some of the best woodland walks in the country are directly accessible from the gardens. Whichever pastime you choose, Whitley Ridge is the perfect setting for a restful holiday. Your hosts Rennie and Sue Law welcome guests for a very pleasant stay.

Places of interest nearby: A number of stately homes, including Broadlands and Wilton House, are within easy reach. Lord Montagu's Motor Museum, Buckler's Hard and historic Stonehenge are also within driving distance. **Directions: M27 junction 1. Situated on the B3055, Brockenhurst – Beaulieu.**

In association with MasterCard

MELBOURN BURY

MELBOURN, CAMBRIDGESHIRE, NR ROYSTON SG8 6DE
TEL: 01763 261151 FAX: 01763 262375

OWNERS: Anthony and Sylvia Hopkinson

S: £50
D: £80

Set in extensive grounds with a lake and wildfowl, Melbourn Bury is an elegant manor house. It has had only two ownerships since the 1500s. The first owners were the Bishops of Ely and then in 1850, the property was purchased by the ancestors of Sylvia Hopkinson.

Gracious reception rooms are furnished with antiques and fine paintings, while the en suite bedrooms are comfortable and have charming views of the gardens. Fresh flowers and log fires are extra touches which guests will appreciate. Adjoining the library is a 19th century billiard room with a full-size table.

Delicious home cooking encompasses traditional English recipes and continental dishes prepared in cordon bleu style. Dinner is by prior arrangement.

Lunches and dinners for up to 22 persons seated; more can be accommodated buffet style – small conferences, receptions and exhibitions. Closed at Christmas & Easter. **Places of interest nearby:** Cambridge, Duxford Air Museum, Audley End, Ely, Wimpole Hall and Hatfield House. **Directions: Off A10, 10 miles south of Cambridge, 3rd turning on left to Melbourn; 2 miles North of Royston 1st turning on right to Melbourn. Entrance is 300 yards on left after the turning. Look for white gate posts and lodge cottage.**

In association
with MasterCard

THE GARDEN HOTEL

167-169 THE STREET, BOUGHTON-UNDER-BLEAN, FAVERSHAM, KENT ME13 9BH
TEL: 01227 751411 FAX: 01227 751801

OWNERS: Allen and Gillian Carr
MANAGER: Karen Carr
CHEF: Allen Carr

10 rms	10 ens	SMALL HOTEL

MasterCard VISA AMERICAN EXPRESS

S: £60
D: £80

The Garden Hotel, a Grade I listed building, is optimally situated for touring the "Garden of England", walking the Downs and enjoying the waterside activities of the resorts at Whitstable and Herne Bay. The channel ports and tunnel are within quick motorway reach.

Attractively decorated and furnished, the hotel provides every modern comfort for the discerning traveller and guest and has been awarded the status of Four Crowns Highly Commended by the English Tourist Board.

All 10 bedrooms are light, airy, comfortable and have full en suite facilities. The pillared restaurant has floor-to-ceiling window areas and is fully air-conditioned.

Diners can enjoy varied à la carte and table d'hôte menus and there are special business lunches. The hotel features regular opera evenings throughout the year

An attractive bar lounge provides a relaxing interlude and a private room is available for meetings and functions. Clay-pigeon shooting, windsurfing, squash and golf can be easily arranged.

Places of interest nearby: The historic city of Canterbury's great Norman cathedral and excellent shopping, Leeds Castle and Sissinghurst are just a short drive away. **Directions: From the M2, exit at junction 6 for Faversham.**

CROSBY LODGE COUNTRY HOUSE HOTEL

HIGH CROSBY, CROSBY-ON-EDEN, CARLISLE, CUMBRIA CA6 4QZ
TEL: 01228 573618 FAX: 01228 573428

OWNERS: Michael, Patricia and James Sedgwick
CHEF: James Sedgwick

11 rms   11 ens   SMALL HOTEL

MasterCard   VISA   AMERICAN EXPRESS

S: £75–£80
D: £98–£120

Crosby Lodge is a romantic country mansion that has been converted into a quiet efficient hotel without spoiling any of its original charm. Grade II listed, it stands amid pastoral countryside close to the Scottish Lowlands and the Lake District.

Spacious interiors are elegantly furnished and appointed to provide the maximum of comfort. The personal attention of Michael and Patricia Sedgwick ensures that a high standard of service is maintained. All of the bedrooms are beautifully equipped, most with antique beds and half-testers. Two bedrooms are situated in the converted courtyard stables overlooking the walled garden and in these rooms guests are welcome to bring their pet dogs.

In the restaurant, extensive menus offer a wide and varied choice of dishes. Traditional English recipes are prepared along with continental cuisine. Tables are set with cut glass and gleaming silver cutlery and, in keeping with the gracious surroundings, gentlemen are requested to wear a jacket and tie for dinner. Crosby Lodge, with its spacious grounds, is a superb setting for weddings, parties, business and social events. Closed 24 December to 20 January.

Places of interest nearby: Hadrian's Wall, Carlisle Cathedral and Castle, and nine miles from Lanercost Priory, the Scottish Borders. **Directions: From M6 junction 44 take A689 Brampton road for three miles; turn right through Low Crosby. Crosby Lodge is on the right.**

NUMBER THIRTY ONE

31 HOWARD PLACE, CARLISLE, CUMBRIA CA1 1HR
TEL: 01228 597080 FAX: 01228 597080

OWNERS: Philip and Judith Parker
CHEF: Philip Parker

3 rms 3 ens

 S: £40–£55
D: £60–£80

This thoughtfully renovated Victorian town house is an ideal, restful retreat situated in a tree-lined avenue in the centre of Carlisle, the ancient and frequently fought over capital of north-west England. Number Thirty One is owned and run by Philip and Judith Parker who aim to make visits peaceful and comfortable. The three bedrooms are equipped to a high standard without destroying their Victorian splendour and have been decorated in a sympathetic way to enhance the natural characteristics of this dignified building in its convenient location.

Philip provides tasteful, home cooked meals with special emphasis on quality local produce. He even has his own "Smokie" where he treats the salmon and trout which he frequently catches. Number 31 is unlicensed so guests are invited to bring their own wine. This is a non smoking house. As well as excellent walks there is good fishing on the rivers Eden and Calder, canoeing, hound trailing, shooting, golf and riding. Closed December to February.

Places of interest nearby: Carlisle cathedral and castle, Hadrian's Wall, the Scottish Borders and the beauty of England's largest National Park. **Directions: From the M6, exit at junction 43 and take the Warwick Road towards Carlisle. Howard Place is the first road on the right after the sixth set of traffic lights.**

Aynsome Manor Hotel

CARTMEL, GRANGE-OVER-SANDS, CUMBRIA LA11 6HH
TEL: 015395 36653 FAX: 015395 36016

OWNERS: Tony and Margaret Varley, Chris and Andrea Varley
CHEF: Victor Sharratt

S: £55–£62
D: £91–£108
(including dinner)

12 rms | 12 ens | SMALL HOTEL

In the beautiful Vale of Cartmel, with views of the priory and beyond to the village of Cartmel itself, stands Aynsome Manor, once the home of Wiliam Marshall, Earl of Pembroke. It is an ideal retreat for anyone seeking peace and quiet. Guests can stroll around the grounds or, in cooler months, relax by log fires in the lounges.

The elegant candlelit dining room is the perfect setting in which to enjoy a five-course dinner. The restaurant has an excellent reputation for its home cooking, from delicious home-made soups such as apple, celery and tomato, to main courses such as roast breast of pheasant with smoked bacon and an orange and chestnut sauce. Fresh, local produce is used wherever possible. A high tea is provided for children under five as they are regrettably not allowed in the restaurant for dinner. There are 12 bedrooms, 2 of which are in Aynsome Cottage, across the courtyard.

Places of interest nearby: Aynsome Manor is a perfect base for touring the Lake District. Lake Windermere is 4 miles away. In summer, Holker Hall organises ballooning and vintage car rallies. There is horseracing in Cartmel on Whitsun and August bank holidays and 5 golf courses nearby. Closed 2nd to 26th January. **Directions: Leave M6 at junction 36 and take the A590 signposted Barrow-in-Furness. At end of dual carriageway (12 miles) turn left into Cartmel. The hotel is on the right.**

In association
with MasterCard

EASTON COURT HOTEL

EASTON CROSS, CHAGFORD, DEVON TQ13 8JL
TEL: 01647 433469 FAX: 01647 433654 E-MAIL: stay@easton.co.uk

OWNERS: Gordon and Judy Parker

8 rms | 8 ens | SMALL HOTEL

S: £65–£70
D: £110–£135
(including dinner)

Easton Court is a 15th century, Grade II listed, thatched Tudor house with many historic connections, particularly literary ones. Both Evelyn Waugh – who wrote *Brideshead Revisited* here – and Patrick Leigh Fermor found inspiration in this rural setting amid the glorious Devon countryside. The sensitive restoration of the hotel has removed none of its old-world charm and period features such as exposed granite walls, oak beams and a great inglenook fireplace, complete with bread oven, have been retained. For those with a literary bent, there is a superb library housing a fascinating collection of old tomes.

The eight tastefully furnished bedrooms have lots of interesting nooks and crannies and offer wonderful rural and moorland views. The menus in the attractive restaurant vary with the seasons and special diets can be catered for by prior arrangement. Special breaks available. **Places of interest nearby:** Dartmoor's mystery and grandeur lie 'on the doorstep' of the hotel, offering an endless variety of breathtaking walks, while Exmoor, Lynton and the rugged North Devon coast are a short journey away. Castle Drogo, Fernworthy Reservoir and Exeter are among the many other local places of interest. Closed January. **Directions: From Exeter, take the A30. At the first roundabout take the A382 signposted Moretonhampstead.**

In association with MasterCard

THE OAK HOUSE HOTEL

THE SQUARE, AXBRIDGE, SOMERSET BS26 2AP
TEL: 01934 732444 FAX: 01934 733112

OWNERS: Amanda and Anthony Saint Claire
CHEF: Martin Ball

10 rms   10 ens

MasterCard VISA AMERICAN EXPRESS

S: £42–£45
D: £57–£69.50

The gleaming, colour-washed Oak House Hotel stands proudly in the spacious old market square of the medieval town of Axbridge in the heart of rural Somerset. It is encompassed by small, ancient streets and a happy mix of 13th century to 19th century buildings including The National Trust's King John's Hunting Lodge.

In summer months there is a distinctive Continental feel about the surroundings as the owners enhance the exterior with colourful hanging baskets, flower-laden wooden tubs and bright table umbrellas.

Partially dating from the 11th century, this elegantly furnished hotel has many beautiful features: exposed beams, stone walls, massive inglenook fireplaces and an ancient well linked to the Cheddar caverns.

The en suite bedrooms are charmingly decorated and comfortably furnished. There is a small intimate bar and unpretentious award-winning Bistro with old pine tables and a wonderful atmosphere where delicious West County cusine is served. Fishing, sailing and golf are within easy reach.

Places of interest nearby: The Cheddar Gorge and caves. Wookey Hole Caves, Cheddar Valley Vineyards, several cider museums, Forde Abbey and Gardens and the cathedral city of Wells. **Directions: From the M5, exit at junction 22 and take the A38 towards Bristol. Join the A371 towards Cheddar/Wells and then turn left at sign for Axbridge.**

In association
with MasterCard

CHARLTON KINGS HOTEL

CHARLTON KINGS, CHELTENHAM, GLOUCESTERSHIRE GL52 6UU
TEL: 01242 231061 FAX: 01242 241900

OWNER: Trevor Stuart
MANAGERS: Bob Seels and Jane Saunders

S: £41–£75.50
D: £62–£94

Surrounded by the Cotswold hills, on the outside of Cheltenham but just a few minutes by car to the heart of town stands Charlton Kings Hotel. If you seek instant peace and solitude follow the footpath running alongside the hotel into the beautiful Cotswold countryside. The famous 'Cotswold Way' escarpment walk passes just half a mile away.

The hotel is attractively furnished with an accent on light woods and pastel colouring. All rooms are en suite, some are reserved for non smokers. The Restaurant is fresh and inviting offering space and privacy for those all important business meetings or perhaps an intimate dinner for two? An à la carte menu is supplemented by a daily table d'hôte, using the finest fresh produce. The bar and conservatory are open throughout the day for snacks and refreshments. A full Sunday Roast Lunch is served 12-2. **Places of interest nearby:** Cheltenham Spa – famous for its architecture festivals and racing also has plenty to offer in the way of theatres, restaurants and a distinguished selection of shops. To the North, East and South lie charming Cotswold Villages, too numerous to mention, and to the West the Forest of Dean, Wye Valley, Malvern Hills and much much more. **Directions: The hotel is the first property on the left coming into Cheltenham from Oxford on the A40 (the 'Welcome to Cheltenham' Boundary Sign is located in their front garden!).**

HALEWELL

HALEWELL CLOSE, WITHINGTON, NR CHELTENHAM, GLOUCESTERSHIRE GL54 4BN
TEL: 01242 890238 FAX: 01242 890332

OWNER: Mrs Elizabeth Carey-Wilson

S: £55.50
D: £83–£85
S: £140

This enchanting manor house is built of warm honey–coloured Cotswold stone. It is the home of Elizabeth Carey-Wilson who has made it a charming venue for guests seeking to stay within the ambience of a private house. The skilful restoration reflects both her affection for Halewell and consideration for those staying with her.

The guest rooms are individual. Two have adjoining rooms so families can be together and a ground floor room has been designed for disabled guests.

Meals are en famille, prepared by the hostess, at one long and lovely table. Breakfast is seldom before 9 o'clock, and early children's meals are provided, as the traditional dinner is around 8 o'clock accompanied by good wine. Lunches and more exotic meals can be found in the attractive pubs close by.

Guests use the Sitting Room which has a games table, and after dinner appreciate joining Mrs Carey-Wilson in her private drawing room, The Solar, with its unusual vaulted ceiling. Within the grounds are delightful terraced gardens, a stretch of the River Colne for fishing, and a large trout lake, in addition to an outdoor swimming pool.

Places of interest nearby: The Cotswolds offer fine walking and there is an old Roman villa within 2 miles walk. Cheltenham has its races and festivals and Blenheim and Sudeley are in easy reach. **Directions: Leave A40 at Andoversford (A436). Take first left to Withington village, then second right and second entrace on the left.**

In association
with MasterCard

CROUCHERS BOTTOM

BIRDHAM ROAD, APULDRAM, NEAR CHICHESTER, WEST SUSSEX PO20 7EH
TEL: 01243 784995 FAX: 01243 539797

OWNERS: Drew and Lesley Wilson
CHEF: Drew Wilson

9 rms | 9 ens

D: £75–£95

Crouchers Bottom Country Hotel is situated just ½ mile from the Yacht Basin and 2 miles from the centre of Chichester. Surrounded by fields, it offers fine views of the Cathedral, Goodwood and the South Downs and aims to create a relaxed and informal atmosphere for its guests.

There are nine en suite rooms, all located in the separate 'coach house' and equipped with a full range of modern amenities, including a telephone, colour TV, hairdryer and tea and coffee-making facilities. The south-facing ground floor rooms open out onto a large patio with a lovely view of the garden and its pond with resident waterfowl. One of the twin-bedded rooms is particularly suitable for wheelchair users. Free-range hens provide the eggs of a full English breakfast, while dinner promises an interesting selection of freshly prepared dishes which changes daily. The area provides guests with a plentiful choice of activities, including boating around Chichester Harbour and visiting the City, with its cathedral, Roman walls, Festival Theatre, art gallery, and museum.

Places of interest nearby: The famous Mary Rose can be seen in Portsmouth, where there are also a number of Maritime museums. Goodwood House and Arundel Castle are both within easy reach. **Directions: From the M27, Junction 12, take the A27 to Chichester and then the A286 south towards Witterings. Crouchers Bottom Hotel is on the left.**

In association
with MasterCard

WOODSTOCK HOUSE HOTEL

CHARLTON, NEAR CHICHESTER, WEST SUSSEX PO18 0HU
TEL: 01243 811666 FAX: 01243 811666

OWNERS: Michael and Elizabeth McGovern
CHEF: Elizabeth McGovern

| 11 rms | 11 ens | 🌳 | SMALL HOTEL |

S: £38.50–£48
D: £66–£92

Nestling below the heights of Charlton Forest in the middle of West Sussex downland, Woodstock House is a perfect example of the small country house hotel. In summer the sun shines all day on its secluded courtyard garden. It was built in the 18th century but the public rooms, which include a bar and two sitting rooms, enjoy a modern feeling of spaciousness.

The dining room, however, retains a more traditional, atmosphere in which the high standard of cooking – set by Mrs McGovern – can be savoured to the full. The 11 bedrooms, all en suite, are comfortable and well-equipped with television and tea-making facilities. One bedroom offers a four-poster bed.

The hotel could not be better placed for offering outside interest from racing at Goodwood, golf at Goodwood and Cowdray Park golf clubs, sailing at Itchenor, Bosham and Dell Quay and Chichester Sea School and yacht basin, bathing at East and West Wittering and the Chichester Festival Theatre.

Places of interest nearby: There are historic houses in the area: Goodwood, Petworth, Parham and Uppark and Arundel Castle. The gardens of Wakehurst Place and Sheffield Park are well worth a visit, also nature reserves at Kingsley Vale and Pagham Harbour. **Directions: From M27 take A27 north of the Goodwood Estate. Charlton can be approached from A285 or A286.**

STANTON MANOR

STANTON SAINT QUINTIN, NR CHIPPENHAM, WILTSHIRE SN14 6DQ
TEL: 01666 837552 FAX: 01666 837022

OWNERS: Philip & Elizabeth Bullock

| 10 rms | 10 ens |

MasterCard VISA AMERICAN EXPRESS

S: £75
D: £95

Near to the M4 just off the beaten track in five acres of leafy gardens, there has been a habitation at Stanton Manor for over 900 years. The original house was listed in the Domesday Book and was later owned by Lord Burghley, Elizabeth I's chief minister. The Elizabethan dovecote in the garden bears witness to that period, although the present building dates largely from the 19th century. The bedrooms are furnished in a homely, country style and several offer views over Wiltshire farmland.

Choices from the menu might include a starter of tasty Homemade soup or chicken liver parfait followed, for a main course, by saddle of spring lamb in a brandy, tomato and tarragon sauce. A variety of light meals is available in either the lounge or the bar.

Proprietors Elizabeth and Philip Bullock are invariably on hand to ensure that a friendly, personal service is extended to all their visitors.

Places of interest nearby: The Roman city of Cirencester, Chippenham, and a wealth of pretty villages all invite exploration. **Directions:** Leave the M4 at junction 17 and join the A429 towards Cirencester. After 200 yards, turn left to Stanton Saint Quintin; Stanton Manor is on the left in the village.

CHIPPING CAMPDEN (Broad Campden)

THE MALT HOUSE

BROAD CAMPDEN, GLOUCESTERSHIRE GL55 6UU
TEL: 01386 840295 FAX: 01386 841334

OWNERS: Nick and Jean Brown
CHEF: Julian Brown

8 rms   8 ens

S: £49.50–£72.50
D: £72.50–£89.50
Suites: £80–£115

Nick and Jean Brown have achieved a blend of warm, relaxed and yet professional service, welcoming guests as part of an extended house party. The idyllic surroundings of The Malt House, a beautiful 17th century Cotswold home in the quiet village of Broad Campden, further enhance the congenial atmosphere.

Rooms, including a residents' sitting room, combine comfortable furnishings with antiques and displays of fresh flowers. Most bedrooms overlook the wide lawns which lead to a small stream and orchard beyond. All of the recently refurbished rooms are individually decorated and have an en suite bathroom. The Windrush Suite has an 18th century four-poster bed and a family suite is also available.

Dinner is served six days a week. The proprietors' son Julian is a highly accomplished chef who uses many ingredients from the kitchen gardens to prepare a table d'hôte menu, accompanied by a choice selection of wines. The English breakfasts are equally good.

The Malt House has earned a Highly Commended award from the English Tourist and most deservedly 2 Rosettes for its food from the AA.

Places of interest nearby: Hidcote Manor Gardens (N.T), Chipping Camden Church, The Cotswolds, Cheltenham, Stratford-upon-Avon, Oxford and Bath. **Directions: The Malt House is in the village of Broad Campden which is just one mile from Chipping Campden.**

In association
with MasterCard

TUDOR FARMHOUSE HOTEL & RESTAURANT

HIGH STREET, CLEARWELL, NR COLEFORD, GLOUCESTERSHIRE GL16 8JS
TEL: 01594 833046 FAX: 01594 837093

OWNERS: Richard and Deborah Fletcher
CHEF: Dean Wassell

S: £47.50
D: £57

Tudor Farmhouse is an idyllic haven away from the hustle and bustle of every day life. A cosy, friendly 13th century stone-built hotel in the centre of the historic village of Clearwell on the peaceful fringe of the Forest of Dean. Clearwell's history dates from Roman times and the village is dominated by the huge ramparts of a fine Neo Gothic castle.

Owners Richard and Deborah Fletcher take pride in the standard of comfort and hospitality at Tudor Farmhouse, whose features include massive oak beams and original panelling. There is a large, roughstone inglenook fireplace in the attractive lounge providing warmth and cheer in winter. A conservatory looks onto the landscaped garden and 14 acres of fields. The bedrooms have been refurbished in traditional style. Those in the house are reached by a wide, oak spiral staircase. Others are in converted stone cider makers' cottages quietly situated in the garden and include three family suites.

The candlelit restaurant, awarded a red Rosette, with its open stonework and exposed beams is the ideal setting in which to enjoy unhurried evening meals.

Places of interest nearby: The Forest of Dean and Wye Valley, Offa's Dyke, Tintern Abbey, Monmouth and Ross on Wye, spectacular Symonds Yat, Raglan and Chepstow Castles. **Directions: From M4 join M48 taking junction 2 to Chepstow then follow A48 and B4231**

ABBOTS OAK

GREENHILL, COALVILLE LE67 4UY
TEL: 01530 832 328 FAX: 01530 832 328

OWNERS: Bill, Audrey and Carolyn White

S: £50–£55
D: £70–£75

This Grade II listed building is on the edge of Charnwood Forest, with 19 acres of gardens, woodland and unusual granite outcrops where guests can stroll or play croquet and tennis. Being in the heart of Quorn country, stables are available for visitors' horses in the hunting season.

Inside is the most spectacular carved oak panelling and stained glass – indeed the staircase goes to the top of the tower from where it is possible to look out over five counties.

The house has four bedrooms available for the use of guests, two of which are en suite. There is a gorgeous drawing room and elegant dining room. Dinner is served en famille by candlelight. The menu is therefore not extensive and the wine list short but good. After dinner enjoy a game of snooker in the superb billiard room. This establishment is not suitable for young children.

Places of interest nearby: Mid-week it is ideal for businessmen with meetings in Loughborough or Leicester. There is excellent golf nearby and shooting can be arranged. Further afield are Stratford-upon-Avon, Warwick Castle and Rutland Water. **Directions: Leave the M1 at junction 22, taking B587 through Copt Oak to Whitwick. Abbots Oak is 1¼ miles on opposite the Bulls Head inn.**

In association with MasterCard

HOCKLEY PLACE

RECTORY ROAD, FRATING, COLCHESTER, ESSEX CO7 7HG
TEL: 01206 251703 FAX: 01206 251578

OWNERS: Helen and Humphrey Bowles

S: £30
D: £60

Hockley Place is renowned for its rhodendendron walk, in full bloom in May and June, just part of the lovely five acres of parkland, orchards and farmland surrounding this 'Lutyens' style house, where no smoking is permitted.

The interior reflects the hostess's talents as an artist, with her paintings around the house. The kitchen is equally creative, as she is also a superb cook, using prime local ingredients for the delicious dinner served in the beamed dining room – and breakfast is substantial.

The charming bedrooms will delight tall guests, for there are extra long beds!

Relaxation facilities include a gymnasium, heated pool and croquet lawn. Highly rated by other guides.

Places of interest nearby: Mystical Constable country, the Essex coastline and Colchester with its Norman Castle and Roman Walls. Beth Chatto's gardens are just three minutes' drive away. Felixstowe, Ipswich, and, beloved of many artists, Dedham, Flatford Mill and Lavenham are all very accessible. **Directions: At major junction A12/A120 take first exit A120 Harwich /Clacton, first exit A133 Clacton. Second exit roundabout. A133 Elmstead Market. First left 'Kings Arms' B1029 Brightlingsea/ First right signposted Elmstead Market, Rectory Road. Turn left at junction Rectory Road/Church Road into Apple Orchard.**

COMBE MARTIN (East Down)

ASHELFORD

ASHELFORD, EAST DOWN, NEAR BARNSTAPLE, NORTH DEVON EX31 4LU
TEL: 01271 850469 FAX: 01271 850862

OWNERS: Tom and Erica McClenaghan
CHEF: Erica McClenaghan

3 rms | 3 ens

S: £55
D: £77–£90

North Devon has over 850 square miles of heritage countryside and coast that are classified as one of the last remaining tranquil areas in England. Ashelford stands in over 60 acres of superb pasture and woodland facing south at the head of its own valley with views beyond the National Trust's Arlington Court to Exmoor.

Formerly a 17th century farmhouse, Ashelford has retained its sense of history with a wealth of oak beams, slate floors and log fires. Owners Tom and Erica McClenaghan offer peace, seclusion and cosy informality where a visitor's comfort is their greatest concern.

Privacy is enhanced by enchanting, warmly decorated and well-appointed bedrooms, each having en suite facilities and extras that include a refrigerator with fresh milk, orange juice and spring water. The lounge and dining room are comfortable and welcoming with superb meals prepared from local produce.

Golf, fishing, riding and carriage driving can be arranged and the residence has an outside bath with hot and cold water for well-behaved dogs after they have completed one of the many surrounding walks with their owners!

Places of interest nearby: The R.H.S. Rosemoor Gardens, Dartington Glass, Arlington Court. **Directions: From Barnstaple take A39 towards Lynmouth. After Shirwell village take second turning on left and follow signs to Churchill. Ashelford is on the right.**

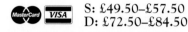

COOMBE HOUSE COUNTRY HOTEL

COLEFORD, CREDITON, DEVON EX17 5BY
TEL: 01363 84487 FAX: 01363 84722 E-MAIL: coombehs@mail.zynet.co.uk

OWNERS: David and Pat Jones
CHEF: Bill Denton

S: £49.50–£57.50
D: £72.50–£84.50

This elegant Georgian manor is listed as a protected building of historic interest and certainly the Cellar Bar has over 700 years of history – reputedly it sheltered Cromwell's men in the Civil War. Now these elegant buildings which offer relaxation in lovely landscaped grounds are being thoughtfully refurbished and up-graded by their caring and welcoming owners.

There are 15 bedrooms in all, the spacious Superior rooms at the front of the house enjoying restful views over the grounds and surrounding countryside with well-equipped bathrooms en suite; the six Standard en suite rooms are equally pleasant but their differing quality is reflected in the price structure.

The restaurant was once a ballroom added on in Victorian times and it provides a gracious, elegant atmosphere in which to enjoy the daily-changed cuisine and wines from the informative list. The grounds provide facilities for those who wish to play tennis, swim in a heated pool or indulge in croquet. For the more adventurous golf, shooting and riding can all be arranged. **Places of interest nearby:** The city of Exeter with its cathedral and university, the Taw and Torridge valleys, Dartmoor, Exmoor and a number of National Trust properties. **Directions: From Exeter join A377 and pass through Crediton. After approximately 1½ miles further on the hotel is signposted**

PRINCE HALL HOTEL

TWO BRIDGES, DARTMOOR, DEVON PL20 6SA
TEL: 01822 890403 FAX: 01822 890676

OWNERS: Adam and Carrie Southwell

S: £57.50–£70.50
D: £115–£125
(including 4 course dinner)

Set high in the heart of Dartmoor National Park, Prince Hall is a unique and peaceful, 18th century country house hotel. Once the summer residence of Lord and Lady Astor, it commands spectacular views over the the West Dart River to rolling open moorland, an idyllic setting for walking, bird watching or simply just relaxing.

Prynse Hall, as the hotel was originally called, is one of the ancient tenements of Dartmoor and a dwelling has stood on the site since 1443.

The Hall is comfortably furnished. Attractive fabrics, interesting pictures, shelves of books and roaring log fires in winter add to the warm welcome. Each of the spacious, en suite bedrooms individually decorated, has its own particular character and offers all modern comforts.

In the delightful restaurant with its granite stone walls and charming ambience, great care and attention is taken with the four course table d'hôte daily changing menu. Quality local produce, including local venison and lamb, Brixham fish and salmon and trout from the River Dart is used. Dogs are welcome free of charge. Closed January.

Places of interest nearby: Buckland Abbey, houses and gardens such as Castle Drogo, Knightshayes and Killerton, Iron Age and prehistoric sites. **Directions: From Exeter take the A38 to Ashburton and follow the signs for Two Bridges and Princetown. Prince Hall is on the left on the B3375 one mile before Two Bridges.**

In association
with MasterCard

GLADWINS FARM

HARPER'S HILL, NAYLAND, SUFFOLK CO6 4NU
TEL: 01206 262261 FAX: 01206 263001 E-MAIL: GladwinsFarm@Compuserve.com

OWNERS: Robert and Pauline Dossor

2 cottages

£215–£685 per week
flexible breaks available

Gladwins Farm stands in 22 acres of rolling Suffolk countryside, commanding stunning panoramic views over the Stour Valley and Constable country. In the local church one of the famous painter's few religious works of art can be viewed.

The cottages, in a group of 6 converted from a Tudor barn and stable, are light and airy and tastefully upgraded to meet modern demands. Bedrooms are fitted with pine furniture and the attractive open-plan beamed living room/dining rooms are furnished to the highest standards. The kitchen areas are equipped with a full range of modern electric appliances. One cottage is "non-allergenic" and the other is adapted to the needs of the less able-bodied. Some bed and breakfast accommodation is available in the main house.

Consideration has been given to entertaining children with the provision of an adventure playground. They are also welcome to feed the animals – the pot-bellied pigs will prove irresistible! A new indoor heated swimming pool features a sauna suite, viewing gallery and changing rooms.

Places of interest nearby: Gainsborough's house in Sudbury and the villages of Long Melford and Lavenham, also Cambridge and Norwich. **Directions: From the A14 at Bury St Edmunds take A134 towards Sudbury, or from A12 (London to Ipswich) take A134 at Colchester. Nayland is halfway between Sudbury and Colchester and the farm is signposted on the road.**

SALISBURY HOUSE

VICTORIA ROAD, DISS, NORFOLK IP22 3JG
TEL: 01379 644738 FAX: 01379 644738

OWNERS: Barry and Sue Davies

| 3 rms | 2 ens | 🌲 |

S: £50–£62
D: £70–£82

This impressive Victorian house is set in pleasant, mature gardens on the edge of Diss, described as 'the perfect market town' by the late Sir John Betjeman. Salisbury House has established an enviable reputation for its individual style of cooking and cellar of 200 wines. The à la carte menu changes monthly to take advantage of the best seasonal produce.

Deciding where and what to eat is a choice which guests will enjoy making. They can self-denyingly opt to have perhaps just one delicious main meal dish with a glass of wine in the new Bistro with its refreshingly modern decor, or elect to relish the superb cuisine off the à la carte menu in the pretty and traditional, non-smoking, dining room, and to end the meal, coffee and original home-made petits fours.

The decoration is principally Victorian and in each individually styled bedroom fresh flowers and pot-pourri add a welcoming touch. During the summer months, guests can sip their drinks in the large conservatory overlooking a pretty garden complete with walled patio, croquet lawn, summerhouse and a duck pond graced by a weeping willow. A private room is available for boardroom meetings and private dining. Closed for 2 weeks in Summer.

Places of interest nearby: Newmarket, Snetterton motor circuit, Norwich, Thetford, Bury St Edmunds, Ipswich and the coast. **Directions: On the A1066 Victoria Road, 1/4 mile outside town centre of Diss. The A143 and A140 lead to the A1066.**

YALBURY COTTAGE HOTEL

LOWER BOCKHAMPTON, DORCHESTER, DORSET DT2 8PZ
TEL: 01305 262382 FAX: 01305 266412

OWNERS: Heather and Derek Furminger
HEAD CHEF: Nick Larby

S: £46
D: £72

Yalbury Cottage Hotel is a lovely thatched property dating back about 300 years. Family run, it offers guests a warm welcome and a friendly, personal service in an atmosphere of peace, relaxation and informality.

The eight spacious bedrooms are attractively decorated and furnished, all having well appointed bathrooms en suite. Each offers a full range of desirable extras, including colour television, hairdryer and tea and coffee making facilities.

A comfortable lounge, complete with large inglenook fireplace and low, beamed ceilings, is the perfect place to relax before dinner. The proprietors pride themselves on the high standard of cuisine served in the attractive dining room. A good variety of imaginative dishes is always available, for example, paupiette of cod filled with crab on a mustard sauce, rack of lamb with a honey and rosemary sauce, local calves liver with a redcurrant and thyme sauce or vegetable Wellington with a pesto sauce. A selection of carefully chosen wines is available to complement any meal.

Places of interest nearby: Thomas Hardy's birthplace, Athelhampton House, Parnham House, Abbotsbury Swannery, Corfe Castle and Sherborne Castle. Yalbury Cottage is an excellent centre from which to explore Dorset, with its superb walking country, pretty villages and magnificent coastline. **Directions: Lower Bockhampton is one mile south of A35 between Puddletown and Dorchester.**

In association with MasterCard

WALLETT'S COURT

WEST CLIFFE, ST MARGARET'S-AT-CLIFFE, DOVER, KENT CT15 6EW
TEL: 01304 852424 FAX: 01304 853430

OWNERS: Chris, Lea and Gavin Oakley

9 rms | 9 ens

S: from £40
D: £65–£85

The Doomsday Book records this listed Grade II house as 'The Manor of Westcliffe'. It was transformed into this lovely hotel by the Oakley family who discovered it in ruins in the late 70s. Wallett's Court invites relaxation, either strolling in the extensive gardens, collapsing into the large leather sofa, listening to the tick of the grandfather clock or enjoying the view from the conservatory.

There are large bedrooms in the main house, some with four-posters and others are in a converted barn, with names such as the Dairy or Stable. All are comfortable and well-equipped.

The Chef-Patron, Chris Oakley, puts history into the restaurant with a Jacobean flavour to the menus, which change every month. Try the Huntsman's Platter, local monkfish, Kentish lamb and syllabub. The wine list is long, mostly French, and there is a good selection of half-bottles, all acceptably priced. Breakfast is another feast, with farm eggs, sausages made by the nearby butcher, and homemade preserves. Awarded 3 AA Rosettes.

Places of interest nearby: Guests enjoy walking on the cliff tops to St Margaret's Bay, exploring the Cinque Ports and playing golf on the nearby championship courses. Some visitors drive 10 miles to the Channel Tunnel for a day in France! **Directions: From the A2 roundabout immediately north of Dover take the A258 signposted Deal. After one mile turn right and the Court is on the right.**

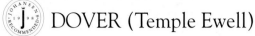

THE WOODVILLE HALL

TEMPLE EWELL, DOVER, KENT CT16 1DJ
TEL: 01304 825256 FAX: 01304 825256

OWNER: Mr A.D.M. Allen
MANAGERS: Sue and Roger Westoby

3 rms 3 ens

Suites: from £95

The owners justifiably boast that this is one of the most beautiful small hotels in England. One cannot believe that this magnificent residence, built in 1820 for Henry Colman (of mustard fame) and set in 40 acres of secluded parkland, is a short drive from Dover and the Channel Tunnel.

The accommodation is superb, three spectacular suites which are all furnished most luxuriously in the greatest detail. Awarded 'Best Small Hotel' by the Welcome to Kent Scheme.

The ambience throughout the entire house reflects the gracious Georgian era, with silver and highly polished antiques, oil paintings and marvellous flowers. Welcoming and friendly hospitality is of the highest standard. Guests enjoy immaculate service and haute cuisine beautifully presented with interesting wines and champagnes. Dinner is served either in the dining room or in the suites.

Places of interest nearby: When not enjoying the extensive grounds with its ancient woodland guests can visit nearby nature reserves, Dover Castle and Hellfire Corner, the Battle of Britain Museum, the Old Town Gaol, the White Cliffs Experience and Walmer Castle, or, further afield, Canterbury Cathedral. **Directions: Take A2 from Dover and at the second roundabout turn left. At the bottom of the hill turn right towards Lydden. Continue for one mile and Woodville Hall is on your right.**

MANOR HOUSE HOTEL AND RESTAURANT

10/15 HIGH STREET, OLD DRONFIELD, DERBYSHIRE SI8 1PX
TEL: 01246 413971 FAX: 01246 412104

OWNERS: Janet and Andrew Coghlan
CHEF: Janet Coghlan

10 rms | 10 ens | SMALL HOTEL

S: £55
D: £75
Suite: £115

Situated in the heart of Old Dronfield, the Manor House offers a professional, yet relaxed environment for both business and social travellers. There are two suites and eight en suite bedrooms combining high standards of modern luxury with the charm and ambience of a building dating from 1540. The Piper-Heidsieck suite is a new addition to the hotel facilities. This opulently restored suite is designed to reflect Piper's long standing relationship with the stars on the big screen and includes complementary champagne Piper. Oak beams and Derbyshire stone are features carried throughout the building.

The restaurant now enjoys an enviable reputation in the locality, serving new English classical cooking with influences from Europe and the Americas. Innovation of ideas and a light touch with sauces coupled with simple yet effective presentation of dishes ensure that the restaurant is often booked some weeks in advance and booking is recommended for weekend visits. Wines are treated with as much importance as food and the cellar is stocked with over 200 bins including wines from Schloss Reinhartshausen and the Millennium Collection.

Places of interest nearby: Chatsworth House, Haddon Hall, Bakewell and the Peak District, Blue John Mines, Chesterfield Spire and Dronfield Church. **Directions: Old Dronfield is three miles south of Sheffield, off the A61. The Manor House is in the centre of the village near the church.**

ASHWICK COUNTRY HOUSE HOTEL

DULVERTON, SOMERSET TA22 9QD
TEL: 01398 323868 FAX: 01398 323868

OWNER: Richard Sherwood
CHEF: Richard Sherwood

S: £73–£82
D: £126–£164
(including dinner)

This small, charming Edwardian Country House stands in six acres of beautiful grounds above the picturesque valley of the River Barle within Exmoor National Park. Sweeping lawns lead to large water gardens where guests can relax in summer shade and breathe in sweet floral scents. Ashwick House offers old world hospitality. Its atmosphere is sunny with flowers in summer and elegantly cosy with candlelight and log fires in winter.

The baronial style hall with its long, broad gallery and cheerful log fire, the restaurant opening onto a terrace where breakfast is served and the comfortably furnished lounge offer a peaceful sanctuary not easily found in today's busy world. All the spacious bedroom suites are pleasantly decorated.

Chef-patron Richard Sherwood presents quality cuisine using fresh local produce. Shooting and riding facilities are close by. **Places of interest nearby:** Dunster's Norman Castle and 17th century Yarm Market, Exmoor Forest, many National Trust houses and gardens. **Directions: From the M5, exit at junction 27 onto the A361 to Tiverton. Take the A396 north until joining the B3222 to Dulverton and then the B3223 signposted Lynton and Exford. After a steep climb drive over a second cattle grid and turn left to Ashwick House.**

THE EXMOOR HOUSE HOTEL

WEST STREET, DUNSTER, SOMERSET TA24 6SN
TEL: 01643 821268 FAX: 01643 821267

OWNERS: David and Karan Howell
CHEF: Karan Howell

6 rms | 6 ens | SMALL HOTEL

S: £48.50–£67.50
D: £65–£95

This enchanting and individual 17th century Grade II listed building is a jewel in a medieval town: it has the atmosphere of a private house, tastefully but comfortably furnished with carefully chosen antiques and pictures. Fresh flowers and generously hospitable owners greet guests on arrival.

Each of the six bedrooms has its own character, from the Hemingway with its 1920's French cane furniture to Haydn's Oak twin four-poster. Five of the rooms have an en suite shower and one an en suite bathroom and all are extremely well-equipped.

The cuisine is in keeping with the individual character of the owners: Mrs Howell is the chef and she uses local fresh produce in her imaginative and tempting menus which are served in first class fashion and can be accompanied by fine wines from a well-chosen list. All meals are enjoyed in the elegant Garden Room overlooking the floodlit courtyard and lion fountain.

Fishing, golf, sailing and riding within a few miles of Dunster are all available through arrangement.

Places of interest nearby: Dunster Castle, Selworthy National Trust village, Rosemoor Gardens and the towns of Lynton and Lynmouth. **Directions: Leave M5 junction 23 (Bridgewater) and join A39 to Dunster. The entrance to Exmoor House is 50 yards from the entrance to the National Trust Castle.**

In association
with MasterCard

OAK LODGE HOTEL

80 VILLAGE ROAD, BUSH HILL PARK, ENFIELD, MIDDLESEX EN1 2EU
TEL: 0181 360 7082

OWNERS: John and Yvonne Brown

| 5 rms | 5 ens | | SMALL HOTEL |

S: £69.50
D: £89.50–£120

Oak Lodge is just nine miles from central London with excellent road and rail connections and conveniently placed for each of the capital's five airports. The hotel is small but it offers a very generous welcome which encompasses charm, courtesy and old-fashioned hospitality.

Each en suite bedroom is highly individual, imaginatively furnished, and with all the facilities found in larger rooms.

Traditional English cuisine, complemented by an exceptionally good wine list, is served in the intimate restaurant which overlooks and opens out onto a delightful evergreen garden. For after-dinner relaxation a pianist regularly entertains guests in a romantic Noel Coward style in the hotel's elegant lounge.

Enfield has excellent shopping facilities and preserves the atmosphere of the country town it once was. There are many fine old houses, particularly in Gentlemen's Row, where the 19th century author Charles Lamb lived.
Places of interest nearby: Forty Hall, built in 1632 for Sir Nicholas Raynton, Lord Mayor of London, now a cultural centre and museum, Capel Manor, St Albans cathedral and the ruins of a Roman amphitheatre. **Directions: From the M25 exit at junction 25 onto the A10 south. Turn right at the eighth set of traffic lights into Church Street, then right again at the next traffic lights into Village Road. Oak Lodge is on the right.**

JOHANSENS RECOMMENDED 1998

THE MILL AT HARVINGTON

ANCHOR LANE, HARVINGTON, EVESHAM, WORCESTERSHIRE WR11 5NR
TEL: 01386 870688 FAX: 01386 870688

OWNERS: Simon and Jane Greenhalgh

21 rms · 21 ens · SMALL HOTEL

MasterCard · VISA · AMERICAN EXPRESS

S: £58
D: £92

From the first glimpse of Simon and Jane Greenhalgh's elegant brochure one is aware that The Mill at Harvington is going to be very special. This delightful small country house hotel set on the bank of the Avon is in the heart of England with easy access to the West, The Cotswolds, Wales and, of course, Shakespeare country.

From inside the welcoming and graceful reception rooms, which are brightened by big open fires in the winter, there are views over the extensive gardens and the river.

The high standards of hospitality and service are evident. The en suite bedrooms are beautifully furnished with all the modern comforts including hairdryers, mineral water, colour television, tea and coffee facilities.

A modestly priced but excellent wine list accompanies the appetising menu which makes maximum use of local and seasonal produce, fish and game (there are also light lunches on the Terrace), reflecting the owners' belief that dining well must be high on the agenda for a successful visit. Guests take away memories of spectacular countryside, superb meals, immaculate service, charming surroundings and perfect hosts. **Directions: The Mill can be reached by a roadbridge over A46 opposite Harvington village, off the Evesham to Bidford road.**

THE LORD HALDON HOTEL

DUNCHIDEOCK, NR EXETER, DEVON EX6 7YF
TEL: 01392 832483 FAX: 01392 833765

OWNERS: Michael and Simon Preece

19 rms   19 ens

S: £38–£54
D: £59–£87

Ideally situated amid rolling Devon countryside between the historic cathedral town of Exeter, dartmoor and the coast stands this imposing country house.

The present building is a fragment of the huge mansion that once stood in this marvellous location, built in 1737. However, the beautiful views planned by Capability Brown can still be enjoyed, as can the peace and tranquillity of this quiet part of Devon.

All the bedrooms are decorated in an individual style, the majority enjoying picturesque rural views, and there are family rooms and four-poster suites for the romantic at heart.

Meals are served in the Chandelier Restaurant, a superb setting to enjoy only the freshest of seasonal produce. Special diets can also be catered for and picnics can be provided on request. A member of Relais Du Silence.

Places of interest nearby: The Maritime Museum at Exeter, Haldon Forest, (designated SSSI) perfect for ornithologists and photographers, and the moorland beauty of Dartmoor, are all just a short drive away from the hotel. **Directions: Exit junction 31 of the M5 onto A30 and leave this dual carriageway at the first available exit signed Marsh Barton and Exeter. Take the first exit at the roundabout signed Ide and then follow local signs for Ide and Dunchideock.**

THE CROWN HOTEL

EXFORD, EXMOOR NATIONAL PARK, SOMERSET TA24 7PP
TEL: 01643 831554/5 FAX: 01643 831665 E-MAIL: bradleyhotelsexmoor@easynet.co.uk

OWNERS: Mike Bradley and John Atkin
CHEF: Andrew Dixon

| 17 rms | 17 ens | SMALL HOTEL |

S: £42–£57
D: £84–£100

This coaching inn, almost three hundred years old, in the Exmoor National Park is surrounded by wonderful countryside, from coastline to valleys, streams and moorland, populated with red deer, ponies, amazing birdlife and salmon.

The hotel has been completely refurbished, to the highest standards of elegance and comfort. Guests can enjoy its comfort in every season – its coolness in summer, its warmth in winter.

The bedrooms, all en suite, have been beautifully decorated and are well-equipped with modern necessities.

There is a lively bar, patronised by the locals, for drinks or informal meals ordered from the extensive menu, or guests may prefer an apéritif in the lounge before entering the delightful dining room for a beautifully presented evening meal from the seasonal menu. Good wines complement the meal. After dinner guests may wish to sroll in the water garden.

Places of interest nearby: Fly fishing (and tuition) in local rivers, riding over the moor and clay pigeon shooting can be arranged. Order a packed lunch and walk the moor or visit Lynmouth and Porlock. **Directions: Exit M5, junction 27. Drive eight miles down the A361, then take the A396 to Wheddon Cross, where Exford is signposted.**

VERE LODGE

SOUTH RAYNHAM, FAKENHAM, NORFOLK NR21 7HE
TEL: 01328 838261 FAX: 01328 838300

OWNERS: Major and Mrs George Bowlby

14 cotts

From £234–£1017
(per cottage per week)

Fourteen spacious, and beautifully decorated self-contained cottages are scattered in seclusion throughout 8 acres of woodlands, paddocks and sweeping lawns surrounding impressive Vere Lodge, a Grade II listed building dating from 1798 and former dower house to Raynham Hall. Some are conversions of old outbuildings, others recently built. All have every home comfort.

Families are particularly well catered for. The grounds are a paradise for children with a playground, a toddlers' play area and unusually tame rabbits, hens, peacocks, dogs, goats, a donkey and a pony to stroke, feed and enjoy.

A grass tennis court and croquet lawn cater for the sports enthusiast and a leisure centre with a 38-foot-long swimming pool, sauna, solarium, table tennis, pool table, sun patios, lounge and a bar serving drinks and alfresco snacks are in a corner of the grounds so as not to intrude upon the peace and seclusion of Vere Lodge. Fresh free-range eggs and a selection of mainly home-cooked frozen foods can be obtained in the leisure centre and there is a launderette. Three night breaks are available.

Places of interest nearby: Norfolk's long sandy beaches, Blickling Hall, Holkham Hall, Sandringham. Riding and fishing can be arranged. **Directions: From Swaffham take A1065 towards Fakenham. After 11 miles enter South Raynham: 100 yards past the village sign turn left. Vere Lodge is the white house 400 yards ahead.**

For hotel location, see maps on pages 266-272

JOHANSENS RECOMMENDED

TRELAWNE HOTEL – THE HUTCHES RESTAURANT

MAWNAN SMITH, NR FALMOUTH, CORNWALL TR115HS
TEL: 01326 250226 FAX: 01326 250909

OWNERS: Paul and Linda Gibbons, Anthony and Jenny Bond
CHEF: Nigel Woodland

12 rms   12 ens   SMALL HOTEL

MasterCard   VISA   AMERICAN EXPRESS   ◊

S: £45–£75
D: £90–£149
(including 4 course dinner)

A very friendly welcome awaits guests, who will be enchanted by the beautiful location of Trelawne Hotel, on the coast between the Rivers Fal and Helford. Large picture windows in the public rooms, including the attractively decorated, spacious lounge, ensure that guests take full advantage of the panoramic vistas of the ever-changing coastline.

The bedrooms are charming, many with views of the sea. The soft colours of the décor, the discreet lighting and attention to detail provide a restful atmosphere, in harmony with the Wedgwood, fresh flowers and sparkling crystal in The Hutches Restaurant, which has been awarded 2AA Rosettes.

The menu changes daily and offers a variety of inspired dishes, including local seafood, game and fresh vegetables. Recreational facilities include an indoor heated swimming pool and a games room. Trelawne Hotel offers its own golf package at no less than ten fine courses. 'Slip Away Anyday' spring, autumn and winter breaks. Closed January. **Places of interest nearby:** The Royal Duchy of Cornwall is an area of outstanding beauty, with many National Trust and English Heritage properties to visit and a range of leisure pursuits to enjoy. **Directions: From Truro follow A39 towards Falmouth, turn right at Hillhead roundabout, take exit signposted Maenporth. Carry on for 3 miles and Trelawne is at the top ovelooking Falmouth bay.**

WHITE WINGS

QUAKER CLOSE, FENNY DRAYTON, NR NUNEATON, LEICESTERSHIRE CV13 6BS
TEL: 01827 716100 FAX: 01827 717191

OWNERS: Ernest and Josephine Lloyd

In association with MasterCard

S: £40–£55
D: £70–£80

This lovely family home provides peaceful and informal accommodation with spacious and traditionally furnished rooms. The well appointed bedrooms all offer private facilities, colour TV and views of the luxuriant garden.

Breakfast and dinner are served on some of the finest collections of china and crystal, in fact Josephine's collection is so vast that you could quite easily not see the same china twice during your stay, and all this in the elegant dining room overlooking the garden. Afterwards guests are invited to relax in the library or the conservatory and to enjoy the use of the Steinway grand piano or go through to the billard room and play on a full sized billard table.

The surrounding villages and towns offer plenty of entertainment, including music, opera, ballet, theatre and exhibitions. For the active, there are golf courses and opportunities for fishing, canal trips and indoor skiing.
Places of interest nearby: Fenny Drayton is an excellent centre from which to visit Stratford-upon-Avon, Warwick, Kenilworth and Leicester, with their ancient castles, historic houses, museums and art galleries. Close by is the village of Twycross with its zoo housing a famous collection of primates. **Directions: On the A444 from Nuneaton, turn left into George Fox Lane (becoming Old Forge Road) and right into Quaker Close.**

CHIPPENHALL HALL

FRESSINGFIELD, EYE, SUFFOLK IP21 5TD
TEL: 01379 588180/586733 FAX: 01379 586272

OWNERS: Barbara and Jakes Sargent

5 rms | 5 ens

MasterCard VISA

S: £53–£59
D: £59–£65

The present manor is a listed Tudor building, although its origins date from Saxon times and is referred to in the *Domesday Book* as Cybenhalla. Secluded at the end of a long leafy drive, the hall enjoys a setting of rural tranquillity amid seven acres of lawns, trees, ponds and gardens.

Every evening, by arrangement, a superb candle-lit dinner is prepared by your hostess and served in convivial surroundings. Proprietors Barbara and Jakes Sargent pride themselves in offering a fine choice of reasonably priced wines from the cellar to complement your meal. A seat beside the copper-canopied inglenook fire in the Shallow .End bar room is the ideal place to enjoy pre-dinner drinks.

The house is heavily-beamed throughout, including the en suite bedrooms which are named after relevant historical associations. During the summer, guests can relax by the heated outdoor swimming pool which is set in the rose-covered courtyard. With attentive service, good food and wine, it is not surprising to learn that Chippenhall Hall is ETB Highly Commended and AA Premier Selected

Places of interest nearby: Snape Maltings, Minsmere Bird Sanctuary, the Otter Trust at Earsham and the towns of Bury St Edmunds and Norwich. **Directions: One mile outside Fressingfield on the B1116 to Framlingham.**

In association with MasterCard

STANHILL COURT HOTEL

STANHILL ROAD, CHARLWOOD, NR HORLEY, SURREY RH6 0EP
TEL: 01293 862166 FAX: 01293 862773

OWNERS: Antonio and Kathryn Colas

13 rms | 13 ens

S: from £89
D: £95–£125

Built in 1881 in the Scottish Baronial style, Stanhill Court Hotel is set in 35 acres of ancient wooded countryside and offers spectacular views over the North Downs. It boasts an original Victorian walled garden and amphitheatre available for concerts or corporate presentations and events.

The hotel is traditionally furnished to provide an intimate, warm and comfortable atmosphere, with rich pitch pine panelling evident throughout the hall, minstrels gallery and barrel roof. There is a wide choice of bedrooms, all decorated and furnished to the same high standards and offering a full range of facilities.

A superb à la carte restaurant offers a menu which is international in flavour and complemented by an excellent range of regional and vintage wines. A choice of vegetarian dishes is always included and old style, friendly personal service is guaranteed.

Versatile conference facilities include small meetings rooms and a choice of five function rooms. Stanhill Court is also an excellent venue for wedding receptions, family celebrations and social gatherings.

Places of interest nearby: Leonardslee, High Beeches, Nymans and Wakehurst Place. **Directions: Charlwood is north west of the airport and reached off the M23/A23 via Hookwood or Lowfield Heath. Go through Charlwood and follow signs towards Newdigate.**

THE WIND IN THE WILLOWS

DERBYSHIRE LEVEL, GLOSSOP, DERBYSHIRE SK13 9PT
TEL: 01457 868001 FAX: 01457 853354

OWNERS: Anne Marsh and Peter Marsh
CHEF: Hilary Barton

12 rms | 12 ens | SMALL HOTEL

S: £65–£88
D: £85–£110

"Not so much a hotel, more a delightful experience" wrote a guest of this charming, small, family-run hotel on the edge of the Peak District. It won the AA Greatest Courtesy and Care in the North of England award 1996/97. The Mother-and-Son team of Anne and Peter Marsh have added lavish care, attention to detail and a sincere courtesy to their recipe of antiques, Victorian bric-à-brac and delightful charm that is characteristic of The Wind in the Willows. If you don't know how it gets its name, stay there and read your bedside book!

The marvellous scenery of the National Park is, literally, at the doorstep. All of the twelve, en-suite bedrooms enjoy superb views, and all are full of character, even the newer ones, opened in 1995, having their share of antique furniture and traditional decor that embellishes the whole house. There are some very special features, too – huge antique mahogany beds, a Victorian style bath and individual touches created by Anne in various rooms.

Anne also supervises in the kitchen from where delicious home-cooking is served to both the private dining room and the purpose-built meeting room. Local activities include pot-holing, riding, gliding and para/hang gliding.

Places of interest nearby: Glossop itself, a historic town mentioned in the *Domesday Book*, Peak District National Park, Derwent and Ladybower Reservoirs and the Pennines. **Directions: One mile east of Glossop on the A57, 400 yards down the road opposite the Royal Oak.**

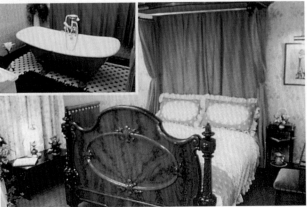

GOLANT BY FOWEY

THE CORMORANT HOTEL

GOLANT BY FOWEY, CORNWALL PL23 1LL
TEL: 01726 833426 FAX: 01726 833426

OWNERS: George and Estelle Elworthy

11 rms | 11 ens | SMALL HOTEL

S: £42–£57
D: £84

The Cormorant Hotel stands high above the beautiful Fowey Estuary with magnificent views over the shimmering waters and the Cornish countryside. A warm, friendly and inviting atmosphere pervades the hotel which is enjoying gradual artistic refurbishment.

There are 11 entirely individual bedrooms, all en suite and with colour television, radio, direct dial telephone and extensive views over the estuary and creeks. Guests can relax in an extremely comfortable lounge which has full length picture windows and a log fire in winter. The bar is small and welcoming. Guests can also enjoy lounging on the terrace by the hotel's heated swimming pool which has a sliding roof for opening on hot summer days.

This corner of Cornwall is a living larder of wholesome produce all made use of by enthusiastic chef-patron George Elworthy and served in a pretty candle lit restaurant. A choice of long and imaginative menus is offered.

Places of interest nearby: Miles of walking along the coastline, quaint fishing villages, Lanhydrock House and gardens, Trelissick garden and many National Trust properties. Fishing, riding and golf can be arranged locally.
Directions: From Exeter, take A30 towards Bodmin and then B3269 towards Fowey. After six miles turn left at a staggered junction to Golant. Bear right as you approach the estuary and continue along the water's edge. The hotel is on the right.

WHITE MOSS HOUSE

RYDAL WATER, GRASMERE, CUMBRIA LA22 9SE
TEL: 015394 35295 FAX: 015394 35516

OWNERS: Peter and Susan Dixon

8 rms | 8 ens | SMALL HOTEL

S: £74–£90
D: £128–£180
(including 5-course dinner)

Set in a fragrant garden of roses and lavender, White Moss House was once owned by Wordsworth, who often rested in the porch here between his wanderings. Built in 1730, it overlooks beautiful Rydal Water. Many famous and interesting walks through fells and lakeland start from the front door. Guests have free use of the local leisure club and swimming pool and free fishing on local rivers and lakes.

It has been described by a German gourmet magazine as 'probably the smallest, most splendid hotel in the world'. Proprietors Peter and Susan Dixon have created an intimate family atmosphere with a marvellous degree of comfort and attention to detail.

The seven bedrooms in the main house and the two in the Brockstone Cottage Suite are individually furnished, and most have lake views. Chef Peter Dixon has won international acclaim for his culinary skills including 2 AA rosettes and a Red Star. The restaurant is deservedly famous for food prepared with imagination and style – 'the best English food in Britain', said *The Times* – and offers an extensive wine list of over 300 bins.

Closed early December to early March.

Places of interest nearby: Dove Cottage and Rydal Mount (Wordsworth's houses) are both one mile away. **Directions: White Moss House is off the A591 between Rydal Water and Grasmere, on the right as you drive north to Grasmere.**

THE OLD RECTORY

GREAT SNORING, FAKENHAM, NORFOLK NR21 OHP
TEL: 01328 820597 FAX: 01328 820048

OWNERS: Rosamund and William Scoles

S: £69.50
D: £91

The Old Rectory, a former manor house, stands in 1¹/₂ acres of walled gardens amid the unspoilt countryside of North Norfolk. It is believed to date back to 1500, when it was the seat of Sir Ralph Shelton. The house was originally hexagonal and the south east façade has stone mullioned windows bordered with frieze designs in terracotta tiles. Development and restoration work during the Victorian era account for its present day appearance.

The timeless tradition of the Old Rectory's décor and furnishings creates an ambience of bygone days, with fresh flowers adding a homely touch to the surroundings. Each bedroom has a private bathroom, colour television and direct dial telephone.

Full English breakfast is served in the dining room and luncheon hampers are provided on request. Traditional English cuisine is a speciality.

For those who like to be cosseted, without the restrictions associated with traditional hotel service, the Sheltons cottage apartments are available. These are serviced and self contained providing guests complete privacy in delightful surroundings, ideal for family use. The house is closed from 24-27 December.

Places of interest nearby: Norfolk coast, nature reserves, Sandringham and Walsingham. **Directions: Great Snoring is 3 miles north-east of Fakenham from the A148 King's Lynn–Cromer road.**

THE OLD RECTORY

NEDGING, NR HADLEIGH, SUFFOLK
TEL/FAX: 01449 740745

OWNERS: Tess and Rupert Chetwynd

3 rms | 3 ens

S: £35–£40
D: £60–£80

If you are looking for peace and quiet, discover secret Nedging, a tiny hamlet surrounded by the beautiful rolling countryside which inspired artist John Constable. The enchanting Old Rectory is an elegant Georgian house standing in 2 acres of mature gardens. the Chetwynds have carefully renovated The Old Rectory, sympathetically adding modern comforts and restoring traditional Georgian features. The house is delightfully furnished and the individually decorated double bedrooms, with en suite bathrooms, all have lovely views over the gardens and adjoining fields. Nedging is near many ancient churches and medieval towns and villages with lovely colour-washed thatched cottages for which Suffolk is famous.

The excellent 3 or 4 course dinner can be enjoyed in an informal dinner party atmosphere en famille. Free range poultry and meat are used whenever possible with vegetables from the garden and breakfast eggs from the Old Rectory's own hens. A No Smoking House

Places of interest nearby: The ancient wool towns of Lavenham and Long Melford with their renowned antique centres; Bury St Edmunds with the remains of a 14th century Benedictine Abbey; Sudbury, birthplace of Thomas Gainsborough; East Bergholt and Dedham Vale, with the scenery of Constable's "Haywain". **Directions: ½ mile south of Bildeston take the small (unmarked) lane on the left. The Old Rectory is the first house (just before the Church)**

HAMPTON COURT (Hampton Wick)

In association
with MasterCard

CHASE LODGE

10 PARK ROAD, HAMPTON WICK, KINGSTON-UPON-THAMES, SURREY KT1 4AS
TEL: 0181 943 1862 FAX: 0181 943 9363

OWNERS: Nigel and Denise Stafford-Haworth

| 11 rms | 11 ens | SMALL HOTEL |

S: from £62
D: £85–£107

Chase Lodge is situated in Hampton Wick, adjacent to Bushy Park, in a conservation area of outstanding architectural and historical merit. Indeed, it is an ideal touring centre for places of historical interest such as Kew Gardens, Hampton Court Palace, Richmond Theatre and Royal Windsor.

Its proximity to so many major events makes Chase Lodge a popular choice for good accommodation. The Wimbledon Tournament, the Oxford and Cambridge Boat Race, racing at Kempton, Epsom, Ascot and Sandown, rugby at Twickenham and summer regattas at Kingston and Richmond are among the attractions within easy reach.

Originally built in 1870, Chase Lodge is a very successful small hotel, run with style and personality by proprietors Nigel and Denise Stafford-Haworth. The interiors have been designed to a high standard with well-chosen items of furniture and striking fabrics. The bedrooms, although not large, are beautifully appointed.

Private parties and functions can be accommodated.
Places of interest nearby: Hampton Court, Windsor Castle and Richmond Park. **Directions: From the centre of Kingston take the A308 towards Hampton Court. Just after Kingston bridge is the Hampton Wick roundabout; take the White Hart exit into High Street (A310), the left at The Forresters into Park Road.**

HAMSTERLEY FOREST (near Durham)

GROVE HOUSE

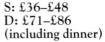

HAMSTERLEY FOREST, NR BISHOP AUCKLAND, CO DURHAM DL13 3ML
TEL: 01388 488203 FAX: 01388 488174

OWNERS: Helene and Russell Close

S: £36–£48
D: £71–£86
(including dinner)

Grove House nestles at the heart of a beautiful garden in the middle of glorious Hamsterley Forest. Two small rivers run, on each side of the property, through 5,000 acres of old oaks and moors. It is an idyllic situation. Peaceful, quiet and historical, the house was built in 1830 as an aristocrat's shooting box and it exudes grandeur. There are fine furnishings and fabrics, stylish decor and open fires. The bedrooms – a double with en suite bathroom, a twin with en suite shower and a twin with private bathroom – have full facilities and are extremely comfortable.

Helene Close prepares five course evening meals from the best fresh ingredients. Often on the set menu are venison and pheasant direct from the forest. Grove House is unlicensed so guests are invited to take their own wine.

Those requiring total seclusion can stay at the adjoining, fully fitted, three-bedroomed Grove Cottage which has a large patio and a hillside rock garden.
Places of interest nearby: Bowes Museum, Raby Castle, High Force waterfall, Killhope Wheel, Beamish Open Air Museum and Durham Cathedral. **Directions: From A1(M) turn off onto A68 and just over two miles after Toft Hill turn left, through Hamsterley Village until the sign for "The Grove". Turn right, then left and continue until right hand turn sign for Hamsterley Forest. Grove House is three miles further on.**

In association
with MasterCard **MasterCard**

THE WHITE HOUSE

10 PARK PARADE, HARROGATE, NORTH YORKSHIRE HG1 5AH
TEL: 01423 501388 FAX: 01423 527973

OWNER: Jennie Forster

| 10 rms | 10 ens | SMALL HOTEL |

MasterCard VISA AMERICAN EXPRESS

S: £68.50–£90
D: £90–£130

The White House enjoys a splendid location overlooking the Stray, 200 acres of parkland just a few minutes from the town centre. You will discover a unique residence in which luxury and comfort have blended with informality creating a relaxed atmosphere. The en suite bedrooms are individually furnished with designer fabrics and antiques together with full facilities.

The Venetian Room Restaurant offers a wide variety of exquisite and original dishes, with a very fine wine list.

Some of the many awards the hotel has achieved recently are 'Which?' County Hotel of the Year, A.C.E. Best Small Hotel, AA two Rosettes for cuisine, RAC Restaurant and Hospitality awards.

A perfect hotel for a private house party or wedding, where attantion to detail is a foregone conclusion.

Places of interest nearby: Harrogate is a spa town with its own Turkish bath, beautiful parks and gardens, numerous shops including antiques. Other attractions include Fountains Abbey, Harewood House and the Yorkshire Dales. **Directions: The White House is situated on The Stray and is set back from the A59. Request a map when booking for detailed directions.**

ROOKHURST GEORGIAN COUNTRY HOUSE HOTEL

WEST END, GAYLE, HAWES, NORTH YORKSHIRE DL8 3RT
TEL: 01969 667454 FAX: 01969 667454

OWNER: Iris Van der Steen

| 5 rms | 4 ens | SMALL HOTEL |

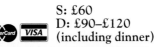

S: £60
D: £90–£120
(including dinner)

Nestling in the midst of Wensleydale, the front gate of this part-Georgian, part-Victorian country house opens onto the 250 mile-long Pennine Way. Visitors to Rookhurst are welcomed as friends by proprietress Iris Van der Steen. The cosy oak-beamed Georgian bedrooms and more spacious Victorian bedrooms are furnished with half-tester or four-poster beds: the Bridal Suite and master four-poster rooms are particularly ornate. Smoking is not permitted in the bedrooms or the dining room.

Iris specialises in traditional home-cooked English dishes, made with fresh produce. Dinner in the restaurant is a candle-lit ceremony.

A wood-burning stove creates a snug atmosphere in the sitting room and bar, where guests can relax with a drink. The hotel is closed during January. Special break rates available.

Places of interest nearby: Rookhurst makes an ideal base for exploring Herriot country – the Yorkshire Dales are a delight for both serious walkers and strollers. Nearby is the Carlisle to Settle railway and you can be collected from Garsdale Station. Just round the corner is the Wensleydale Creamery, and in Hawes the Upper Dales folk museum. **Directions: Take A684 Sedbergh–Bedale road. At Hawes take Gayle Lane to Gayle. At the top of the lane turn right and the hotel is 300 yards further on the right.**

SIMONSTONE HALL

HAWES, NORTH YORKSHIRE DL8 3LY
TEL: 01969 667255 FAX: 01969 667741

HOSTS: John and Christine Simmons
CHEF: Steven Faulkner

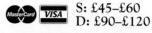 S: £45–£60
D: £90–£120

20 rms   20 ens

Fine cuisine, comfort, peace and tranquillity combine with breathtaking scenery to make any stay at Simonstone Hall totally memorable. This former Tudor hunting lodge has been lovingly restored and furnished with antiques to create an idyllic retreat for its guests. The Hall, which stands in 5 acres of beautiful landscaped gardens, has recently been totally refurbished. The very best has been retained being rich in period features such as panelled dining room, maghogany staircase with ancestral stained glass windows and a lounge with ornamental fire place and ceilings. The 20 bedrooms have been redecorated to the highest standards and offer every modern comfort. The culinary delights include tempting dishes such as escalope of salmon, gently grilled with lemon butter; prime fillet of beef wrapped with bacon coated with a Burgundy wine sauce. An excellent wine list is available to complement any dish. Fine meals served in the Game Tavern which provides a particularly warm and local atmosphere. Simonstone Hall, with its spectacular views, is the perfect base for enjoying and exploring the hidden Yorkshire Dales.

Places of interest nearby: The area abounds with ancient castles, churches and museums, and Hardraw Force, England's highest single drop waterfall which can be heard from the gardens, is only a walk away. **Directions: Hawes is on the A684. Turn North on the Buttertubs Pass towards Muker. Simonstone Hall is 1½ miles on the left.**

BEL ALP HOUSE

HAYTOR, NR BOVEY TRACEY, SOUTH DEVON TQ13 9XX
TEL: 01364 661217 FAX: 01364 661292

OWNERS: Jack, Mary and Rachael Twist
CHEF: Ian Davidson

In association with MasterCard

8 rms | 8 ens | SMALL HOTEL

S: £60
D: £120–£130

Peace and seclusion are guaranteed at the Bel Alp House with its spectacular outlook from the edge of Dartmoor across a rolling patchwork of fields and woodland to the sea, 20 miles away.

Built as an Edwardian country mansion and owned in the 1920s by millionairess Dame Violet Wills, Bel Alp has been lovingly restored and the proprietors' personal attention ensures their guests' enjoyment and comfort in the atmosphere of a private home.

The set dinner is changed nightly, using only the best local produce, and the meals are accompanied by a well-chosen and comprehensive wine list.

Of the eight en suite bedrooms, two still have their original Edwardian basins and baths mounted on marble plinths, and all bedrooms have views over the gardens.

An abundance of house plants, open log fires and restful colours complements the family antiques and pictures to create the perfect environment in which to relax. Awarded an AA Rosette.

Places of interest nearby: Bel Alp is ideally situated for exploring Devon and parts of Cornwall. Plymouth, famed for Drake and the Pilgrim Fathers, Exeter with its Norman cathedral, and National Trust properties Castle Drogo and Cotehele Manor House are all within an hour's drive. **Directions: Bel Alp House is off the B3387 Haytor road, 2½ miles from Bovey Tracey.**

TREGILDRY HOTEL

GILLAN, MANACCAN, HELSTON, CORNWALL TR12 6HG
TEL: 01326 231378 FAX: 01326 231561

OWNERS: Huw and Lynne Phillips

10 rms · 10 ens · SMALL HOTEL

S: £55–£60
D: £100–£120
(including dinner)

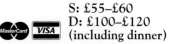

This elegant small hotel with charm and style lies in a tranquil corner of the Lizard Peninsula overlooking the Helford River with spectacular, panoramic views across Falmouth Bay and the Cornish Coastline. The home of Huw and Lynne Phillips, who manage the hotel in true country house style, Tregildry is for those who enjoy relaxed comfort in away from it all surroundings for this is a magically unspoilt, uncrowded corner of Cornwall.

The lounges are elegant and spacious with panoramic seaviews, comfy sofas, fresh flowers and the latest books and magazines. The restaurant, awarded 2 Rosettes by the AA, continues the large, light, glamourous theme and features modern British dishes with a French influence and fresh local produce.

The ten en suite bedrooms, mostly with seaviews, are pretty and bright with elegant cane furnishings and exotic, colourful fabrics.

The area has been designated one of Outstanding Natural Beauty and the hotel's private path to the coast makes it an ideal starting point for glorious coastal walks

Places of interest nearby: Trebah, Glendurgan, Heligan and many other celebrated Cornish gardens. Art galleries, quaint fishing villages, uncrowded beaches. **Directions: From Helston join A3083 towards Lizard and take first left for St Keverne. Follow signs for Manaccan and then Gillan.**

NANSLOE MANOR

MENEAGE ROAD, HELSTON, CORNWALL TR13 0SB
TEL: 01326 574691 FAX: 01326 564680

OWNERS: The Ridden Family

 7 rms | 6 ens | SMALL HOTEL

 S: £45–£59 D: £75–£120

This enchanting Georgian manor stands in romantic Daphne du Maurier country, and guests are instantly aware they are coming to somewhere very special, as they approach the house along the tree lined drive.

Discovering Nansloe is serendipity – peaceful, surrounded by verdant, rural countryside, the hotel is owned (and managed) by the Ridden family, who have personally added so much to its warm ambience.

The bedrooms have lovely views across the Loe Valley. Each differs from the next, all are spacious and luxurious, with curtains and covers in gorgeous fabrics.

The drawing room has a fine Victorian fireplace, a welcome sight on cool evenings. It is charmingly furnished, big bowls of fresh flowers adding colour; the overall effect is relaxing – the ideal spot for a traditional Cornish tea or aperitif, in summer enjoyed al fresco on the croquet lawn.

The restaurant is famed for its inspired menus, featuring local specialities including fish fresh from the sea, and the cellar contains excellent wines.

Places of interest nearby: Helston, Falmouth, St Ives and many gardens. Golf and sailing. Special breaks are available. **Directions:** The Manor is well signed close to the junction of A394 from Falmouth and A3083 to the Lizard.. **Directions: At the end of a well signed drive some 300 yards from junction of A394 from Falmouth and A3083 to the Lizard.**

THE BOWENS COUNTRY HOUSE

FOWNHOPE, HEREFORDSHIRE HR1 4PS
TEL: 01432 860430 FAX: 01432 860430

OWNERS: Carol and Tony Hart

S: from £30
D: from £60

Surrounded by one-and-a-half acres of mature garden and the outstanding natural beauty of the peaceful Wye Valley this stone-built 17th century renovated farmhouse provides every modern comfort while retaining its bygone charm and character. It stands on the eastern edge of the village of Fownhope, nestling beneath wooded slopes once the sites of Iron Age hill forts, of which there are many in the area. The fish filled River Wye meanders through meadows south of the village.

The hotel's spacious lounge opens onto the garden and features a magnificent inglenook discovered during recent alterations. There is a cosy sitting room with log fires in winter and the en suite bedrooms offer every up-to-date facility and superb views over the garden and the village's 11th century church.

Traditional English cuisine is served in the compact restaurant. Tucked away in the garden are a putting green, croquet lawn and tennis court. Golf, riding, canoeing, fishing and horse racing are within easy reach.

Places of interest nearby: Hereford, Ross-on-Wye and the beauties and attractions of the Wye Valley.
Directions: From the M50, exit at junction 4 and join the A449 towards Ledbury. After approximately two-and-a-half miles turn onto the B4224 to Fownhope.

THE STEPPES

ULLINGSWICK, NR HEREFORD, HEREFORDSHIRE HR1 3JG
TEL: 01432 820424 FAX: 01432 820042

OWNERS: Henry and Tricia Howland

6 rms | 6 ens

S: from £45
D: from £80

A Grade II listed 17th-century yeoman's house, The Steppes is located in Ullingswick, a *Domesday Book* hamlet set in the Wye Valley. The gleaming whitewashed exterior conceals a host of original features. Cobble and flag-flooring, massive oak timbers and an inglenook fireplace were part of the ancient dairy and cider-making cellars, which form the splendid cellar bar and lounge.

Winner of the Johansens 1996 "Value for Money Award, the ambience of the house has been applauded by *The Sunday Telegraph*, *The Guardian* and *The Independent* newspapers – all of which praise the enthusiasm and hospitality of owners Henry and Tricia Howland and, in particular, Tricia's cooking. The candle-lit dinners are compiled from medieval recipes, revived local dishes, Mediterranean delicacies and French cuisine. The interesting breakfast menu is complemented by generous service. Exceptionally high standard en suite accommodation is provided in either the Tudor Barn or Courtyard Cottage, both located within the grounds. Closed for two weeks before Christmas and three weeks after New Year.

Places of interest nearby: River Wye (salmon fishing), Black Mountains, Malvern Hills (Elgar's birthplace), Welsh Marches, Gloucester and Worcester. Riding can be arranged. **Directions: A mile off A417 Gloucester-–Leominster, signed Ullingswick.**

THE BELFRY COUNTRY HOTEL

YARCOMBE, NR HONITON, DEVON EX14 9BD
TEL: 01404 861234 FAX: 01404 861579

OWNERS: Tony and Jackie Rees
CHEF: Jackie Rees

| 6 rms | 6 ens |

S: £44
D: £68

This flint and Portland stone building, originally the local school, was a gift to the village from the Drake family, whose coat of arms is carved above one of the stained glass windows. The foundation stone was laid by Lady Eliott Drake, a direct descendant of Sir Francis.

The building exudes warmth and welcome, comfort and relaxation. The six bedrooms have a country cottage atmosphere, are fully en suite, comprehensively equipped, and have lovely countryside views. The public rooms are cosily furnished and the Chimes Restaurant is totally pine-clad, with corner bar and bench seats around a log fire. Guests return time and time again for Jackie's scrumptious home-cooking which has been awarded an AA rosette, and the wine list is carefully selected and modest in price.

The unusual design of the building is unsuitable for children, but the 2 ground floor bedrooms are easily accessible for the elderly or disabled. Restaurant and bedrooms are non-smoking. There is much to see and do, especially for garden lovers – complimentary entry to 11 classic gardens is available to residents. Honiton has nearly 40 Antique shops and 3 Salerooms; there are 4 National Hunt racecourses close by, and all the usual country sports. Special two-day plus breaks are available all year.

Places of interest nearby: Forde Abbey, Killerton House, Montacute House. **Directions: On A30 midway between Honiton and Chard.**

UNDERLEIGH HOUSE

OFF EDALE ROAD, HOPE, HOPE VALLEY, DERBYSHIRE S33 6RF
TEL: 01433 621372 FAX: 01433 621324

OWNERS: Barbara and Tony Singleton

| 5 rms | 5 ens | |

S: £40–£45
D: £60–£66

Underleigh House is set on a hillside, less than 2 miles from the centre of the ancient Saxon village of Hope in the glorious Peak District National Park. Every bedroom in the house has either a countryside view or one over the lovely award winning garden which in summer displays colourful tubs and baskets, roses. and honeysuckle. A full range of modern amenities makes guests feel at home, including a colour TV, radio alarm clock, hair dryer, tea and coffee making facilities and a resident teddy bear! Underleigh has a 5Q Premier Award from the AA.

Breakfast and evening meals are served in "house party" style around the scrubbed top kitchen table or the oak refectory table in the stone flagged dining hall. There is a choice of a hearty English breakfast or, for the smaller appetite, a continental breakfast, while an interesting and the daily changing menu has a wide selection of dishes available for the evening.

Half day pony treks start from the Edale centre and there is an abundance of golf courses. Cycle hire centres cater for those who wish to enjoy the scenery on wheels.
Places of interest nearby: Chatsworth, Haddon and Hardwick. The historic villages of Hope, Castleton, Hathersage and "Plague" Eyam are within a five mile radius. **Directions: From Hope take turning opposite church to Edale, one mile on where road bears right take left lane. Underleigh House is ¹/₃ mile on right.**

DALE HEAD HALL LAKESIDE HOTEL

THIRLMERE, KESWICK, CUMBRIA CA12 4TN
TEL: 017687 72478 FAX: 017687 71070 FREEPHONE: 0800 454166 E-MAIL: daleheadho@aol.com

OWNERS: Alan and Shirley Lowe and family

9 rms 9 ens SMALL HOTEL

S: £78–£95
D: £105–£160
(including 5 course dinner)

On the edge of Thirlmere, "the lake in the hollow", with only the sound of the birds breaking the silence stands Dale Head Hall. It is a truly scenic gem. At the foot of Helvellyn, almost completely surrounded by lush woodlands, this glorious 16th century house reigns alone on the shores of the lake and must surely command one of the most tranquil settings in the Lake District. Hosts Alan and Shirley Lowe and family, having restored the 16th century authenticity of the house, now offer exceptional accommodation and service. The hotel was deservedly runner-up for the Johansens 1995 Most Excellent Country House Hotel.

Bar and lounge are both delightful, sharing views over lake and mountains. The oak panelled dining room is the ideal place to enjoy the hotel's superb cuisine (Michelin; Good Food Guide; AA Red Rosette; RAC Restaurant Award). The bedrooms are extremely welcoming, warm and spacious and have all the things that you will expect to find, plus those little extras that make your stay so very special. Dale Head is one of those wonderful secrets which you would like to keep for yourself. Internet: WWW:http://home.aol.com/daleheadho

Places of interest nearby: All the splendours of the Lake District: Helvellyn is on the doorstep and Borrowdale is close by. **Directions: On the A591, halfway between Keswick and Grasmere. The hotel is situated along a private driveway overlooking Lake Thirlmere.**

In association with MasterCard

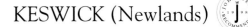

SWINSIDE LODGE HOTEL

GRANGE ROAD, NEWLANDS, KESWICK, CUMBRIA CA12 5UE
TEL/FAX: 017687 72948

OWNER: Graham Taylor

9 rms | 9 ens | SMALL HOTEL

S: £72–£85
D: £128–£160
(including dinner)

Swinside Lodge, situated at the foot of Catbells, is a Victorian lakeland house, surrounded by hills, valleys and woodland, and close to the shores of Derwentwater.

The house has nine attractive en suite bedrooms, each offering a high degree of comfort and equipped with colour TV, radio, hairdryer, tea making facilities plus a wealth of extras. Begin your day with a hearty Cumbrian breakfast and later return to the comfort of the charming sitting rooms before enjoying your five-course dinner in the intimate candle-lit dining room. Menus change daily and a typical meal could include fillet of cod on a bed of salad of crushed potatoes with a dill vinagrette, a delicious soup with home-baked rolls followed by pan-fried breast and stuffed leg of guinea fowl with a red wine and shallot sauce with freshly cooked vegetables. A choice of puddings or a variety of British farmhouse cheeses is followed by coffee.

An AA Red Star hotel with 2 Rosettes for food and ETB 3 Crown De Luxe, Swinside Lodge is non-smoking and unlicensed but guests are welcome to bring wine of their own choice. Closed from mid-December to mid-February.
Places of interest nearby: Keswick Pencil Museum, Castlerigg Stone Circle, Wordsworth's birthplace, excellent walks from the house. **Directions: M6 junction 40 take the A66 bypassing Keswick – over main roundabout – take second left. Go through Portinscale towards Grange; hotel is two miles further on the right.**

THE GRANGE COUNTRY HOUSE HOTEL

MANOR BROW, KESWICK-ON-DERWENTWATER, CUMBRIA CA12 4BA
TEL: 017687 72500

OWNERS: Duncan and Jane Miller

10 rms | 10 ens | SMALL HOTEL

S: £57–£64
D: £94–£108
(including 5 course dinner)

Standing in its own secluded grounds, The Grange commands views over Keswick-On-Derwentwater and the surrounding fells. The imposing lakeland house dates from the 1840s and is furnished with numerous antiques. The bedrooms all have en suite bathrooms or showers and some have romantic half-tester beds.

The award-winning restaurant has a varied menu which may include crab and asparagus tart and coronation chicken with Waldorf salad followed by a wonderful home-made soup, duck breast with a red plum sauce or medallions of pork fillet with apple and cider. Tempting sweets include hot puddings like spiced apple tart with an almond crunch top or mango and passion fruit crème brulée. The wine list includes labels from Europe, Australia and South America.

The hotel also has a cocktail bar, a quiet reading lounge and a coffee lounge. The garden is lovely. Closed mid-November to mid-March.

Places of interest nearby: Many spectacular walks are to be had across the fells. Local attractions include numerous National Trust Properties, the Castlerigg Stone Circle, Mirehouse, Wordsworth's Dove Cottage, the Pencil Museum and all the beauties of the Lake District.

Directions: Leave M6 at junction 40. Take A66 into Keswick then go left on to A591 to Windermere for ¹/₂ mile. Take first right, hotel 200 yards on right.

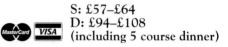

In association with MasterCard

THE WHITE HOUSE

CHILLINGTON, KINGSBRIDGE, DEVON TQ7 2JX
TEL: 01548 580580 FAX: 01548 581124

OWNERS: Michael Roberts and David Alford

8 rms	8 ens	SMALL HOTEL

S: £43–£60
D: £68–£94

Standing in lawned and terraced gardens in rural South Devon, The White House has an atmosphere reminiscent of a quieter and less hurried age. A period Grade II listed building of great charm, the hotel is an ideal base for exploring the countryside and coastline.

To the west is the busy market town of Kingsbridge and the Salcombe Estuary famous for its sailing. To the north are Totnes, Dartington and the wild expanses of Dartmoor. Historic Dartmouth, Torquay and the English Riviera are to the east, and south is the spectacular South Hams coastline with its rugged cliffs, sandy beaches and quiet coves.

The White House offers the utmost comfort with well-proportioned bedrooms, two of which are spacious suites.

Guests can relax in the elegant Brockington Room and Doctor Smalley's Drawing Room which opens onto the south-facing terrace and garden. The Bar Lounge is another comfortable meeting place.

The Garden Room Restaurant makes a delightful setting for enjoying appetising cuisine prepared by chef David Alford who makes the maximum use of local and seasonal produce.

Places of interest nearby: Kingsbridge, Totnes, Salcombe, Dartmouth, numerous picturesque villages and several National Trust properties. **Directions: Leave Totnes on the A381 to Kingsbridge and then turn left onto the A379 Dartmouth road to Chillington.**

HIPPING HALL

COWAN BRIDGE, KIRKBY LONSDALE, CUMBRIA LA6 2JJ
TEL: 015242 71187 FAX: 015242 72452

OWNERS: Ian and Jocelyn Bryant

7 rms 7 ens

MasterCard VISA AMERICAN EXPRESS

S: £69
D: £84

Hipping Hall is a 17th century country house set in three acres of walled gardens on the Cumbria/North Yorkshire borders, so an ideal centre from which to tour both the Lake District and Yorkshire Dales. Having just five double rooms and two cottage suites, this is an especially suitable venue for small groups wanting a place to themselves – families or friends celebrating an anniversary, golfing parties, corporate entertaining etc – and these house parties (available throughout the year) are a feature of Hipping Hall's success.

But from March to November it is mostly individual guests who enjoy the comfort and informality of staying with Ian and Jocelyn. The well-equipped bedrooms are largely furnished with antiques and all have attractive bathrooms. Guests help themselves to drinks from a sideboard in the conservatory before dining together at a large table in the Great Hall in a very informal dinner party style. Dinner is a set five course menu (including vegetarian dishes by prior request), served with three wines (optional) selected by Ian for that particular menu. All dishes are freshly prepared by Jocelyn, whose cooking draws so many people back to Hipping Hall.

Places of interest nearby: The Lake District, The Yorkshire Dales, The Settle to Carlisle Railway, Brontë country, Sizergh Castle. **Directions: Hipping Hall lies on the A65, two miles east of Kirkby Lonsdale towards Settle & Skipton, eight miles from M6 junction 36.**

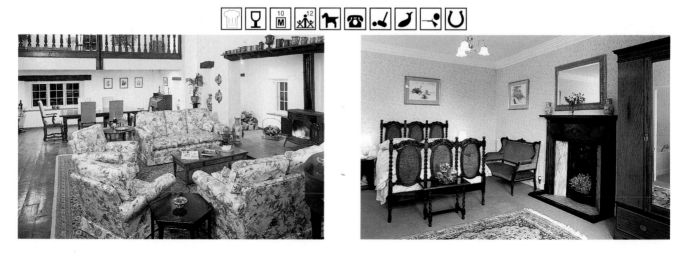

LAVENHAM PRIORY

WATER STREET, LAVENHAM, SUFFOLK CO10 9RW
TEL: 01787 247404 FAX: 01787 248472

OWNERS: Tim and Gilli Pitt

| 3 rms | 3 ens | |

S: £45–£55
D: £60–£90

The magnificent timber-framed Priory was originally a 13th-century hall house and the home of Benedictine monks. Over succeeding centuries it passed through a number of illustrious families, including the Earls of Oxford. Although considerable alterations have been made through the ages, The Priory retains many original features. Ceilings are high and mullioned windows, exposed beams, flagged and oak boarded floors abound.

The Priory stands as a historical and intriguing bridge between past and present, a comfortable family home with modern furnishings and amenities.

At its heart is the heavily beamed Great Hall with a massive Tudor inglenook fireplace and a solid Jacobean staircase leading to the principal bedchambers decorated with Elizabethan wall-paintings. The bedrooms are spacious and comfortably furnished.

Guests can enjoy summer breakfast or a quiet drink in the sheltered herb garden surrounded by three acres of grounds. Dinner is by arrangement.

Places of interest nearby: Medieval Lavenham, the market town of Sudbury, birthplace of painter Thomas Gainsborough and many National Trust properties.
Directions: From Bury St Edmunds join A134 towards Sudbury then A1141 to Lavenham. From Colchester join A134 signed Sudbury. Take by-pass, signed Long Melford, right onto B1115 which becomes B1071 to Lavenham.

LOWER BACHE

KIMBOLTON, NR LEOMINSTER, HEREFORDSHIRE HR6 OER
TEL: 01568 750304

OWNERS: Rose and Leslie Wiles

| 4 rms | 4 ens | |

S: £31.50
D: £53

A Johansens award winner 4 miles from historic Leominster, Lower Bache is an oasis for nature lovers in 14 acres of a gentle Herefordshire valley. This substantial 17th century stone farmhouse has been restored by Rose and Leslie Wiles. While retaining its exposed stone walls, wealth of oak beams and flagstone flooring, it incorporates all the comforts of modern living. ETB Highly Commended. An annexe of three en suite bedrooms is furnished in a charming cottage style. Each bedroom has its own private sitting room. Also available is a similar suite at ground floor level. Watercolours, original prints, plants, books and ornaments create an atmosphere of quality and comfort. With its vaulted ceiling and original cider press, the dining room is unique. Rose and Leslie are acclaimed gourmet cooks: the four-course set menu is superb value. Bread, ice-cream and preserves are all home-made; fish, game and poultry are smoked on the premises and most of the vegetables are grown organically in the garden. The breakfast menu offers an exceptional choice including laverbread, kedgeree, sautie bannocks, floddies and scrambled eggs with smoked salmon. Organic wines are also available.

Places of interest nearby: Welsh Marches, Ludlow, Tenbury Wells, Hereford, Worcester and Hay-on-Wye. **Directions: Kimbolton village is 2 miles north-east of Leominster (which is off the A49). Lower Bache is signposted at the top of the hill on the Leysters road A4112.**

THE THATCHED COTTAGE
COUNTRY HOTEL AND RESTAURANT

SPRYTOWN, LIFTON, DEVON PL16 0AY
TEL: 01566 784224 FAX: 01566 784334

OWNERS: Garth and Rita Willing and Victoria Bryant and Janet Purr

S: £38.50–£49.50
D: £77–£99

Nestling on the edge of Dartmoor in 2½ acres of landscaped gardens, The Thatched Cottage Country Hotel & Restaurant is just 1 mile from the Saxon village of Lifton. The bedrooms are situated in a converted coach house a few yards from the main thatched house. All rooms are decorated in a charming cottage style and have lovely views of the surrounding countryside.

The 16th century thatched cottage houses the restaurant, where a leisurely breakfast is served until 10am. The restaurant has been awarded two stars and a rosette by the AA for food and service. The menu which changes regularly plus an extensive wine list offers a varied and imaginative choice for the gourmet.

The lounge, with its inglenook fireplace, comfortable armchairs and cosy atmosphere, is the ideal place to enjoy apértifs, after-dinner coffee, liqueurs and petits fours.

The premises are unsuitable for very young children.

Places of interest nearby: Well placed for exploring Exmoor, Bodmin Moor and Dartmoor. This is an area rich in sites of historical, architectural and archaeological interest. **Directions: From Exeter follow A30 for about 35 miles. Leave A30 at Stowford Cross. At the top of the slip road at the T-junction turn left (the hotel is signposted) and travel to Sprytown Cross, straight across, the hotel drive is 100 yards on right.**

LINCOLN

D'ISNEY PLACE HOTEL

EASTGATE, LINCOLN, LINCOLNSHIRE LN2 4AA
TEL: 01522 538881 FAX: 01522 511321

OWNERS: David and Judy Payne

S: £56.50–£65
D: £72–£93

The D'Isney Place Hotel lies in the heart of the old city of Lincoln, with its steep, cobbled streets and historic buildings. Just 100 metres away is the famous triple-towered Cathedral – the ancient Cathedral Close Wall forms the southern boundary of the hotel's gardens.

Built in 1735 for John D'Isney, the house was extended in Queen Victoria's reign and now offers elegant and luxurious accommodation in well-proportioned single, double, twin and family bedrooms. These light and airy rooms are highly individual in style and offer full modern facilities – as well as some nice personal touches such as fluffy towelling bathrobes. Several have a Jacuzzi bath.

An English or Continental breakfast is served in the bedroom on Minton china and, although there are no dining facilities, many good restaurants and bistros are just minutes away.

A spacious self-catering cottage with two double en suite bedrooms, living room, dining room and modern kitchen is also available.

Places of interest nearby: Lincoln Cathedral, Lincoln Castle, Burghley House, and Belvoir Castle. The city is world famous for its Christmas market, usually held in early December, and nearby Horncastle is excellent for antiques' shopping. **Directions: From A1 take the A57 or A46 and continue to north entry of city and follow signs for cathedral and Eastgate.**

WASHINGBOROUGH HALL

CHURCH HILL, WASHINGBOROUGH, LINCOLN LN4 1BE
TEL: 01522 790340 FAX: 01522 792936

OWNERS: Mary and Brian Shillaker

S: £56.50–£69
D: £79.50–£91.50

This listed Georgian Manor House is set in three acres of secluded grounds, containing many mature trees and some wonderful displays of fuchsias and begonias. There is also a large lawned area where guests can play croquet.

The individually and prettily furnished bedrooms offer a full range of modern comforts, with some having a four-poster bed, some a spa bath.

A good selection of real ales is served in the bar, while the Wedgwood Dining Room overlooks the garden and provides the perfect setting for a meal. The imaginative menu caters for all tastes and is complemented by an extensive list of carefully selected wines. RAC Restaurant Award and RAC Hospitality, Comfort and Restaurant Award. Guests at Washingborough Hall have access to the Canwick Golf Club and hard tennis courts.

Places of interest nearby: The city of Lincoln is just two miles away and has a magnificent 11th century cathedral and castle. A short drive away is the beautiful rolling countryside of the Lincolnshire Wolds with many unspoilt villages and market towns to visit. Aircraft buffs should head for The Battle of Britain Memorial Flight, The Aviation Heritage Centre and The Newark Air Museum.

Directions: From Lincoln take the B1188 towards Branston and then turn left onto the B1190 towards Bardney. Turn right (approx two miles) opposite telephone box. The Hall is 200 yards on the left.

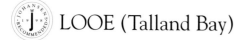

ALLHAYS COUNTRY HOUSE

TALLAND BAY, LOOE, CORNWALL PL13 2JB
TEL: 01503 272434 FAX: 01503 272929 E-MAIL: allhayscountryhouse@BTinternet.com

OWNERS: Brian and Lynda Spring

S: £28–£38
D: £56–£76

Set in its own gardens, just a few minutes' walk from the sea, Allhays stands on a gently sloping hillside overlooking Talland Bay. Situated between Looe and the fishing village of Polperro, it lies on a spectacular stretch of rugged coastline, much frequented by smugglers for many years. As a quiet retreat, Allhays is as attractive to those who wish to relax in comfort as it is to guests with a more energetic holiday in mind. Allhays is closed 24 December to 7 January.

The bedrooms, most of which offer magnificent views, have a radio alarm, tea/coffee making facilities and electric over-blankets for the out-of-season months. Until the arrival of summer a log fire blazes in the lounge, where drinks are served from the bar.

This corner of Cornwall is a living larder of wholesome produce – early vegetables, dairy cattle, Cornish cream, farmhouse cheese, garden herbs, soft fruits and fresh seafood are all made use of by chef-patronne, Lynda Spring. Food is cooked with an Aga in the traditional way, using recipes that have become an integral part of West Country life, and she has been awarded an AA rosette for her cuisine.

Places of interest nearby: Miles of walking along National Trust coastline, quaint fishing villages and the smugglers museum of Polperro. Water sports, riding and golf can be arranged locally. **Directions: From Looe take the A387 signposted to Polperro. After approximately 2 miles you will see Allhays signposted on the left-hand side.**

In association with MasterCard

COOMBE FARM

WIDEGATES, NR LOOE, CORNWALL PL13 1QN
TEL: 01503 240223 FAX: 01503 240895

OWNERS: Alexander and Sally Low

9 rms 9 ens

S: £26–£36
D: £52–£72

Coombe Farm was originally part of a large estate and the house was built in 1928 for a nephew of the landowner. It enjoys magnificent views down an unspoilt wooded valley to the sea and is set in 10½ acres of lawns, meadows, woods, streams and ponds.

A warm, friendly and relaxed atmosphere pervades the house, which has been carefully furnished with antiques and paintings. Open log fires in the winter months add to the sense of comfort and cosiness. All the bedrooms offer lovely country views and are cheerfully decorated and centrally heated.

A full English breakfast is served at Coombe Farm and in the evening a four-course dinner is available in the lovely candlelit dining room. The traditional menu is changed daily and vegetarians are well catered for.

There are over three acres of lawns where guests are invited to soak up the sun, play croquet or swim in the heated outdoor swimming pool and there is a snug stone outhouse for snooker and table tennis. The farm is closed to guests from 1 November to 1 March.

Places of interest nearby: Coombe Farm is ideal for visiting all parts of Cornwall and most of Devon – The Coastal Path, fishing villages, old smuggling coves and beaches. Dartmoor and Bodmin Moor, many superb National Trust houses and gardens. **Directions: B3253 just south of Widegates village, 3½ miles east of Looe.**

DELBURY HALL

DIDDLEBURY, CRAVEN ARMS, SHROPSHIRE SY7 9DH
TEL: 01584 841267 FAX: 01584 841441 E-MAIL: wrigley@delbury.demon.co.uk

OWNERS: Patrick and Lucinda Wrigley

| 3 rms | 1 ens |

S: £50
D: £80–£90

Delbury, built in 1753 and probably Shropshire's most beautiful Georgian mansion, faces south across water meadows to medieval Ludlow, with a backdrop of the Clee Hills and the Wenlock Edge. Approached through 80 acres of landscaped parkland, the house is in a tranquil setting, surrounded by flower-filled gardens and overlooking a lake with ornamental ducks.

Delbury is a family house with bedrooms available for guests, one with a four-poster, one with a half-tester, all with private bathrooms (one en suite) and all recently restored to a high standard. The large entrance hall has the original oak staircase, leading up to a first floor gallery on three sides and there is a large drawing room and sitting rooms for guests' use.

Guests dine at one large table in the dining room, where Patrick, an enthusiastic cook, who has completed an advanced course at Leith's School of Food and Wine in London, serves the finest home produced food; smoked salmon from the house smoker, home cured prosciutto, fresh vegetables from the walled garden, eggs and hand-churned butter.

Places of interest nearby: Ludlow Castle. Offa's Dyke (built centuries ago to fend off the Welsh), Stokesay Castle, a 13th century manor house five miles away, and the Severn Valley Steam Railway. **Directions: On the B4368 between Craven Arms and Much Wenlock.**

Overton Grange Hotel

OVERTON, LUDLOW, SHROPSHIRE SY8 4AD
TEL: 01584 873500 FAX: 01585 873500

OWNERS: Grange Hotels Ltd

16 rms | 16 ens

S: £55
D: £81-£92

The setting of Overton Grange Hotel, which stands in 2½ acres of peaceful gardens overlooking the scenic Shropshire countryside, would be hard to rival for guests seeking to relax and refresh their spirits. A genuinely friendly and courteous staff delivers a first class personal service.

Most of the generously sized and elegant bedrooms offer excellent views over the landscape and have been individually designed with the highest standards of comfort in mind. Similar attention to detail has ben paid in the spacious and attractive public rooms. For a quiet drink there is a choice of location – the cosy cocktail bar or the conservatory, which opens out onto the gardens and patio.

A comfortable oak-panelled restaurant is the setting in which to enjoy the gastronomic delights of the chef – slowly roasted rabbit with sun dried tomatoes and bubble and squeak; lobster and scallops with asparagus and coriander; or grilled lamb, beef and quail with mustard mash.

Sporting facilities such as tennis, swimming, fishing, golf and riding are all available within the local area.

Places of interest nearby: The hotel is only 1½ miles from the centre of the beautiful country town of Ludlow with its impressive castle and interesting museum. Stokesay Castle and Berrington Hall are also within easy reach. **Directions: From A49 take B4361 Ludlow-Richard Castle road. The hotel is about ¼ mile along this road.**

 In association with MasterCard

LITTLE OFFLEY

HITCHIN, HERTFORDSHIRE SG5 3BU
TEL: 01462 768243 FAX: 01462 768243

OWNERS: Martin and Lady Rosemary French

 S: £50
D: £65

Set in 800 acres of farmland in the Chiltern Hills, Little Offley is a beautiful 17th century house with wonderful views over the garden and surrounding countryside. One complete wing of the house has been set aside for guests, and it provides a quiet haven comprising a large drawing room with a listed carved fireplace, dining room and 3 double bedrooms with bathrooms. The rooms are spacious and comfortable and there is an outdoor swimming pool and croquet lawn available for guests' use in summer.

Accommodation is offered on a bed-and-breakfast basis. Lunch and dinner for larger groups can be provided, as can meetings, small exhibitions and receptions.

Alternatively, there are 5 pubs – 4 of them with excellent restaurants – in the nearby village of Great Offley, 1½ miles away. Guests may leave their car at the house when flying from Luton Airport. No children under 12.

Places of interest nearby: Little Offley is an ideal touring base from which to visit Hatfield House, Luton Hoo and Whipsnade Zoo, Woburn Abbey and Cambridge. The nearest town is Hitchin, which has large open-air markets on Tuesdays and Saturdays. London is 30 minutes by train. **Directions: Take A505 Luton–Hitchin road. At Great Offley, turn off for Little Offley.**

MOOR VIEW HOUSE

VALE DOWN, LYDFORD, DEVON EX20 4BB
TEL: 01822 820220

OWNERS: David and Wendy Sharples
CHEF: Wendy Sharples

4 rms | 4 ens | SMALL HOTEL

S: £45–£55
D: £74–£98

This small country house was built in 1869 and has offered hospitality to the traveller throughout its life. In the early years the Victorian writer Eden Phillpotts was a regular visitor and it was here that he was inspired to write his most successful play, "A Farmer's Wife", and also "Widdicombe Fair". The property faces Dartmoor from the front, while to the rear are spectacular views across the Devon and Cornwall countryside. Wonderful vistas of the landscape are lit by the setting sun.

Always putting their guests' comfort first, the Sharples family has created a friendly hotel with a genuinely relaxing ambience. The reception rooms reflect the cheery glow of open fires, and tasteful furnishings are a feature throughout. A Victorian decorative theme characterises the well-appointed bedrooms.

Sparkling crystal, bone china and gleaming silver in the dining room ensure that each meal is a special occasion. The daily four-course dinner menu embodies traditional country-style recipes using the finest local seasonal meat, fish and game, complimented by sound, sensibly priced wines.

Places of interest nearby: Lydford Gorge and Castle, Tavistock, Clovelly and Exeter. **Directions: From Exeter take A30 Okehampton bypass to Sourton Cross. Then take A386 signposted to Tavistock; Moor View's drive is situated four miles along on the right.**

THATCH LODGE HOTEL

In association with MasterCard

THE STREET, CHARMOUTH, NR LYME REGIS, DORSET DT6 6PQ
TEL: 01297 560407 FAX: 01297 560407

OWNERS: Christopher and Andrea Worsfold
CHEF: Andrea Ashton-Worsfold

| 7 rms | 7 ens | | SMALL HOTEL |

D:£72–£80
Four Poster/Half-Tester:£90

For more than 600 years Thatch Lodge has been part of the village of Charmouth, where a Dorset river enters Lyme Bay. To the east is Golden Cap, the highest cliff on the south coast, and to the west Lyme Regis, with its romantic Cobb which featured both in 'The French Lieutenant's Woman' and Jane Austen's 'Persuasion'.

Thatch Lodge itself makes its own unique contribution to an Area of Outstanding Natural Beauty – thatched roofs, pink cobb walls, hanging baskets, oak beams, antiques, walled gardens and a 200 year old vine. Each of the bedrooms has its own character, some have four poster and half tester beds. Luxury toiletries, crisp sheets, courtesy tray, television and thoughtful extras add to your comfort. E.T.B.

3 Crowns Highly Commended. Totally non-smoking.

An outstanding feature of the 'Thatch' is the dining. Andrea, a qualified chef, cooks to order, using the freshest seasonal produce, resulting in a meal that will delight the eye and the palate. The Daily Mail comments "I have never tasted a soufflé as good/delicious/perfect". Awarded AA Rosette for cuisine.

Places of interest nearby: Dorset Heritage Coast, Thomas Hardy Trail, Abbotsbury Swannery and sub-tropical gardens, Montacute House (NT). Golf, tennis, riding, fishing, bird watching, walking and world renowned for fossil collecting on the beach. **Directions: Charmouth is off the A35, two miles east of Lyme Regis.**

THE GORDLETON MILL HOTEL

SILVER STREET, HORDLE, NR LYMINGTON, HAMPSHIRE SO41 6DJ
TEL: 01590 682219 FAX: 01590 683073

OWNER: William F. Stone
MANAGER: Toby Hill

| 7 rms | 7 ens | SMALL HOTEL |

MasterCard VISA AMERICAN EXPRESS

S: from £97
D: from £112

Hidden in the countryside between the New Forest National Park and the sea lies an ivy-clad 17th century Water Mill, now privately owned and sympathetically renovated to make a seven bedroomed luxury hotel. It is set in 5½ acres of landscaped, natural garden, with woods, fields, millpond, sluice gates, rustic bridges and lily pond creating a perfect riverside retreat.

Gordleton Mill is renowned too for the gastronomique delights of Toby Hills' nationally acclaimed 'Provence Restaurant', which has won a star from Egon Ronay, two red stars and four rosettes from the AA for its excellent food. Also rated 'Restaurant of the Year', Good Food Guide 1997.

This idyllic hotel boasts seven exquisitely furnished bedrooms all en suite including whirlpool baths and showers along with luxury towelling robes, flowers, bottled water, fruit and a complimentary half bottle of champagne to greet guests on their arrival. Four of the bedrooms are exclusively reserved for non-smokers.

Prices include a full English or continental breakfast, and unlimited tea and coffee throughout a guest's stay.

Places of interest nearby: Beaulieu. Bucklers Hard, Exbury Gardens, Romsey and Broadlands. **Directions: M27 junction 1. A337 south for 11 miles near Lymington after the railway bridge and mini roundabout turn sharp right before Toll House Inn, head towards Hordle and hotel is on right in about 1½ miles.**

LYNTON

HEWITT'S HOTEL

NORTH WALK, LYNTON, DEVON EX35 6HJ
TEL: 01598 752293 FAX: 01598 752489

OWNERS: Richard and Pat Stagg

S: £33–£36
D: £70–£88

Once the home of a distinguished Victorian, Sir Thomas Hewitt, this elegant and secluded 19th century country house hotel stands statuesquely high on the cliffs overlooking the sea to Wales. Its 27 acres of woodland and garden are a haven for wildlife, and visitors can enjoy breathtaking vistas as they stroll down through the grounds to Lynmouth Harbour 500 feet below.

Hewitt's is just minutes from the centre of Lynton and behind the hotel's grey stone walls there is only the Coastal Path, which meanders for miles through Exmoor.

Although having every modern facility, the Victorian character of the house has been beautifully retained. A sweeping oak staircase leads from the imposing reception area past a superb stained glass window by Burne-Jones. The ornate fire places and panelling in the lounges and bar provide a warm and friendly ambience.

All bedrooms are well furnished. Some have balconies and all but one face seawards. Visitors can also enjoy the wonderful views from the hotel's terrace and from the intimate dining room. Ample parking.

Places of interest nearby: Valley of the Rocks, Watersmeet, Arlington Court, the Rosemoor Gardens, Barnstaple and numerous National Trust properties.
Directions: From the M5 exit at junction 23, signposted Minehead, follow the A39 to Lynton.

MAIDSTONE (Boughton Monchelsea)
TANYARD

WIERTON HILL, BOUGHTON MONCHELSEA, NR MAIDSTONE, KENT ME17 4JT
TEL: 01622 744705 FAX: 01622 741998

OWNER: Jan Davies

 SMALL HOTEL

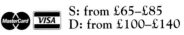 S: from £65–£85
D: from £100–£140

Standing within its own ten acres of garden with gently flowing stream, Tanyard is situated in the heart of rural Kent, with far-reaching views across the Kentish Weald. The features and ambience of this medieval farmhouse have been extremely well preserved – exposed beams and inglenook fireplaces abound.

The interiors have been decorated and furnished in a style sympathetic to the age and character of the house. Antique accoutrements are combined with up-to-date facilities to ensure guests' comfort. As well as the five bedrooms, a heavily beamed suite complete with spa bath is available. Occupying the whole top floor of the house, this suite affords particularly fine views.

Dating from about 1350AD the restaurant is the oldest part of the building previously used as a tannery. An imaginative menu is offered for dinner on seven evenings a week.

Winner of the Johansens Recommended Country Houses Award 1993.

Places of interest nearby: Optimally located for touring the 'Garden of England', Leeds Castle and Sissinghurst. The Channel ports, tunnel and Gatwick Airport are within an hour's drive. **Directions:** From the B2163 at Boughton Monchelsea turn opposite The Cock into Park Lane, right into Wierton Road, right again for Tanyard.

In association
with MasterCard

NEWSTEAD GRANGE

NORTON-ON-DERWENT, MALTON, NORTH YORKSHIRE YO17 9PJ
TEL: 01653 692502 FAX: 01653 696951

OWNERS: Pat and Paul Williams

S: £40–£48
D: £66–£82

Enclosed in 2½ acres of gardens and grounds, Newstead Grange is an elegant Georgian country house with wonderful views of the Wolds and Moors. Resident owners Paul and Pat Williams extend a warm welcome to their guests, who are assured of personal attention.

The Grange maintains the quality and style of a country house restored. It has antique furniture and original features including working shutters and fine fireplaces. Open fires are lit in cooler months in one or both of the lounges. Bedrooms, all individual in character, have period furniture, paintings and prints. The Celebration Room contains an antique mahogany half-tester bed. Menus are prepared from the extensive organic kitchen garden and the best local produce, recognised by the AA rosette award for fine food. Wines are selected to complement the food. Special diets are catered for.

Newstead Grange is an entirely non-smoking house. ETB Highly Commended. Closed mid-November to mid-February. Special break rates available.

Places of interest nearby: The ancient market town of Malton, York, the North York Moors National Park and the East Coast. Stately homes (including Castle Howard), abbeys, scenic walks and drives. **Directions: Follow signs out of Malton and Norton-on-Derwent to Beverley. Newstead Grange is on the left, ½ mile beyond the last houses and at the junction with the Settrington Road**

THE MANOR FARMHOUSE

DETHICK, MATLOCK, DERBYSHIRE DE4 5GG
Tel: 01629 534246

OWNERS: Harold and Ruth Groom

3 rms | 2 ens

S: £30
D: £50

In the unspoilt hamlet of Dethick at the gateway to the beautiful Peak District, The Manor Farmhouse provides an ideal setting for relaxing breaks. It is surrounded by rolling Derbyshire countryside with enchanting walks, elegant stately homes and picturesque villages. Partly Tudor it has connections with Anthony Babington, whose misguided plot to assassinate Queen Elizabeth I cost him his own head. It is also the house featured in Alison Uttley's book "A Traveller in Time".

Guests will find a friendly welcome and an informal atmosphere. With its stunning views and lovely garden it is perfect for those seeking seclusion.

There are three charming bedrooms, including two en suite with television. All have central heating and are comfortably furnished. English or Continental breakfast is served in a pretty room, with separate tables. There is a cosy upstairs sitting room with television. Evening meals can occasionally be provided by arrangement. Closed at Christmas.

Places of interest nearby: The Peak National Park, Matlock, the Heights of Abraham, the stately homes of Chatsworth, Hardwick Hall, Haddon Hall and the Crich Tramway Museum. **Directions: From the M1, exit at junction 28. Take A38 to Alfreton and then A615 towards Tansley and Matlock. Dethick is signposted left before Tansley.**

MIDDLECOMBE (Minehead)

PERITON PARK HOTEL

MIDDLECOMBE, NR MINEHEAD, SOMERSET TA24 8SW
TEL: 01643 706885 FAX: 01643 706885

OWNERS: Richard and Angela Hunt

8 rms | 8 ens | SMALL HOTEL

S: £65
D: £96

As you climb the winding drive through the woods, rhododendrons and azaleas to this Victorian country house hotel on the edge of the Exmoor National Park, it is not hard to see why Periton Park is described as a place "where time stands still". Richard and Angela Hunt run the hotel in an efficient and friendly way ensuring that, while their guests are staying with them, they will be carefully looked after. All the rooms are spacious and well proportioned, enlivened with warm autumn colours to create a restful atmosphere.

The wood panelled restaurant, with its double aspect views over the grounds, is the perfect place to enjoy some of the finest food on Exmoor. Menus change with the seasons to reflect the best of West Country produce – fresh fish, local game, delicately cooked vegetables, local cheeses and Somerset wine.

Exmoor is for country lovers with miles of varied, unspoilt, breathtaking landscape. A perfect retreat from the trials of everyday life. Riding is available from stables close to the hotel. Shooting is also available in season. Internet: http://www.SmoothHound.co.uk/hotels/periton.html **Places of interest nearby:** Dunster Castle and Gardens, Knightshayes, Rosemoor, Selworthy, Arlington Court and Exmoor. **Directions: Exit M5 junction 24. Take the A39 towards Minehead. Follow signs to Porlock and Lynmouth. Hotel is on the left hand side.**

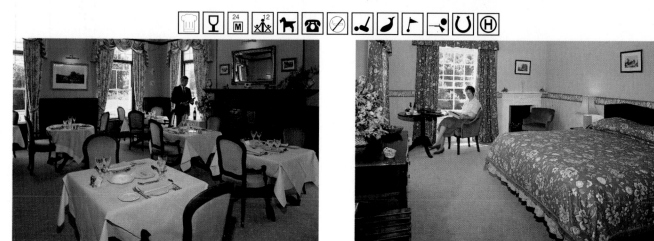

In association with MasterCard

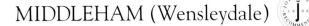

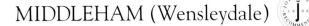
JOHANSENS 1998 RECOMMENDED

MIDDLEHAM (Wensleydale)

MILLERS HOUSE HOTEL

MIDDLEHAM, WENSLEYDALE, NORTH YORKSHIRE DL8 4NR
TEL: 01969 622630 FAX: 01969 623570 E-MAIL: hotel@millershouse.demon.co.uk

OWNERS: Judith and Crossley Sunderland

7 rms | 6 ens | SMALL HOTEL

MasterCard VISA

S: £37–£48
D: £75–£90

The peaceful village of Middleham nestles in the heart of the Yorkshire Dales and the Millers House Hotel is a perfect base from which to explore James Herriot country. This elegant Georgian house has been decorated in period style, including a magnificent, fully canopied four-poster bedroom. A recent addition is an attractive conservatory. Voted Hotel of the Year runner up in the Yorkshire and Humberside Tourist Board White Rose Awards.

The restaurant has won an AA Red Rosette for the last few years. Extensive use is made of fresh local produce, complemented by a fine selection of sensibly priced wines. Especially popular are the gourmet wine-tasting weekends.

Close by is Middleham Castle, once the seat of Richard III. The village is now better known as a racehorse training centre and guests can combine enjoyment of the glorious views across Wensleydale and Coverdale with watching racehorses exercising on the moorland gallops. Racing breaks with a day at the races and a visit to a training yard are also popular. Millers House is open for Christmas and New Year breaks and is available for house parties.

Places of interest nearby: Bolton and Richmond Castles, Jervaulx Abbey, Aysgarth Falls, York, Harrogate and several golf courses. **Directions: Approaching from A1 take the A684 to Bedale and Leyburn; the left turning immediately before Leyburn takes you to Middleham. Millers House Hotel is in the centre of the village.**

THE OLD PRIORY

CHURCH SQUARE, MIDSOMER NORTON, NR BATH, SOMERSET BA3 2HX
TEL: 01761 416784 FAX: 01761 417851

OWNERS: Rudi and Jill Birk
CHEF: Rudi Birk

6 rms | 6 ens | SMALL HOTEL

S: £47.50
D: £65–£80

The mellow Old Priory, with origins dating back to the 12th century, nestles in a quiet corner of the small town of Midsomer Norton almost equidistant from the cities of Bath, Bristol and Wells and surrounded by an area abundant with historical and cultural interest.

Originally believed to have been some kind of "travellers' rest" it was later home to the order of monks who founded Christ Church, Oxford, and was owned by the college until 1712. Today it is a charming olde worlde haven of tranquillity offering a hospitable welcome to visitors. Heavy antique furniture, huge open fires, rich panelling, artefacts and exposed beams abound.

Owners Rudi and Jill Birk give high priority to the provision of friendly and unobtrusive service. Rudi, awarded two AA rosettes at their previous hotel near Bristol, produces European cuisine to appeal to every palate in the delightful restaurant. In keeping with the hotel's history and tradition, the bedrooms are charming, heavily beamed and pleasantly furnished.

Places of interest nearby: Bath, the National Trust village of Laycock, Wells cathedral. **Directions: From the M4, exit at junction 18 onto the A46 to Bath. Join the A367 towards Exeter and at Radstock turn right to Midsomer Norton. Turn left to town centre. At traffic lights turn right and then right again at mini roundabout. The Old Priory is straight ahead, near the church.**

BURLEIGH COURT

MINCHINHAMPTON, GLOUCESTERSHIRE GL5 2PF
TEL: 01453 883804 FAX: 01453 886870

OWNERS: Ian and Fiona Hall

S: £85
D: £115
(including dinner)

Burleigh Court is a very special hotel, where a warmth reminiscence of an era long forgotten greets all guests from the moment they arrive at this beautiful 18th century Gentleman's Manor House. Situated amidst 3.5 acres of lovingly restored landscape gardens with terrace, pools and hidden pathways, every visitor is beguiled into enjoying all the pleasures of a tranquil Cotswold life.

All of the 17 characterful and individual bedrooms recreate the atmosphere of staying in a family home with friends. Indeed the house is still owned and operated by a close knit family. In the dining room the thoughtfully prepared dishes offer an ideal blend of traditional cooking, with simplicity, freshness and purity. Many of the herbs and salad vegetables are home grown.

Places of interest nearby: Burleigh Court's setting in an area of outstanding natural beauty near Minchinhampton and Rodborough Commons affords the ideal location for touring the Southern Cotswolds, the Regency Spa towns of Bath and Cheltenham a short distance away and the picture postcard Cotswold villages on the doorstep.
Directions: Leave Stroud on the A419, heading towards Cirencester. 2½ miles outside Stroud take a right turn, signposted Burleigh and Minchinhampton, about 500 yards along this road there is a sharp left turn signposted Burleigh Court, the house will be on your right after a further 400 yards.

In association
with MasterCard

THE BEACON COUNTRY HOUSE

BEACON ROAD, MINEHEAD, SOMERSET TA24 5SD
TEL: 01643 703476 / 07071 222133 FAX: 01643 707007 E-MAIL: Beacon@globalnet.co.uk

OWNERS: David and Gina Twist
CHEF: Keith Wearing

S: £58–£68
D: £86–£96
suite: £136

An elegant Edwardian country house hotel perched high above the coastline, embraced by its own 20 acres of land, gardens, orchard, livery and home farm, nestling peacefully amid the rolling countryside, the hotel has direct access onto Exmoor and the Coastal Path, yet is only minutes from Minehead town centre.

All bedrooms are en suite, individually decorated, some with sea view and all overlooking the landscaped gardens and countryside beyond. There are two attractive lounges with open fireplaces, a domed glass conservatory and a stylish restaurant and bar serving superb food and drink. Riding, golfing, hiking, cycling, fishing, sailing, sightseeing and shopping are all close by. The hotel is highly reputed for its friendly staff and thoughtful personal service.

Places of interest nearby: The Beacon Country House Hotel is an ideal base for touring Exmoor and the West Country. **Directions: From M5, turn off to Bridgewater at J23 then take A39 to Minehead. At Minehead follow signs into Town Centre. Turn right at T-junction onto The Parade, take second left into Blenheim Road, then first left into Martlet Road. Proceed uphill and turn straight across at the memorial into Burgundy Road. Carry on round the hairpin bend and follow Beacon Road to the end. The hotel is on the left with its own car park.**

In association
with MasterCard

CHANNEL HOUSE HOTEL

CHURCH PATH, MINEHEAD, SOMERSET TA24 5QG
TEL: 01643 703229

OWNERS: Jackie and Brian Jackman
CHEFS: Jackie and Brian Jackman

| 8 rms | 8 ens | SMALL HOTEL |

S: £60–£80
D: £97–£120
(including dinner)

The owners pride themselves on offering their guests the gracious living of the Edwardian era in which the house was built. This is evident from the warm and personal welcome received on arrival and the first impressions of the tasteful furnishings. This warm and friendly atmosphere pervades throughout the whole hotel.

On the lower slopes of Minehead's picturesque North Hill, the hotel is secluded within award winning gardens where visitors can enjoy magnificent views of the sea and Exmoor.

All eight bedrooms are furnished to a high standard and beautifully decorated in soft pastel shades which with the views they enjoy gives one the feeling of total peace. All have en suite bathrooms which are excellently appointed.

The restaurant continues this beautiful ambience; it is furnished in soft pinks with sparkling crystal, shining silver and Royal Doulton china. The cuisine is of the highest quality and is created with great care by the owners using only the finest of local produce. Everything is prepared and cooked on the premises, including the bread. Channel House is ETB Highly Commended.

Places of interest nearby: Knightshayes Court, West Somerset Steam Railway and Exmoor National Park.

Directions: On reaching Minehead follow signs to sea front then turn left into Blenheim Road. Take first right up Northfield Road. Church Path is on the left and first right is into Channel House.

WIGHAM

MORCHARD BISHOP, NR CREDITON, DEVON EX17 6RJ
TEL: 01363 877350 FAX: 01363 877350
FROM USA TOLL FREE: 1 800 805 8210

OWNERS: Stephen and Dawn Chilcott

5 rms   5 ens

S: £65–£82
D: £98–£138
(including dinner)

A picturesque, 16th century, thatched Devon longhouse, Wigham adjoins its own 30-acre organic farm which supplies the kitchen with fresh lamb, beef and pork, eggs and dairy products. Good honest home cooking, complemented by an excellent wine list, are hallmarks of this delightful country house.

After dinner, guests may take coffee in the lounge. Please note Wigham is a no-smoking house.

Proprietors Stephen and Dawn Chilcott have created a warm and welcoming atmosphere at this charming retreat. The interiors are characterised by low ceilings, exposed beams, massive fireplaces and original wall panelling. The bedrooms are individually furnished in cottage style and have pretty, co-ordinated fabrics. In the honeymoon suite there is a rustic four-poster bed. All the bedrooms are en suite and have a TV and video. There is also a self contained cottage which sleeps six – details available on request. For further entertainment there is a snooker lounge with a 7-foot table, a heated outdoor swimming pool with a barbecue and a well-equipped 'honour' bar. Special breaks available on request.

Places of interest nearby: Exmoor, Dartmoor, Exeter, Tiverton and Barnstable. **Directions: From Morchard Bishop, take the road marked Chawleigh–Chumleigh, fork right after ¾ mile, and ¾ mile on, on the right, is a small private road marked Wigham.**

ROMNEY BAY HOUSE

COAST ROAD, LITTLESTONE, NEW ROMNEY, KENT TN28 8QY
TEL: 01797 364747 FAX: 01797 367156

OWNERS: Jennifer and Helmut Gorlich

S: from £45
D: £70–£110

This spectacular house was built in the 1920s for the American actress and journalist, Hedda Hopper, by the distinguished architect, Sir Clough Williams-Ellis.

The gracious drawing room overlooks the English Channel, panoramically surveyed through the telescope in the first floor library. There is access to the beach, a tennis court, croquet lawn and golf course. A 5 minute drive to Lydd airport and you can fly to Le Touquet for lunch.

The owners have completed an impressive refurbishing programme. Upstairs, designated non-smoking, the charming en suite bedrooms are furnished with antiques.

Wonderful cream teas can be enjoyed on the terrace in the sun-lit sea air, and traditional four-course dinner is served. The hotel is fully licensed and guests will strongly approve of the short but excellent wine list. Less than 20 minutes drive from the Channel Tunnel Terminal

Places of interest nearby: There is so much history in Romney Marsh, renowned years ago for its smuggling. Caesar landed here in 55BC at Port Lympne and the famous Cinque Ports stretch along the coast. Canterbury Cathedral is a reasonable drive inland. Littlestone Golf Course is close to the hotel and wind-surfing is popular.

Directions: From New Romney head for the coast by Station Road leading to Littlestone Road – pass the miniture railway station – at the sea, turn left and follow signs for Romney Bay House for about a mile.

In association with MasterCard

BEECHWOOD HOTEL

CROMER ROAD, NORTH WALSHAM, NORFOLK NR28 0HD
TEL: 01692 403231 FAX: 01692 407284

OWNERS: Don Birch and Lindsay Spalding
CHEF: Steven Norgate

9 rms | 9 ens | SMALL HOTEL

S: £39–£49
D: £60–£70

The combination of an elegant, spacious, ivyclad house, surrounded by well laid-out gardens, dating back to 1800, with a lovely ambience generated by the proprietors' warm welcome and the attentive staff has created a very special country house hotel in East Anglia.

For many years residents in North Walsham knew it as the doctor's house, then it was extended and transformed to accommodate guests, including Agatha Christie, who was a regular visitor.

The bedrooms are delightful, with big windows, individually decorated, and filled with traditional and antique furniture. The comfortable drawingroom is well supplied with books and magazines and residents enjoy the intimate bar, mingling with local folk. The atmosphere in the Dining Room reflects the contentment of diners appreciating a menu that includes classic English dishes and the Chef's personal suggestions, incorporating the excellent local produce available, together with fine wines, many from the New World, personally selected by the owners.

Places of interest nearby: Sandringham, Blickling Hall, and Holkham Hall. Bird watchers head for Cley Marches and the Nature Reserves; others enjoy the Norfolk Broads or explore Norwich Cathedral. **Directions: Leave Norwich on B1150, driving 13 miles to North Walsham. Pass under the railway bridge, then left at the first traffic lights and right at the next set, finding the hotel 150m on the left.**

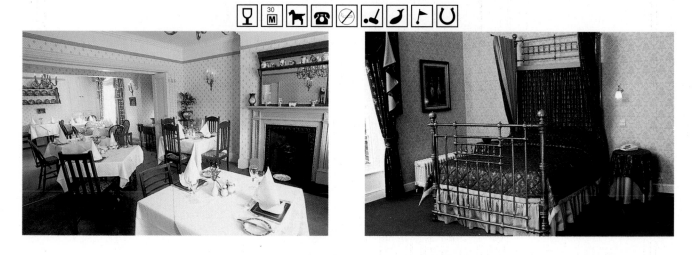

ELDERTON LODGE

GUNTON PARK, THORPE MARKET, NR NORTH WALSHAM, NORFOLK NR11 8TZ
TEL: 01263 833547 FAX: 01263 834673

OWNERS: Christine and Martin Worby

11 rms   11 ens

S: £55
D: £80

Quietly grazing red deer, proudly strutting pheasants and cooing wood pigeons provide memorable awakening viewing to guests gazing from their bedroom windows over the vast and tranquil Gunton Park that is the scene of this 18th century, Grade II listed hotel.

Standing in the heart of unspoiled countryside yet only four miles from the coast, the impressive Elderton Lodge Hotel and Restaurant, with its own six acres of mature gardens, was once the Shooting Lodge and Dower House to Gunton Hall Estate.

Gunton Hall, home of the Earls of Suffield, was a favoured retreat for Lillie Langtry, the celebrated Victorian beauty, who according to legend entertained Edward VII here when he was Prince of Wales. Owners Christine and Martin Worby are restoring the hotel to its original country house splendour, complete with gun cupboards and elegant panelling. Bedrooms are attractive and comfortable, the bar informal and welcoming, and the excellent cuisine featuring local game and seafood specialities– fit for a King, not only the Prince of Wales.
Places of interest nearby: The cathedral city of Norwich, National Trust properties, including Blickling Hall, Felbrigg Hall, Sheringham Park, and the Norfolk Broads National Park. **Directions: Leave Norwich on A1151. Join A149 towards Cromer and the hotel is on the left prior to entering Thorpe Market.**

For hotel location, see maps on pages 266-272

129

THE BEECHES HOTEL AND VICTORIAN GARDENS

4-6 EARLHAM ROAD, NORWICH, NORFOLK NR2 3DB
TEL: 01603 621167 FAX: 01603 620151 E-MAIL: beeches.hotel@paston.co.uk

OWNERS: Keith and Elisabeth Hill

25 rms 25 ens SMALL HOTEL

S: £50–£60
D: £65–£80

With three acres of English Heritage Victorian Gardens, this hotel offers discerning guests a warm welcome and exceptionally high standards of comfort in a relaxed, informal atmosphere. Two separate Grade II listed Victorian mansions which have been beautifully restored, extended and attractively decorated and are collectively known as the Beeches. (Plantation House pictured).

When the houses were built in the mid-1800s, an idyllic Italianate garden was created in the deep hollow it overlooks. In 1980, this 'secret' garden now known as The Plantation Garden was rediscovered. It is being restored to its former glory and guests are free to wander through this enchanting and extraodinary reminder of our Victorian heritage with its ornate Gothic fountain and amazing terraces. All bedrooms feature charming individual decor, seperate modern facilities and are non smoking.

A varied selection of tempting dishes is cooked to order and served in the Bistro Restaurant which overlooks a delightful patio garden. Residents and diners can enjoy a pre-dinner drink in the comfortable lounge bar.

Places of interest nearby: The city of Norwich, with its castle containing a famous collection of the Norwich school of painting and its fine cathedral, the Norfolk coast and Broads. **Directions: From the A11 take the inner ring road west and turn onto the B1108 (Earlham Road) to the city centre. The hotel is near the Roman Catholic cathedral.**

In association
with MasterCard

CATTON OLD HALL

LODGE LANE, CATTON, NORWICH, NORFOLK NR6 7HG
TEL: 01603 419379 FAX: 01603 400339

OWNERS: Roger and Anthea Cawdron

5 rms 5 ens

S: £42.50–£48
D: £60–£95

Catton Old Hall was built in 1632 and has been sympathetically restored to its former glory. It lies just 2½ miles north east of Norwich city centre and within easy reach of the airport. The Hall, once a farmhouse, retains a wealth of oak beams and one of the largest inglenooks in Norwich. Now the family home of Roger and Anthea Cawdron, it provides luxurious accommodation for its guests. The en suite bedrooms are spacious, tastefully decorated and furnished to the highest standards. The dining room and lounge have a homely atmosphere and are ideal places in which to enjoy quiet comfort.

Full English breakfast is served at the Hall and evening meals are available if booked in advance. A typical evening meal might be a choice between breast of Barbary duck, cooked in blackberry and blueberry sauce laced with Crème de Mûre, or fillet of beef Wellington, a steak with a mushroom and onion farce wrapped in crisp pastry served with a rich port and thyme jus.

A full range of office facilities is available and arrangements can be made to visit local sporting events.
Places of interest nearby: The ancient cathedral city of Norwich, with its 12th century castle, fine museums and many other historic buildings. Also the Norfolk Broads and the long sandy beaches on the Norfolk coastline.
Directions: 2½ miles north east of Norwich centre. Lodge Lane is just off Spixworth Road.

In association with MasterCard

THE MOAT HOUSE

RECTORY LANE, HETHEL, NORWICH, NORFOLK NR14 8HD
TEL: 01508 570149 FAX: 01508 570149

OWNERS: Lesley and Colin Rudd

S: £40
D: £60
Suite: £75

A tiny bridge takes you over a well maintained moat surrounding this peaceful and lovely Georgian house situated in pastoral countryside just south west of Norwich. All the rooms are spacious and classically elegant. Old portraits hang in the welcoming hall while the walls of the comfortable sitting room are decorated with equestrian pictures and memorabilia reflecting the owners' interest in eventing. There is a secluded meeting-room. Breakfast is nourishing and dinner en famille is available by arrangement.

The hotel is surrounded by 50 acres of grounds and garden with areas left wild to encourage the growth of butterfly-attracting flowers.

A well equipped leisure centre includes a swimming pool dominated by a peacock wall sculpture which at night reflects a myriad of tiny lights onto the water. Golf and shooting are close by and there is horseracing at Fakenham, Great Yarmouth and Newmarket. Stables and grazing are available.

Places of interest nearby: The cathedral city of Norwich with its many historic buildings, Wymondham Abbey and the roman site at Caistor. **Directions: From the A11 W Direction of Norwich, exit at the Wymondham by-pass onto the B1135 signposted to Bungay. Turn right from the slip road, travel over the dual carriageway and then take the first left, then first right and second right. Rectory Lane is on the right after one mile.**

In association with MasterCard

THE NORFOLK MEAD HOTEL

COLTISHALL, NORWICH, NORFOLK NR12 7DN
TEL: 01603 737531 FAX: 01603 737521

OWNERS: Donald and Jill Fleming

9 rms | 9 ens

S: £55–£75
D: £69–£95

This elegant Georgian manor house, dating back to 1740, sits on a quiet edge of the Norfolk Broads, standing in 12 acres of lovely gardens and rolling lawns which sweep down to the River Bure. Guests can stroll down to the water to catch a glimpse of a kingfisher or heron and enjoy the variety of birdlife. The new owners have added a host of personal touches to create a homely atmosphere, the fragrance of fresh flowers pervades the hotel.

The delightful restaurant which overlooks the gardens and the river, offers a constantly changing menu thoughtfully selected by the chef to utilise the abundance of local produce, which includes fish caught off the Norfolk coast, game from the local estates, vegetables and herbs from the gardens. An extensive wine list has been carefully selected. Relax with a drink before dinner in the bar, where a log fire burns in winter and French windows open onto the old walled garden in the summer. The hotel boasts a well-stocked fishing lake, off-river mooring and a 60 foot outdoor swimming pool. Situated only 7 miles from the centre of Norwich and 12 miles from the coast, the Norfolk Mead is ideally situated for both business trips and leisurely breaks

Directions: On reaching Norwich take outer ring road to B1150 signposted North Walsham. After Horstead/ Coltishall bridge, bear right on the B1354, signposted Wroxham. Entrance signposted on right just before church.

In association
with MasterCard

THE OLD RECTORY

103 YARMOUTH ROAD, THORPE ST ANDREW, NORWICH, NORFOLK NR7 OHF
TEL: 01603 700772 FAX: 01603 700772

OWNERS: Chris and Sally Entwistle

S: £52.50–£55
D: £68–£78

Situated in just over an acre of mature gardens and overlooking the River Yare on the outskirts of Norwich, The Old Rectory offers discerning guests a warm welcome and exceptionally high standards of comfort in a relaxed and informal atmosphere.

Dating back to 1745, this attractive, Virginia Creeper clad Grade II listed hotel is within reach of the city centre and the Norfolk Broads and is an ideal base for those wishing to explore the beautiful Broadland countryside. The comfortable, spacious and well furnished bedrooms in the hotel and adjacent Coach House, all have en suite bath or shower rooms and every amenity. Guests can unwind after a busy day over a pre-dinner drink in the elegant drawing room and make a choice from a four course table d'hôte menu prepared from fresh local produce. The Wellingtonia Room, which together with an attractive conservatory looks onto the sun terrace and heated swimming pool, is an excellent venue for private dining or business meetings.

Places of interest nearby: The cathedral city of Norwich with its 12th century castle, fine museums and many historic buildings. The Norfolk Broads and the sandy beaches on the Norfolk coastline. **Directions: Follow the A47 Norwich bypass towards Great Yarmouth. Take the A1042 exit and follow the road into Thorpe St Andrew. Bear left onto the A1242 and the hotel is approximately 50 yards on the right after the first set of traffic lights.**

THE STOWER GRANGE

SCHOOL ROAD, DRAYTON, NORFOLK NR8 6EF
TEL: 01603 860210 FAX: 01603 860464

OWNERS: Paul and Sarah McCoy

S: £47.50
D: £62.50
Four-poster: £80

Built of mellow old Norwich bricks, this former rectory dates back to the 17th century. The Stower Grange is set in delightful lawned gardens with mature trees and offers its guests a peaceful retreat from the busy world. Its atmosphere is friendly and informal – open fires in the reception rooms are particularly welcoming in the cooler months.

There are a variety of bedrooms to choose from, all well proportioned and prettily decorated. The pine four-poster bedroom will appeal especially to those in a romantic mood. An abundance of flowers adds a colourful personal touch to the unpretentious comfortable surroundings.

Overlooking the garden is the dining room, offering a renowned à la carte menu and imaginative four-course dinner menus. Steak and salads are served in the lounge bar on Sunday evenings.

Places of interest nearby: Norwich, Norfolk Broads, Holkham Hall, Houghton Hall, Blickling Hall, Sandringham and the Norfolk Coast. **Directions: From A11 left on to inner ring road proceed to ASDA junction with A1067 Norwich–Fakenham Road. Approximately two miles to Drayton turn right at Red Lion public house. After 80 yards bear left. The Stower Grange is on the right.**

In association with MasterCard

THE COTTAGE COUNTRY HOUSE HOTEL

EASTHORPE STREET, RUDDINGTON, NOTTINGHAM NG11 6LA
TEL: 01159 846882 FAX: 01159 214721

OWNERS: Christina and Tim Ruffell
CHEFS: Christina Ruffell and Penny Brash

13 rms · 13 ens

S: £70
D: £95
Suites: £115

Roses and honeysuckle ramble over the walls of The Cottage Country House Hotel, a unique restoration of 17th century cottages; it lies tucked away in the village of Ruddington, yet only a few minutes drive from the bustling city of Nottingham. It is the imaginative concept of the designer proprietors and with its private, gated courtyard and delightful walled garden it has won three major awards, including the Conservation Award for the best restoration of an old building in a village setting.

Christina and Tim Ruffell are proud of their attention to detail and they engaged local leading craftsmen to renovate and refurbish the hotel in keeping with its original features. Their aim was to provide quality, style and comfort in tranquil surroundings. They have succeeded in every way.

All the hotel's rooms are individually designed and furnished to reflect the needs of discerning guests. The bedrooms are all en suite, with thoughtfull extra touches, and each room is individually named. The superb restaurant serves excellent cuisine and fine wines, there's a sitting room with an original inglenook fireplace, a charming bar with niche seating and oak beams, and a terrace patio leading into the garden. Golf, tennis and water sports are within easy reach. **Directions: Ruddington is three miles south of Nottingham on the A60 Loughborough road. The hotel is situated at the heart of the village.**

In association with MasterCard

PEN-Y-DYFFRYN COUNTRY HOTEL

RHYDYCROESAU, NR OSWESTRY, SHROPSHIRE SY10 7JD
TEL: 01691 653700 FAX: 01691 653700

OWNERS: Miles and Audrey Hunter

| 8 rms | 8 ens | 🌲 | SMALL HOTEL |

MasterCard VISA AMERICAN EXPRESS

S: £42–£50
D: £66–£74

Pen-y-Dyffryn Country Hotel is a haven of peace and quiet, set in five acres of grounds in the unspoilt Shropshire hills, midway between Shrewsbury and Chester. And while civilisation is close at hand, buzzards, peregrine falcons, badgers and foxes regularly delight the guests with their unscheduled appearances. The stream in front of the hotel marks the border with neighbouring Wales.

All the bedrooms have modern amenities and overlook the attractively terraced hotel gardens. In the cooler months, log fires burning in the two homely lounges help to create a cosy and informal atmosphere in which to relax and forget the pressures of everyday life. The best of British cuisine is served in the hotel's renowned restaurant.

Adventurous menus offer dishes using the finest fresh ingredients and traditional English puddings are a speciality. The hotel is fully licensed and has an extensive wine list.

Although Pen-y-Dyffryn provides the perfect setting for total relaxation, for more active guests there are facilities for hill walking and riding on the doorstep and six 18-hole golf courses within 15 miles. There is also a private trout pool just yards from the hotel.

Places of interest nearby: Four major National Trust properties; Powys and Chirk Castles, Erddig and Attingham. Historic towns of Shrewsbury and Chester. Excursions to Snowdonia. **Directions: From Oswestry town centre take B4580 Llansilin road for three miles.**

In association with MasterCard

IVY HOUSE FARM

IVY LANE, OULTON BROAD, LOWESTOFT, SUFFOLK NR 33 8HY
TEL: 01502 501353 FAX: 01502 501539

OWNERS: Paul Coe and Caroline Sterry
CHEF: Richard Pye

 S: £59–£65
D: £79–£89

A long, leafy drive leads to attractive Ivy House Farm, tucked away in a beautiful conservation area beside Oulton Broad with its fine fishing and abundance of sailing, cruising and motor craft. Spacious lawned gardens lead to meadows and marshes grazed by rare breed sheep. Turkeys, ducks, hens and peacock strut the grounds.

The prettily furnished bedrooms offer a full range of modern comforts and a plentiful supply of books and magazines. These rooms and the excellent restaurant with its lofty beams and splendid minstrels gallery have been created from an 18th century thatched barn and outbuildings and they surround a courtyard featuring a pebble and water garden. Two of the bedrooms have bathrooms specially adapted to suit the needs of the disabled. The conservatory lounge is the ideal place to enjoy aperitifs, after-dinner coffee and liqueurs. Packed lunches are available.

Places of interest nearby: Lowestoft, the easternmost town in England, has quaint old houses, museums, a fishing harbour and a beach. Five miles along B1074 is Somerleyton Hall, a Victorian architectural extravaganza with spectacular gardens. The cathedral city of Norwich, the renowned RSPB bird sanctuary at Minsmere and the Suffolk Heritage Coast are short drives away. **Directions: From Lowestoft take the A146 towards Beccles. Ivy House Farm is in Ivy Lane on the right as you leave Oulton Broad.**

For hotel location, see maps on pages 266-272

OWLPEN

OWLPEN MANOR

NR ULEY, GLOUCESTERSHIRE GL11 5BZ
TEL: 01453 860261 FAX: 01453 860819 E-MAIL: Nicky@owlpen.demon.co.uk

OWNERS: Nicholas and Karin Mander
CHEF: Karin Mander

9 cotts   9 ens

From:
£50-£150
(minimum stay conditions may apply)

Set in its own remote and picturesque wooded valley in the heart of the South Cotswolds, Owlpen Manor is one of the country's most romantic Tudor manor houses. It is steeped in peace and timeless English beauty with the surrounding estate leading the wildlife lover through miles of private woodland paths. Scattered along the valley are distinctive historic cottages, sleeping from two to eight and managed in the style of a country house hotel. There are snug medieval barns and byres, a watermill first restored in 1464, the Court House of the 1620s, weavers' and keepers' cottages and even a modern farmhouse.

All are equipped with every home-from-home comfort, from antiques and chintzes to prints and plants. They are individually furnished in traditional English style and stand in their own secluded gardens. Some have open fireplaces or four-poster beds. An atmospheric restaurant in the medieval cyder house serves seasonal produce from the estate. For sporting visitors fly-fishing and shooting can be arranged. Riding, gliding and golf are nearby.

Places of interest nearby: Owlpen Manor, Uley Tumulus, Westonbirt Arboretum, Berkeley Castle and the Wildfowl Trust at Slimbridge. **Directions: From the M4, exit at junction 18, or M5 junctions 13 or 14, and head for the B4066 to Uley. Owlpen is signposted from the Old Crown opposite the church, or follow the brown signs.**

FALLOWFIELDS

KINGSTON BAGPUIZE WITH SOUTHMOOR, OXON OX13 5BH
TEL: 01865 820416 FAX: 01865 821275

OWNERS: Peta and Anthony Lloyd

5 rms   5 ens

S: £75–£95
D: £90–£120

Fallowfields, once the home of Begum Aga Khan, dates back more than 300 years. It has been updated and extended over past decades and today boasts a lovely early Victorian Gothic southern aspect. The house is set in two acres of gardens, surrounded by 10 acres of grassland.

The guests' bedrooms, which offer a choice of four poster or coroneted beds, are large and well appointed and offer every modern amenity to ensure maximum comfort and convenience. The house is centrally heated throughout and during the winter months there are welcoming log fires in the elegant main reception rooms.

Home cooked cuisine is imaginative in style and presentation and there is a good choice of menu available.

The walled kitchen garden provides most of the vegetables and salads for the table and locally grown organic produce is otherwise used wherever possible. Weekend house parties are ever popular and additional accommodation can be arranged. Five new bedrooms are due for completion in February '98.

Places of interest nearby: Fallowfields is close to Stratford, the Cotswolds, Stonehenge, Bath and Bristol to the west, Oxford, Henley on Thames, the Chilterns and Windsor to the east. Heathrow airport is under an hour away. **Directions: Take the Kingston Bagpuize exit on the A420 Oxford to Swindon. Fallowfields is at the west end of Southmoor.**

In association with MasterCard

MIDSTONE HOUSE

SOUTHORPE, STAMFORD, LINCOLNSHIRE PE9 3BX
TEL: 01780 740136 FAX: 01780 740136

OWNERS: Chris and Anne Harrison-Smith

3 rms | 1 ens

S: £30–£40
D: £40–£65

This delightful farm house, built in the attractive local stone in the 18th century, is in Southorpe village on the Cambridge and Lincolnshire borders. Not far from Peterborough and Stamford, business people find it a peaceful haven after a busy day and, as it is also a farm, a place where they might like to bring their families – who would not enjoy meeting 'George', a Pot Bellied Pig, and the Midstone herd of tiny Dexter cattle?

The pretty bedrooms are comfortable and overlook the countryside. One room is en suite with Jacuzzi bath, the others have a bathroom close by. The lounge has a relaxing atmosphere. Non-smoking prevails.

Alternatively guests may prefer to stay in the lovely Bridle Cottage, the original coach house, which has self-catering facilities.

The Harrison-Smith breakfast is a great start to the day with fresh eggs from the farm and homemade jams. Dinner is by arrangement – however there are many pleasant places to eat in the neighbourhood.

Places of interest nearby: Midstone House is ideally situated for the East of England Show, Newmarket Races and Burghley House. It is a fascinating area to explore – interesting gardens and castles to visit, boating on Rutland Water, good golf courses nearby and the Nene Valley Steam Railway. **Directions: From A1 exit A47 towards Peterborough, after a mile turn left, signed Southorpe.**

In association
with MasterCard

THE COTTAGE HOTEL

PORLOCK WEIR, PORLOCK, SOMERSET TA24 8PB
TEL: 01643 863300 FAX: 01643 863311 E-MAIL: cottage@netcomuk.co.uk

OWNERS: Christopher and Ann Baker
CHEF: Ann Baker

5 rms | 5 ens

MasterCard VISA
S: £55–£95
D: £65–£110

Guests will be enchanted by the lovely location of The Cottage Hotel, overlooking a tiny harbour where Exmoor meets the rugged coastline and sea. It is wonderful walking country abounding in history and scenic delights. With origins dating back to the 18th century, the hotel is surrounded by colourful, terraced gardens where visitors can relax in summer shade and breathe in sweet floral scents.

Owners Christopher and Ann Baker offer a very friendly welcome and excellent value for money. The bedrooms are a delight, comfortable, beautifully decorated and well-equipped with all modern necessities.

Drinks can be taken in the attractively draped lounge with its deep, soft sofas and chairs before dining in the elegant restaurant where delightfully presented meals are served using the finest local produce, including lamb, venison, fish and cheeses.

Places of interest nearby: Dunster's Norman castle, the smallest church in England at Culbone, Lynmouth's picturesque harbour, Minehead, the scenic, wild delights and attractive stone cottage villages of Exmoor.
Directions: From the M5, exit at junctions 23 or 24 and join the A39 towards Minehead, Porlock and Porlock Weir.

In association with MasterCard

TYE ROCK HOTEL

LOE BAR ROAD, PORTHLEVEN, NR HELSTON, SOUTH CORNWALL TR13 9EW
TEL/FAX: 01326 572695

OWNERS: Richard and Pat Palmer

| 7 rms | 7 ens | 🌲 | SMALL HOTEL |

S: £40–£45
D: £60–£66

This family run hotel with its magnificent location offers a wonderful warm, relaxing and welcoming atmosphere as you walk in the door. Whether you choose self-catering or hotel accommodation, you can be sure that Tye Rock's superb elevated position, with views extending from The Lizard to Land's End, will be hard to surpass. Set in 3½ acres surrounded by National Trust land, Tye Rock has an air of seclusion, yet the fishing village of Porthleven is only a short walk away.

The hotel's seven en suite bedrooms all have sea views. Relax and enjoy a traditional, home-cooked meal served in the dining room, offering magnificent views of Mounts Bay. In the hotel grounds there are also eight apartments which offer guests the independence of their own front door.

In a sheltered sun-trap at the bottom of the garden is the large, outdoor heated swimming pool. Open from May to September, the pool, built into the cliff top, is unusually large for a small hotel. Thanks to the mild Cornish climate, spring starts early here and the warm days last well into the autumn. Open all year round, the hotel offers out of season, Christmas and theme weekends and breaks.

Places of interest nearby: St Michael's Mount, Land's End, Goonhilly Earth Satellite Station and many Cornish gardens. **Directions: From Helston take the Porthleven road, then follow signs for Loe Bar; take first left, first right and left at the T-Junction.**

 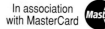

THE BEAUFORT HOTEL

71 FESTING ROAD, SOUTHSEA, PORTSMOUTH PO4 ONQ
TEL: 01705 823707 FAX: 01705 870270 fREEPHONE: 0800 919237

OWNERS Anthony and Penelope Freemantle
CHEF: David Hinds

18 rms 18 ens

MasterCard VISA AMERICAN EXPRESS

S: from £48
D: from £78

Conveniently located in the heart of Southsea, just one minute's walk from the sea, lies The Beaufort Hotel. A relaxed and friendly atmosphere pervades this comfortable and spotless hotel, creating an ideal setting for relaxation. Owners Penny and Tony Freemantle and their staff pride themselves on providing guests with a personal service that is second to none.

The 18 bedrooms have all been designed to give them individual character, from the magnificent Oxford Room, decorated in royal blue and gold, to the bright and sunny Cambridge Room which is tastefully decorated in Burgundy and overlooks the Canoe lake. All the attractive bathrooms feature porcelain and gold fittings and include a selection of luxurious toiletries.

A comfortable cocktail bar is the ideal place to enjoy a pre-dinner drink before moving on to the charming restaurant, with its splendid view of the garden. Here à la carte and table d'hôte menus offer delicious cuisine which is created using only the finest of fresh produce.

Places of interest nearby: The Mary Rose, H.M.S Warrior, H.M.S Victory and the Royal Naval Museum provide a fascinating insight into life on board Britain's most famous warships. The Isle of Wight and Le Havre and Cherbourg in France are all within easy cruising distance. **Directions: Festing Road is off St Helen's Parade at the eastern end of the seafront.**

CHEQUERS HOTEL

CHURCH PLACE, PULBOROUGH, WEST SUSSEX RH20 1AD
TEL: 01798 872486 FAX: 01798 872715

OWNER: John Searancke
CHEF: Anton Goodwin

| 11 rms | 10 ens | SMALL HOTEL |

S: £49.50–£59.50
D: £79–£89

A warm welcome awaits visitors to this historic hotel built in 1548 and Grade II listed. Situated on a sandstone ridge, Chequers has enviable views across the beautiful Arun Valley to the South Downs beyond.

Mindful of the needs of today's traveller, owner John Searancke has ensured that modern amenities have been carefully blended with old world charm and comforts. The hotel has recently enjoyed a programme of refurbishment further to enhance its appeal. All 11 bedrooms have private facilities, 10 of which are en suite. There are 4 bedrooms on the ground floor and three family rooms. Public rooms are comfortably furnished, with a log fire in the lounge on winter evenings.

In warmer weather, guests may linger over an apéritif on the patio or in the secluded garden, before dining in the restaurant, where the traditional English menu changes daily. The hotel is set in the heart of the local conservation area and its nine acre adjacent meadow is an ideal spot for walking your dog.

Places of interest nearby: Chequers Hotel is conveniently placed for the Roman city of Chichester, Goodwood, Arundel Castle and the Sussex coast. Packed lunches can be provided. ETB 4 Crowns Highly Commended, 2 RAC Merit Awards and 2 AA Rosettes. **Directions: At the top of the hill, at the northern end of the village, the hotel is opposite the church.**

REDDITCH (Ipsley)

In association
with MasterCard

THE OLD RECTORY

IPSLEY LANE, IPSLEY, REDDITCH, WORCESTERSHIRE B98 0AP
TEL: 01527 523000 FAX: 01527 517003

OWNERS: The Moore Family
MANAGERS: Greg Underwood and Elaine Biddlestone

| 10 rms | 8 ens | SMALL HOTEL |

S: £55–£65
D: £75–£85

The Old Rectory at Redditch dates back to the 15th century, although well before that the Romans built Icknield Street which forms one boundary of the grounds. The house was substantially modernised in 1812 by the great grandson of Sir Christopher Wren, who lived in the house for 40 years.

In this historic setting surrounded by beautiful and secluded gardens you will find an atmosphere of peace, tranquility and comfort.

The bedrooms are of different shapes and sizes: some with exposed beams, one with a barrel ceiling, and are all tastefully decorated. In the 17th century connecting stable block is the working mechanism of the 100 year old clock.

Meals are served in the conservatory. The surroundings are delightful in the early morning sun whilst you enjoy fresh fruit juices, cereals and your light or full English breakfast. The three-course evening meal (which should be ordered by 1pm), followed by coffee in the lounge, will have been specially prepared for you that day in the large farmhouse kitchen.

Places of interest nearby: Stratford-upon-Avon, Warwick, Leamington Spa, the Cotswolds, Oxford, Worcester, the NEC and Birmingham. **Directions: Arriving in Redditch, follow the signs for 'All Other Redditch Districts' to Ipsley. Ipsley Lane is off Icknield Street Drive.**

GLEWSTONE COURT

NR ROSS-ON-WYE, HEREFORDSHIRE HR9 6AW
TEL: 01989 770367 FAX: 01989 770282

OWNERS: Bill and Christine Reeve-Tucker

7 rms | 7 ens | SMALL HOTEL

MasterCard VISA AMERICAN EXPRESS

S: £40–£60
D: £60–£94

Glewstone Court is set in three acres of orchards, lawns and flowerbeds. Although secluded, it is only three miles from Ross-on-Wye. Furnishings and décor reflect the hospitable personality of the owners and the variety of prints, antiques and bric-à-brac always excites curiosity.

Most country pursuits can be arranged, including canoeing, hot-air ballooning, fishing and riding. This is marvellous country for walking – or just lazing around, too!

Christine's food is always pleasing and both the restaurant and extensive bar menus feature local recipes using only the freshest of ingredients. Dishes are both traditional and unusual and are always prepared and served with care and attention to detail. Now in their twelfth year,

accolades recently awarded are a rosette for good food from the AA and the Which? Hotel Guide Hotel of the Year for Hereford and Worcester 1997. The restaurant and the drawing room bar feature log fires and, like the rest of the hotel, are furnished for comfort.

The bedrooms are large and comfortable too. Each has en suite facilities, a hospitality tray, direct dial phone and colour TV. Closed Christmas Day and Boxing Day.

Places of interest nearby: Ross-on-Wye, Hay-on-Wye, the Welsh Marches, Hereford Cathedral and the Brecon Beacons. **Directions: From M50 junction 4 follow A40 signposted Monmouth. One mile past Wilton roundabout turn right to Glewstone; the Court is ¹/₂ mile on left.**

WHITE VINE HOUSE

HIGH STREET, RYE, EAST SUSSEX TN31 7JF
TEL: 01797 224748 FAX: 01797 223599

OWNERS: Geraldine and Robert Bromley

6 rms	6 ens	SMALL HOTEL

MasterCard VISA AMERICAN EXPRESS

S: From £60
D: From £86

This timber framed house, built over one of the medieval vaulted cellars in the Ancient Town of Rye, is described by its owners as 'a non-smoking haven for grown-ups'. On the site of the original Whyte Vyne Inn, for all its central location, it retains a unique character and restful atmosphere.

In the morning guests can savour the pleasant surroundings while enjoying a generous country breakfast in the Garden Room. The Parlour, where drinks are served, is also an excellent place for quiet relaxation.

There are six comfortable bedrooms – of the five doubles, two have four poster beds. Each is individually styled and well provided with modern amenities.

Healthy cooking styles are used to prepare lunch, which is created from the finest locally sourced ingredients and complemented by a carefully chosen wine list. White Vine House is particularly proud of its exceptional New World house wines. The proprietors will happily recommend good restaurants from the many available in the locality and make dinner reservations on behalf of their guests.

Places of interest nearby: Rye is a town of great historical interest and boasts many art galleries, potteries, antique dealers and book sellers. **Directions: Take the A21 to Flimwell, then the A268 to Rye. Telephone first for parking advice.**

For hotel location, see maps on pages 266-272

THE COUNTRYMAN AT TRINK HOTEL AND RESTAURANT

OLD COACH ROAD, ST IVES, CORNWALL TR26 3JQ
TEL: 01736 797571 FAX: 01736 797571

OWNERS: Howard and Cathy Massey

6 rms | 6 ens | SMALL HOTEL

S: £38
D: £60–£70

Five minutes drive from the quaint town of St Ives is the Countryman Hotel and Restaurant at Trink. St Ives has become a mecca for artists and one of the latest attractions is the new Tate Gallery with its collection of modern paintings and contemporary exhibits. Cornwall has a wealth of interesting things to see not least its dramatic coastline ideal for lovers of nature and walkers.

The Countryman dates from the 17th century. Today the small hotel has been renovated to meet the needs of the modern visitor, all rooms have en suite shower and toilet, colour T.V. and tea making facilities.

The atmosphere of the hotel is friendly and inviting, the emphasis being on cheerful service and good value for money. This is a totally no smoking hotel. In the restaurant, Howard Massey, the chef-patron, likes cooking to order from his varied and interesting menu containing cornish fish supported by a sensibly priced wine-list. St Ives has always had a tradition for generous hospitality. A former mayor, the legendary John Knill, bequeathed £10 for an annual banquet. Prices may have altered a little but the high quality of the local cooking has not changed.

Places of interest nearby: Tate Gallery, Lands End. Barbara Hepworth's house, St Michael's Mount. Golf, riding and the sea. **Directions: A30, A3074 to St Ives, then B3311 for about two miles.**

OLIVER'S LODGE HOTEL AND RESTAURANT

NEEDINGWORTH ROAD, ST IVES, NR CAMBRIDGE, CAMBRIDGESHIRE PE17 4JP
TEL: 01480 463252 FAX: 01480 461150

OWNERS: Christopher and Elizabeth Langley
CHEF: Brian Couzens

15 rms | 15 ens

S: £62–£66
D: £75–90

Originally a Victorian building which has been sympathetically extended, Oliver's Lodge is centrally situated in a quiet residential area of the historic market town of St Ives. It is just a few minutes walk from the River Ouse, which for thousands of years was one of the main highways of Britain.

Oliver Cromwell farmed here in the 1630's and his statue, in which he is booted and wearing an unpuritanically rakish hat, stands in the market-place.

Privately owned and run, the hotel offers a warm, friendly welcome with the emphasis on individual attention and high quality food and service. An extensive à la carte menu, which also features daily specials, is served in the elegant, candle-lit restaurant which overlooks the trim garden. Lighter meals can be enjoyed in the comfortable lounge and new conservatory. The bedrooms, some of which are on the ground floor, include 3 suites/family rooms. There are several function/conference rooms for 6 to 100 people. Special bargain 2 day breaks available.

Places of interest nearby: Cambridge, Huntingdon, Newmarket, the American Cemetery at Madingley, Burghley House Stamford, Imperial War Museum Duxford.
Directions: From Cambridge take A14 towards Huntingdon. Turn right onto A1096 for St Ives.

THE HUNDRED HOUSE HOTEL

RUAN HIGHLANES, NR TRURO, CORNWALL TR2 5JR
TEL: 01872 501336 FAX: 01872 501151

OWNERS: Mike and Kitty Eccles

S: £53–£60
D: £106–£120
(including dinner)

Situated on Cornwall's beautiful Roseland Peninsula is The Hundred House Hotel, an 18th century Cornish country house set in three acres of gardens. It commands panoramic views over the countryside and is close to the sea and the lovely Fal estuary.

Once inside the wide hall with its handsome Edwardian staircase, there is the feeling of an elegant English home. Mike and Kitty Eccles have created a delightful hotel where guests can relax in the pretty sitting room, furnished with antiques and browse among the books of local interest. On cooler days they can enjoy a Cornish cream tea by a log fire and in the summer a game of croquet on the lawn. Each bedroom is individually decorated and has full en suite bath or shower room.

Guests regularly return to enjoy the delicious imaginative dinners and the hearty Cornish breakfast prepared by Kitty Eccles who has been awarded a Red Rosette by the AA. She uses fresh seasonal ingredients and specialities include baked avocado, fillet of lemon sole with a salmon mousse and a honey and lavender ice cream.

Places of interest nearby: Picturesque fishing villages, superb cliff walks and sandy beaches. Cornwall Gardens Festival, mid March to 31 May. Boat trips on Fal Estuary. Lanhydrock House (NT). Cathedral city of Truro 12 miles away. **Directions: A390 from St Austell, left on B3278 to Tregony, then A3078 to St Mawes. Hotel is then 4 miles on.**

BROOM HALL

RICHMOND ROAD, SAHAM TONEY, THETFORD, NORFOLK IP25 7EX
TEL: 01953 882125 FAX: 01953 882125

OWNERS: Nigel and Angela Rowling
MANAGER: Simon Rowling

| 8 rms | 8 ens | 🌲 | SMALL HOTEL |

S: £40
D: £60–£80

Situated in 15 acres of mature gardens and parkland Broom Hall is a charming Victorian country house offering peace and tranquillity. Airy and spacious bedrooms each individually furnished and most offering lovely views provide guests with both comfort and a range of modern amenities.

A feature of the public rooms are the ornate ceilings and in the lounge a large open fire can be enjoyed in the winter months. An indoor heated swimming pool and full size snooker table are available for guests' use.

Fresh vegetables, from Broom Hall's own garden when in season, and many old fashioned desserts ensure that dinner in the dining room overlooking the garden is an enjoyable occasion. Small conferences can be arranged and the entire house can be 'taken over' for your family reunion or celebration.

Places of interest nearby: Within easy reach are Norwich, Cambridge, Ely and Bury St Edmunds. Sandringham and many National Trust properties, Thetford Forest, Norfolk Broads and coastline offering nature reserves and bird sanctuaries. **Directions: Half mile north of Watton on B1077 towards Swaffham.**

SAUNTON

PRESTON HOUSE HOTEL

SAUNTON, BRAUNTON, NORTH DEVON EX33 1LG
TEL: 01271 890472 FAX: 01271 8990555

OWNERS: Andrew and Timothy Flaherty
CHEF: Timothy Flaherty

12 rms | 12 ens | SMALL HOTEL

S: £45–£60
D: £60–£95

Miles of flat, golden sands and white-capped Atlantic rollers greet guests seeking peace, quiet and relaxation at Preston House, standing high on the glorious coastline of North Devon. Terraced, lawned gardens sweep down to the sea and an atmosphere of undisturbed continuity and tranquillity surrounds and influences the hotel which dates back to the Victorian era. The views are spectacular.

Eleven of the 12 en suite bedrooms face seawards. All are individually decorated, tastefully furnished and contain all modern amenities from colour television and direct direct dial telephone to tea and coffee facilities. Some have a four-poster bed, balcony and the added luxury of a Jaccuzzi.

A spacious and comfortable lounge provides the perfect leisured environment. Breakfast can be leisurely enjoyed in the hotel's conservatory which overlooks the garden, sands and ocean and chef Timothy Flaherty serves delicious and imaginative dinners under glittering chandeliers in the elegant restaurant or overlooking the magnificent view in the conservatory.

Places of interest nearby: Lynton, Lynmouth, Exmoor and many National Trust properties. **Directions: From the M5, exit at junction 27 and take the A361 towards Barnstaple. Continue on to Braunton and when there turn left at the traffic lights towards Croyde. The hotel is on the left after approximately two miles.**

THE PHEASANT HOTEL

SEAVINGTON ST MARY, NR ILMINSTER, SOMERSET TA19 0HQ
TEL: 01460 240502 FAX: 01460 242388

OWNERS: Mark and Tania Harris
CHEF: Danny Kilpatrick

8 rms | 8 ens | SMALL HOTEL

MasterCard VISA AMERICAN EXPRESS
S: from £70
D: from £90
Suite: from £100

Visitors to The Pheasant are immediately captivated by the distinctive charm and character of this sumptuously furnished old-world style hotel and restaurant. Set in the heart of Somerset and surrounded by landscaped lawns and splendid gardens, it conveys a restful warmth and welcome. The charming bedrooms are individually styled and very comfortably furnished.

Sympathetic décor and furnishings complement the traditional character of the bar and highly acclaimed restaurant, with their oak-beamed ceilings and large inglenook fireplaces. The cooking is recommended by many hotel and food guides. An extensive menu of imaginatively prepared dishes includes a good choice for vegetarians, while delicious home-made desserts are irresistibly displayed on the sweet trolley.

Places of interest nearby: Being situated near the Somerset border close to both Dorset and Devon, there are many attractions to suit all age groups, including Montacute House, the abbey town of Sherborne, the Fleet Air Museum at Yeovilton and Cricket St Thomas, where the BBC TV series *To The Manor Born* was filmed. **Directions: Leave the A303 at South Petherton roundabout by Ilminster bypass. Take the left spur, (Seavington St Michael), followed by Seavington exit at the next roundabout. Left by the Volunteer Inn and The Pheasant is 200 yards further on the right.**

THE SEDGEFORD ESTATE

BORDERING ROYAL SANDRINGHAM, SEDGEFORD, NR HUNSTANTON, NORFOLK PE36 5LT
TEL: 01485 572855 FAX: 01485 572592

OWNERS: Professor and Mrs Bernard Campbell

Cottage:
£246–£1530pw

Sedgeford Hall, one of Norfolk's finest examples of the Queen Anne period, nestles in a sheltered valley surrounded by 1,200 acres of rolling parkland, lush meadows and ancient woods 5 miles from the coast.

Four spacious cottages are scattered around the elegant Grade II listed Hall, each sleeping four to six. There is also accommodation for two guests in a self-contained wing of the house.

The cottages are over 200 years old and have highly individual styles. They are furnished and equipped to extremely high standards, enabling guests to ejnoy peacefully a traditional country estate and its gardens. Accommodation for up to 14 guests is also available in a fine Georgian house standing in five acres of gardens and meadows with sea views at nearby Heacham. Special weekend breaks are available.

The Hall has a beautiful heated indoor swimming pool, there is shooting, fishing, golf and tennis locally and a range of watersports within easy reach.

Places of interest nearby: Royal Sandringham, the stately homes of Holkham, Houghton, Oxbrough, Felbrigg and Blickling. **Directions: From King's Lynn, A149 north towards Hunstanton. At Norfolk Lavender turn right onto the B1454 to Sedgeford Village. Fork right at war memorial signposted Fring. Large iron gates ½ mile from village, close to farm buildings.**

In association with MasterCard

STAINDROP LODGE HOTEL & RESTAURANT

LANE END, CHAPELTOWN, SHEFFIELD, SOUTH YORKSHIRE S35 3UH
TEL: 0114 284 6727 FAX: 0114 284 6783

OWNERS: The Bailey Family
MANAGERS: Mark and Sue Bailey

13 rms | 13 ens | SMALL HOTEL

S: £45–£65
D: £58–£83

Ivy-clad Staindrop Lodge dates back to 1806 when it was built as the family home of George Newton, a founding father of the famous Yorkshire firm Newton Chambers. Now it has been sympathetically converted into a country hotel with all 20th century facilities. Surrounded by secluded mature gardens on the north side of Sheffield the hotel is five minutes from the M1 and only a few minutes drive from the city centre and within easy reach of Derbyshire's Peak District.

Each of the 13 en suite bedrooms is individually designed, tastefully furnished and has every comfort. The light, pastel coloured restaurant with its fine, flowing drapes has a reputation for good modern English cuisine blended with traditional and classical French influences. Apéritifs can be enjoyed in a small cocktail bar or in the conservatory style lounge. The Thorncliffe Suite is ideal for weddings, dances and business meetings. Special weekend breaks available.

Places of interest nearby: Sheffield Arena and the Meadowhall shopping centre are just a short car journey away. 20 minutes from the Peak District National Park and Chatsworth is within easy reach. **Directions: From the M1, exit at junction 35 and take the A629 for one mile to Chapeltown. Turn right at the second roundabout into Loundside Road and the hotel is on the right after half-a-mile.**

THE EASTBURY HOTEL

LONG STREET, SHERBORNE, DORSET DT9 3BY
TEL: 01935 813131 FAX: 01935 817296

OWNERS: Tom and Alison Pickford

| 15 rms | 15 ens | SMALL HOTEL |

MasterCard VISA AMERICAN EXPRESS

S: from £49.50
D: £79–£89

The Eastbury Hotel is a traditional town house which was built in 1740 during the reign of George II. During its recent refurbishment great care was taken to preserve its 18th century character. In fine weather guests can enjoy the seclusion of the hotel's private walled garden, which encompasses an acre of shrubs and formal plants and a noteworthy listed walnut tree.

Bedrooms are individually named after well-known English garden flowers and each is equipped with a full range of modern comforts and conveniences. The Eastbury is ideal for parents visiting sons or daughters who board at the Sherborne schools.

Traditional English cooking is a feature of the Eastbury restaurant and the dishes are complemented by an extensive list of the world's fine wines.

Places of interest nearby: Sherborne is rich in history and has a magnificent 15th century Perpendicular Abbey Church and two castles, in one of which Sir Walter Raleigh founded the national smoking habit. At Compton is a silk farm and a collection of butterflies. Beyond Yeovil is Montacute House (N.T.) and at Yeovilton is the Fleet Air Arm Museum. **Directions: Long Street is in the town centre, south of and parallel to the A30. Parking is at the rear of the hotel.**

THE SHAVEN CROWN HOTEL

HIGH STREET, SHIPTON-UNDER-WYCHWOOD, OXFORDSHIRE OX7 6BA
TEL: 01993 830330 FAX: 01993 832136

OWNERS: Mr and Mrs Robert Burpitt

In association
with MasterCard

S: £53
D: £75–£100

Built of honey-coloured stone around an attractive central courtyard, The Shaven Crown Hotel dates back to the 14th century, when it served as a monks' hospice. The proprietors, have preserved the inn's many historic features, such as the medieval hall with its ancient timbered roof. This is now the residents' lounge. Each of the bedrooms has en suite facilities and has been sympathetically furnished in a style befitting its own unique character. Rooms of various style and sizes are available, includeing a huge family room and ground-floor accommodation. Dining in the intimate, candle-lit room is an enjoyable experience, with meals served at the tables beautifully laid with fine accessories. The best ingredients are combined to create original dishes with a cosmopolitan flair. The table d'hôte menu offers a wide and eclectic choice with a daily vegetarian dish amoung the specialities. An imaginative selection of dishes is offered every lunchtime and evening in the Monks Bar.

Places of interest nearby: The Shaven Crown is ideal for day trips to the Cotswolds, Oxford, Stratford-upon-Avon and Bath. There are three golf courses and tennis courts close by. Trout fishing and antiques hunting are popular activities in the area. **Directions: Take the A40 Oxford–Cheltenham road. At Burford follow the A361 towards Chipping Norton. The inn is situated directly opposite the village green in Shipton-under-Wychwood.**

SIMONSBATH HOUSE HOTEL

SIMONSBATH, EXMOOR, SOMERSET TA24 7SH
TEL: 01643 831259 FAX: 01643 831557

OWNERS: Mike and Sue Burns

S: £44–£60
D: £78–£90

Simonsbath House was built by James Boevey, Warden of the Forest of Exmoor, in 1654, on rising ground facing due south across the beautiful valley of the River Barle. You are welcomed with log fires in the oak-panelled lounge, and with mineral water, fresh fruit and flowers in the bedrooms. A relaxing atmosphere pervades throughout the house, which is still essentially a home, with welcoming owners and caring staff to pamper you with old-fashioned hospitality.

The bedroom windows overlook beech forests of everchanging hue, a crystal river bubbling through the valley and fold after fold of heather-clad hills. Guests can saddle up and gallop off to Exmoor's highest point – Dunkery Beacon – or set out on foot. The surrounding forests are ideal for strollers; hikers will enjoy the challenge of the high moorlands. Sue Burns is the chef and she uses only fresh local produce. Vegetarian meals by arrangement. Closed during December and January.
Places of interest nearby: The cathedral cities of Exeter and Wells; Glastonbury, Bath and Devon's beautiful coast. **Directions: Simonsbath is on the B3223, situated within the village, nine miles south of Lynton.**

SOUTH MOLTON

In association
with MasterCard

MARSH HALL COUNTRY HOUSE HOTEL

SOUTH MOLTON, NORTH DEVON EX36 3HQ
TEL: 01769 572666 FAX: 01769 574230

OWNERS: Tony and Judy Griffiths

S: £45–£65
D: £75–£95

Marsh Hall is the perfect place for a refreshing and relaxing holiday and is also ideal for business travellers who require a special overnight stay.

Tony and Judy Griffiths took over ownership of the hotel in 1993 and have created a friendly and informal atmosphere that has guests returning time after time.

The hotel is set in three acres of attractive gardens, and was reputedly built by the local squire for his mistress. Here guests can relax in either the elegant chandelier-lit lounge or the friendly bar, both of which have log fires burning during winter. The large hall and stairway light the gallery which leads to the seven en suite bedrooms, all of which are individually furnished and have country views.

The highlight at Marsh Hall is the food. In the delightful award winning restaurant great attention is paid to the quality of the cuisine with the four course table d'hôte menu changing daily. The finest fresh local produce is used together with vegetables, herbs and fruit from the hotel's kitchen gardens. Special diets are catered for.

Places of interest nearby: Exmoor National Park, beaches and cliffs of North Devon, many houses and gardens open to the public. **Directions: Leave the M5 at junction 27 and take the A361 to North Devon, continue for 25 miles then turn right at junction signposted North Molton, after ½ mile turn right then sharp right into hotel drive.**

THE OLD MILL

MILL LANE, TALLINGTON, STAMFORD, LINCOLNSHIRE PE9 4RR
TEL: 01780 740815 FAX: 01780 740280 MOBILE: 0802 373326

OWNERS: Sue and John Olver

S: £30–£40
D: £45–£75

Surrounded by lush water meadows and farmland, The Old Mill is four miles east of the historic town of Stamford on the original Great North Road. The present structure was built in 1682, although there are records of the Mill in the Doomsday Book.

The Old Mill has been renovated to provide spacious and comfortable accommodation to meet all the needs of the modern visitor without losing any of its bygone character and atmosphere. Many of the its original features are intact, including the huge mill workings in the attractive and cosy dining room where dinner can be served by arrangement.

Heavy, exposed beams abound throughout and the five pretty en suite bedrooms have beautiful panoramic views overlooking a footbridge spanning the River Welland to the mill pond and water meadows beyond. These teem with wildlife and are a birdwatcher's paradise. Cross the covered bridge to a delightfully secluded romantic double room, set beside the mill pond with its own private patio – a honeymooners' idyll. The Old Mill is excellent value for money.

Places of interest nearby: Stamford, the ancient market towns of Oakham, Oundle and Uppingham. Majestic cathedrals at Lincoln and Peterborough, Burghley House, the Fens and Rutland Water. Golf and fishing. **Directions: From the A1, exit at Stamford and take the A16 towards Spalding. The Old Mill is on the right.**

THE PRIORY

CHURCH ROAD, KETTON, STAMFORD, LINCOLNSHIRE PE9 3RD
TEL: 01780 720215 FAX: 01780 721881 E-MAIL: Priory.a0504924@infotrade.co.uk

OWNERS: John and Moya Acton
CHEF: Liz Stevenson

| 3 rms | 3 ens | |

S: £55–£58
D: £69–£80

The Priory is an oasis off the A1, a listed country house which has the ambience of a family home offering rooms for guests. The manor house dates back to the 16th century and has been meticulously restored. The magnificent gardens include a terrace by the River Chater, formal rosebeds and a croquet lawn.

The graceful reception rooms are well proportioned. An attractive conservatory has been added where a full English breakfast and dinner may be served as an alternative to eating in the dining room. The evening menu, changing daily, has a choice of meat, fish and vegetarian dishes. Most of the beautifully decorated and spacious guest rooms overlook the gardens and all have colour TV, telephone and tea and coffee making facilities. **Places of interest nearby:** Rutland Water offers sailing and fishing with cycling and walking around a 25 mile perimeter. Burghley House and Belvoir Castle are close by. Cambridge is only 45 minutes drive away. House Party Weekends can be arranged filling The Priory with ones friends. Theme weekends such as Murder Mystery are also featured. Internet: www.rutland-on-line.co.uk/Priory **Directions: Leave the A1 at Stamford. Take the A6121 to Ketton. Follow the sign Ketton Station, Collyweston. The entrance to The Priory is opposite the Churchyard, down some steps. There is a large car- park for guests' use.**

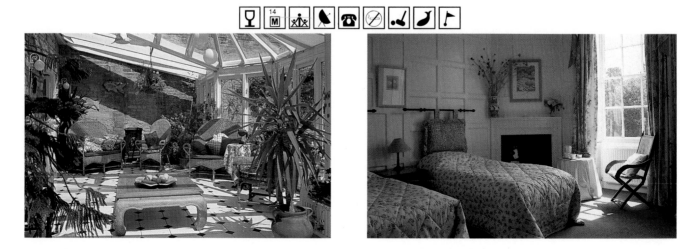

KINGSTON HOUSE

STAVERTON, TOTNES, DEVON TQ9 6AR
TEL: 01803 762 235 FAX: 01803 762 444 E-MAIL: kingston–estate.demon.co.uk

OWNERS: Michael, Elizabeth and Piers Corfield

S: £67.50–£77.50
D: £105
Suite: £115–£125

The Kingston Estate nestles amongst the rolling hills and valleys of the South Hams region of Devon, bounded by Dartmoor and the sea, with the focal point, Kingston House, commanding sweeping views of the moor.

The Mansion, together with the superb self-catering cottages, have been sympathetically restored by the Corfield family to their former glory, and now offer some of the highest standard accommodation to be found in the South West. The House boasts three period suites, (reached by way of the finest example of a marquetry staircase in England), which are hung with authentic wall papers and fabrics, and include a 1735 Angel tester bed, and an 1830 four-poster.

Dinner guests dine by candlelight in the elegant dining room at tables set with sparkling crystal, shining silver and starched linen. In winter, log fires crackle in the hearths, whilst in the summer pre-dinner drinks may be taken on the terrace overlooking the formal 18th century gardens. For every visitor to Kingston, hospitality and comfort are assured in this magnificent historic setting.

Places of interest nearby: Dartington Hall, Dartmouth, Totnes, Dartmoor & Devon's famous coastline.
Directions: Take A38 from Exeter or Plymouth, at Buckfastleigh take A384 Totnes road for two miles. Turn left to Staverton. At Sea Trout Inn, take left fork to Kingston and follow signs.

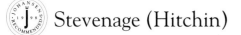

REDCOATS FARMHOUSE HOTEL AND RESTAURANT

REDCOATS GREEN, NEAR HITCHIN, HERTS SG4 7JR
TEL: 01438 729500 FAX: 01438 723322

OWNERS: The Butterfield Family
CHEF: John Ruffell

S: £70–£85
D: £80–£95

This 15th century farmhouse has been in the Butterfield family's possession for generations and in 1971 Peter and his sister converted it into a hotel. They preserved its traditional character of original beams, exposed brickwork and inglenook fireplaces and furnished it in a comfortable and inviting fashion.

It is set in tranquil gardens – one of the larger rooms has its own garden – in the middle of rolling countryside, not far from A1(M). There are 14 rooms, 12 with en suite bathrooms, diverse in character: those in the main house retaining period charm and those in the stable block more modern.

Meals are served in four dining rooms: the Oak Room and the Old Kitchen, log fire cosiness; the Victorian Room, elegant and formal and the Conservatory, garden room atmosphere. Redcoats has a good reputation for its cuisine, which uses much local produce, and a wine list which is as wide ranging geographically as it is in prices.

Places of interest nearby: Redcoats is close to several historic houses including Knebworth House, Hatfield House, Luton Hoo and Woburn. The Roman city of St Albans, the traditional market town of Hitchin and Cambridge University are all within a 30 minute drive.
Directions: Leave the A1(M) at Junction 8 for Little Wymondley. At mini-roundabout turn left. At T-Junction go right, hotel is on left.

In association with MasterCard

STONOR (Henley-on-Thames)

THE STONOR ARMS

STONOR, NR HENLEY-ON-THAMES, OXFORDSHIRE RG9 6HE
TEL: 01491 638866 FAX: 01491 638863

OWNERS: Stonor Hotels Ltd
MANAGER: Guy Hodgson

S: £90
D: £105

This small hotel is not too far from London, and perfectly located for those going to Henley or Ascot. It is in a pretty village on the edge of Stonor Park and restoration has not diminished its 18th century elegance.

The interior of the house has been beautifully decorated in the style of that era, combining grace with comfort. The bedrooms are enchanting, very spacious, furnished with French and English antiques and colourful yet harmonious fabrics.

The hotel has won a high reputation for its first-class food. The restaurant consists of a formal dining area and a conservatory where the atmosphere is more relaxed. The cooking is traditional English and French. Snacks are served in Blades the flagstoned bar where rowing memorabilia adorn the walls. **Places of Interest Nearby:** Windsor and Oxford are easily accessible and sporting activities nearby include boating and golf or walking in the countryside. **Directions: Leave the M40 at junction 6, following B4009 to Watlington, then turn left onto B480 through Stonor.**

CONYGREE GATE HOTEL

KINGHAM, OXFORDSHIRE OX7 6YA
TEL: 01608 658389 FAX: 01608 659467

OWNER: Judy Krasker
CHEF: Andrew Foster

In association
with MasterCard

| 9 rms | 8 ens | SMALL HOTEL |

S: £27.50–£37.50
D: £65–£75

This beautiful Cotswold stone, Grade 11 listed building began life as a 17th century farmhouse. Situated in the centre of the peaceful village of Kingham, it is an ideal retreat from the hustle and bustle of the modern world.

All the bedrooms are individually decorated and several feature original leaded light windows and window seats. A number open directly onto the walled garden where afternoon tea and evening drinks are served.

Leading off the flagstoned hall are two lounges with log fires, original beams and cosy armchairs – perfect for reading and relaxing.

The young chef, Andrew Foster, winner of the 1997 Académie Culinaire Annual Award of Excellence, prepares the delicious dishes offered on the three, four or five course menu. Served in the spectacularly decorated dining room, the meals include starters such as terrine of smoked salmon and anchovy butter with sauce gribiche and main dishes including loin of lamb baked in an olive bread with a beetroot jus, and fillet of salmon on a bed of saffron risotto with a white wine sauce.

Places of interest nearby: Burford, Bourton-on-the-Water and many other typical Cotswold towns and villages are all close by. Blenheim Palace, Stratford-upon-Avon and Oxford are also within easy reach. **Directions: The hotel is in the centre of Kingham, which lies between the B4450 and A436 to the west of Stow.**

GLEBE FARM HOUSE

LOXLEY, WARWICKSHIRE CV35 9JW
TEL/FAX: 01789 842501 E-MAIL: ScorpioLimited@msn.com

OWNER: Kate McGovern

| 2 rms | 2 ens | |

S: £69.50
D: £80

The pleasure of staying at this delightful country house is like that of visiting a private home. Just three miles from historic Stratford-upon-Avon and eight miles from Warwick, Glebe Farm is surrounded by a superb expanse of secluded lawned garden which opens onto 30 acres of beautiful farmland where one can ramble and enjoy the sounds and sights of local wildlife.

Owner Kate McGovern is an accomplished cook and her dinners, served in the attractive surroundings of a conservatory overlooking the gardens, will tempt every palate. Whenever possible fresh produce from the kitchen garden are used. Kate is a talented water colour artist and many of her paintings adorn the walls throughout the house which is furnished and decorated with immaculate taste.

There are two pretty en suite bedrooms with four-poster beds and television and tea and coffee facilities. From both bedrooms and the lounge there are splendid views of the countryside. Local sporting activities include golf, shooting and riding.

Places of interest nearby: The hotel is an ideal base for visiting Shakespeare's Stratford-upon-Avon, Warwick's imposing castle, Ragley Hall, the Heritage Motor Museum and the Cotswolds. **Directions: From the M40, exit at junction 15. Join the A429 and follow the signs to Wellsbourne and then Loxley. Glebe Farm is on the right as you leave Loxley.**

TARANTELLA HOTEL AND RESTAURANT

SUDBURY HALL, MELFORD ROAD, SUDBURY, SUFFOLK CO10 6XT
TEL: 01787 378879 FAX: 01787 378879

OWNER: Domenico Gargiulo
CHEF: Agnello Gargiulo

S: £48.50
D: £74.50

The Gargiulo family have brought the joy of Sorrento to Sudbury, the small Suffolk town where Gainsborough was born and painted his landscapes and portraits.

The Tarantella first opened as a restaurant, set in a splendid Georgian house, with the ambience of a romantic Italian villa. It is surrounded by terraces, statues and landscaped gardens leading down to the River Stour. Marble floors, high ceilings, colourful flowers reminiscent of the Mediterranean add to its charm, and now twelve delightful bedrooms have been added. The quilts and curtains are in gorgeous fabrics and great comfort, country air and peace together ensure a good night's sleep.

Guests enjoy aperitifs in the smart and spacious Sorrento Bar and then indulge themselves with Southern Italian specialities and good Italian wines in the Garden Restaurant, which extends onto the terrace. The Bellavista Banqueting Room is spectacular, with arched Roman windows overlooking the gardens and river – a new and exciting venue for corporate and social events, seating up to 150 people for a conference or a feast.

Special arrangements with a local club, fishing in the river and racing at Newmarket to suit sporting visitors; others explore Cambridge, buy antiques in Long Melford and paintings in Lavenham. **Directions: From M11 take A131, through Sudbury, heading North towards Long Melford. The Tarantella is on the left.**

MARSTON FARM COUNTRY HOTEL

BODYMOOR HEATH, SUTTON COLDFIELD, WARWICKSHIRE B76 9JD
TEL: 01827 872133 FAX: 01827 875043

OWNERS: Brook Hotels PLC
MANAGER: Stephen Quigley
CHEF: Darren Long

S: £39.50–£85
D: £75–£95

Sir Robert Peel and Lord Norton were both previous owners of the lovely 17th century farmhouse building which is now Marston Farm Country Hotel. Set amid nine acres of meadowland, the grounds are bordered by the Birmingham Fazeley canal which bustles with bright coloured barges and upon which the hotel has six moorings. Within the grounds are mature gardens, a tennis court, croquet lawn and well-stocked fishing lake. Inside, discreet, subtle décor, deep armchairs, inglenook fireplaces and cosy snugs combine to create an intimate, welcoming atmosphere.

The service and personal attention offered to all guests are in keeping with English country house tradition. The bedrooms are well-designed and quite spacious: those in the main house have beams, and four poster beds are available. Some rooms are specially equipped for the lady guest. Remote-control teletext, satellite TV, direct-dial telephones, tea/coffee facilities, hairdryer and trouser press are provided.

There are conference and banqueting facilities with syndicate rooms and audio-visual equipment. Weekend, Christmas and speciality breaks available. The courtyard room overlooking the original farm courtyard garden makes a relaxed setting in which to savour succulent country fare. **Places of interest nearby:** Belfry Golf Centre, Middleton Hall and Drayton Manor Park. **Directions: Junction 9, M42 follow signs to Tamworth; Kingsbury Water Park.**

In association
with MasterCard

HIGHER VEXFORD HOUSE

HIGHER VEXFORD, LYDEARD ST LAWRENCE, NR TAUNTON, SOMERSET TA4 3QF
TEL: 01984 656267 FAX: 01984 656707

OWNERS: Nigel and Finny Muers-Raby

3 rms 3 ens

S: £35
D: £56

This traditional Quantock stone country house was built in the 17th and 18th centuries and is a listed building. Today it is a family home which extends a warm welcome to guests who are guaranteed a touch of luxury.

The house stands in 10 acres of grounds, protected by walled gardens. Its spacious bedrooms are traditionally furnished in a style designed to create an atmosphere of homeliness, with plenty of books and magazines around to be enjoyed while relaxing in the comfortable chairs. All the rooms offer stunning views of the surrounding countryside.

A traditional English breakfast is served in the flag stone floored dining room, while a four course evening meal can be prepared by prior arrangement. There are many excellent inns and restaurants in the locality.

Guests may use a heated outdoor swimming pool during May to September, by arrangement, and there are numerous activities available, such as sailing on Wimbleball Lake, pony trekking and horse riding.

Places of interest nearby: Exmoor National Park and the Quantocks are within a few minutes drive and the area is rich in National Trust properties. **Directions: Take the A358 Taunton to Minehead road and then, at Cedar falls, turn left onto B3225. Follow this road for 4½ miles until the signpost on right for Higher Vexford and Lower Vexford. Follow lane for 1.5m and turn right into Higher Vexford House yard.**

 In association with MasterCard

LANGFORD MANOR

FIVEHEAD, TAUNTON, SOMERSET TA3 6PH
TEL: 01460 281674 FAX: 01460 281585

OWNERS: Peter and Fiona Willcox
CHEF: Fiona Willcox

 3 rms 3 ens

S: £50
D: £70–£80

A beautiful Grade II listed 13th-century manor house standing in nine acres of formal gardens and grounds on the edge of the Somerset Levels, offering peace, charm and seclusion. The criteria of owners Peter and Fiona Willcox are good food, faultless service, value for money and an ideal ambience.

Visitors strolling through the immaculate grounds will find a stream and pond with resident ducks and moorhens and orchards used by the family for cider and apple juice production, which you can enjoy with your meals.

The house is named after Roger de Langford, owner from 1309 to 1372. It was gifted to Exeter Cathedral by Sir John Speke in 1518 and remained in the diocese ownership until 1904. Whilst offering every modern day comfort, Langford Manor retains its original character with a magnificent Tudor staircase, extensive Elizabethan panelling, attractive mullioned windows, massive fireplaces and lovely antiques and paintings. The bedrooms are charming, the drawing room elegant and superb and tempting dishes are served in the delightful dining room.

Places of interest nearby: Wells, Bath, Sherborne and Glastonbury. Country Houses: Hatch Court and Montacute. **Directions: From M5 junction25 turn left onto A358 then follow A378 towards Langport. On entering Fivehead turn right just before garage. At foot of hill turn left, then left past Post Office.**

UPPER COURT

KEMERTON, NR TEWKESBURY, GLOUCESTERSHIRE GL20 7HY
TEL: 01386 725351 FAX: 01386 725472

OWNERS: Bill and Diana Herford

4 rms	4 ens	🌲

S: £60
D: from £75

A fine Grade II listed Georgian manor house, Upper Court is the home of antique dealers Bill and Diana Herford and their family. They are happy to welcome all guests, whether visiting on holiday or for business. Antiques, open fires and dried flowers abound. The beautiful four-poster and twin-bedded rooms all have en suite bathrooms, TV and tea trays.

The main feature of the National Garden Scheme garden is the lake: it is perfect for boating, fly-fishing or romantic picnics. In the walled garden there is a heated pool or enjoy a game of croquet or tennis. Riding stables, golf, clay-pigeon shooting and windsurfing are all nearby. Dinner is served in the candle-lit dining room. The coach house and stables have been converted into three self-catering cottages from £230 per week for two people in low season. Kemerton is a beautiful village on Bredon Hill, surrounded by footpaths and riding tracks which offer wonderful views.

Places of interest nearby: Stratford, Sudeley and Warwick Castles, Hidcote, Snowshill Manor, Oxford, Bath, Cheltenham and Broadway. **Directions: From Cheltenham north on A435/B4079. One mile after A46 crossroads sign to Kemerton on the right. Turn off main road at War Memorial. House behind church. From M5 junction 9, go east on A46 to the B4079 crossroads, then left and one mile as above.**

TREBREA LODGE

TRENALE, TINTAGEL, CORNWALL PL34 0HR
TEL: 01840 770410 FAX: 01840 770092

OWNERS: John Charlick and Sean Devlin

| 7 rms | 7 ens | 🌲 | SMALL HOTEL |

MasterCard VISA   S: £55–£60
D: £78–£88

Winner of the Johansens 1994 Country House Award, Trebrea Lodge overlooks the beauty and grandeur of the North Cornish coast and is set in 4½ acres of wooded hillside. This Grade II listed house was built on land granted to the Bray family by the Black Prince in the 14th century and has been lived in and improved by successive generations of the Brays for almost 600 years.

All the bedrooms are individually decorated with traditional and antique furniture and they offer uninterrupted views across open fields to the Atlantic Ocean. The elegant first-floor drawing room also boasts spectacular views, while there is a comfortable smoking room downstairs with an open log fire.

A full English breakfast and four-course dinner are served in the oak-panelled dining room and the menu changes daily. The cooks use the finest local ingredients, including sea trout and wild salmon from the River Tamar, and they have been awarded an AA Rosette.

Places of interest nearby: Tintagel Island and Boscastle. Bodmin Moor, Lanhydrock House and gardens, Pencarrow House and extensive coastal walks. **Directions: From Launceston take Wadebridge–Camelford road. At A39 follow Tintagel sign – turn left for Trenale ½ mile before reaching Tintagel.**

TITCHWELL MANOR HOTEL

TITCHWELL, BRANCASTER, KING'S LYNN, NORFOLK PE13 8BB
TEL: 01485 210221 FAX: 01485 210104

OWNERS: Margaret and Ian Snaith

| 15 rms | 15 ens | |

MasterCard VISA AMERICAN EXPRESS D

S: £35–£55
D: £70–£110

Titchwell Manor Hotel is situated in an area of outstanding natural beauty and is the perfect location for anyone wanting to explore the lovely coastline or to enjoy the flora and fauna of rural Norfolk. The hotel's front offers an excellent view over the salt marshes to the sea, while attractive gardens at the rear provide ideal surroundings in which to enjoy a relaxing stroll.

The bright and attractive bedrooms offer every modern comforts – as well as some extra company for the young or young-at-heart in the guise of a bunny or teddy bear!

A cheerful open fire in the homely lounge promises a warm welcome in all but the hottest weather, helping to create perfect surroundings for relaxation.

The hotel enjoys an excellent reputation for the quality of its food, with its restaurants offering varied and extensive menus. Wholesome and tasty bar meals are also provided, along with morning coffee, packed lunches and afternoon teas. Local seafood a speciality.

A range of outdoor activities is available, including golfing, sailing, cycling, horse-riding and fishing. Closeby is the famous RSPB Titchwell reserve where marsh harriers, avocets and migrating birds can be sighted.
Places of interest nearby: Holkham Hall, Blickling Hall, Sandringham and a host of ancient churches, museums and monuments. **Directions: Situated on the A149 coast road that runs from King's Lynn to Cromer.**

THE ROYAL HOTEL

LEMON STREET, TRURO, CORNWALL, TR1 2QB
TEL: 01872 270345 FAX: 01872 242453

OWNER: Lynn Manning
MANAGER: Martin Edwards
CHEFS: Mike Smith and Bryan Hatton

S: £49–£75
D: £65–£90

Visitors to this elegant, 17th century hotel, situated in the heart of the cathedral city of Truro, cannot but be impressed by the king-size royal coat of arms above the entrance door and the rich, deep blue carpet enhanced with large red and gold crowns in the reception area. These commemorate a visit to the hotel by Queen Victoria's husband, Prince Albert, in 1846.

The Royal Hotel regally exemplifies some of the most dignified and best preserved examples of Georgian architecture in Britain that surround it. It has style, character and comfort. The carefully appointed bedrooms are all fully en suite and have everything expected from a quality hotel. Business facilities in executive bedrooms include a work desk and fax machine.

Superb international cuisine is imaginatively created and presented. Guests wishing to work off a heavy meal and stay trim can take advantage of a mirrored fitness studio.

Places of interest nearby: Falmouth, St Ives, the Seal Sanctuary at Gweek, several heritage sites and many magnificent gardens and National Trust properties.
Directions: From the A30 turn left onto the A3074 at Garland Cross towards the city centre dual carriageway. Go all the way round the second roundabout to drive back up the dual carriageway. Take the first left and the hotel is ahead of you.

In association
with MasterCard

HOOKE HALL

HIGH STREET, UCKFIELD, EAST SUSSEX TN22 1EN
TEL: 01825 761578 FAX: 01825 768025

OWNERS: Alister and Juliet Percy

9 rms	9 ens	SMALL HOTEL

S: from £50
D: from £80

Uckfield lies on the borders of Ashdown Forest, near the South Downs and resorts of Brighton and Eastbourne and 40 minutes from Gatwick Airport. Hooke Hall is an elegant Queen Anne town house, the home of its owners, Juliet and Alister Percy, who have carried out extensive renovations.

The comfortable bedrooms are individually decorated to a high standard with private facilities. In the panelled study guests can relax by the open fire before having dinner at 'La Scaletta' known for its high quality North Italian regional cuisine. The food has earned 2 AA rosettes and small lunch and dinner parties are arranged in other rooms and are looked after by Juliet, herself a Cordon Bleu chef.

Places of interest nearby: Within easy reach are Leeds, Hever and Bodiam Castles, Penshurst Place and Battle Abbey. The gardens of Sissinghurst, Nymans, Great Dixter, Sheffield Park, Wakehurst Place and Leonardslee are no distance nor is Batemans, Rudyard Kipling's home. Glyndebourne Opera is only 15 minutes by car. There are several English vineyards nearby to be visited. Closed for Christmas. **Directions: From M25 take the exit for East Grinstead and continue South on the A22 to Uckfield. Hooke Hall is at the northern end of the High Street.**

In association
with MasterCard

VENN OTTERY BARTON

VENN OTTERY, NR OTTERY ST MARY, DEVON EX11 1RZ
TEL: 01404 812733 FAX: 01404 814713

OWNERS: Shân Merritt and Dan Fishman
CHEF: Andy Witheridge and Annette Sharples

15 rms 15 ens

S: £37–£47
D: £70–£95

Venn Ottery Barton is a superb country house hotel built in 1530 and extended in Georgian and modern times. Set in the midst of unspoilt East Devon, it boasts an old world charm while providing every creature comfort.

The bedrooms are tasteful, roomy and simple and there is an oak-beamed residents' lounge in which to relax and unwind. Next door is the Bar, with its enormous open fireplace making it a warm and inviting place to enjoy a drink.

Imaginative English food is the order of the day in the restaurant. Tempting main courses include dishes such as duck breast served pink with red berry glaze; fillet of salmon in a pool of saffron and vermouth sauce; and chargrilled aubergine and cream cheese quiche. A choice of delicious home-made desserts follows.

The hotel is an excellent base for touring the Devon Heritage Coast, Exeter, and beyond to the South Hams and Dartmoor. For the golfing enthusiast, there are at least six excellent courses close by, including the famous Budleigh Salterton links. Antique-hunters will enjoy browsing around the South-West's nearby antique centres of Honiton and Topsham.

Places of interest nearby: Killerton and Bicton Gardens, Aylesbeare Bird Sanctuary. **Directions: From M5 junction 30 join A3052 towards Sidmouth. On approaching Newton Poppleford turn left at signpost to Venn Ottery. The hotel driveway is a mile along this lane on left at bottom of hill.**

In association with MasterCard

KEMPS COUNTRY HOUSE HOTEL AND RESTAURANT

EAST STOKE, WAREHAM, DORSET BH20 6AL
TEL: 01929 462563 FAX: 01929 405287

OWNERS: Jill and Paul Warren

S: £52–£73
D: £74–£116

This small and welcoming country house hotel, surrounded by unspoilt Dorset countryside, overlooks the Frome Valley and offers lovely views of the Purbeck Hills. The house was originally a Victorian Rectory and its tasteful extension was undertaken with great care to preserve Victorian atmosphere.

There are five bedrooms in the main house, while the Old Coach House has been converted to include four en suite rooms. More recently, six spacious new bedrooms have been added in an annexe, all facing the Purbecks. Decorated and furnished to equally high standards, one of these rooms has a traditional four-poster bed and a whirlpool bath.

Before dinner guests are invited to enjoy a drink in the lounge and bar whilst ordering their meal. The bar features the ornate wallpaper and heavy hangings of the Victorian period. The comfortable dining room extends into the conservatory, from which there are picturesque views of the hills as dusk falls. Kemps restaurant, which has been awarded an AA Rosette, enjoys an excellent local reputation for first-rate cuisine. The table d'hôte menu changes daily and there is also an à la carte menu. Food is prepared to order, everything possible is home-made, and the service is second to none.

Places of interest nearby: Lulworth and Corfe Castles, Athelhampton House and gardens. **Directions: On the A352 main road between Wareham and Wool.**

THE ARDENCOTE MANOR HOTEL AND COUNTRY CLUB

LYE GREEN ROAD, CLAVERDON, WARWICKSHIRE CV35 8LS
TEL: 01926 843111 FAX 01926 842646

MANAGER: Paul Williams
CHEF: Jonathan Stallard

| 18 rms | 18 ens | SMALL HOTEL |

S: £85
D: £135

Situated deep in the Warwickshire countryside yet just minutes from the motorway network, this charming, historic gentleman's residence is a tranquil retreat with an extensive range of sports and leisure facilities. There is an indoor swimming pool with Jacuzzi, solarium and steam rooms, a fully-equipped gymnasium, two all-weather tennis courts, four squash courts, pitch and putt and a jogging trail.

Alternatively, guests can pamper themselves with one of the range of head-to-toe beauty treatments in the hotel's Health and Beauty Suite.

The en suite bedrooms are spacious and tastefully furnished. A creatively designed table d'hôte menu is served in the large, stylish conservatory which opens onto the gardens and has a cosy cocktail bar and dance area. More intimate dining can be enjoyed in the gourmet Oak Room restaurant with its elegant country house atmosphere.

A traditional log cabin Sports Lodge overlooking a large, trout filled lake, and incorporating a separate and informal bar restaurant, nestles gracefully within the 40 acres of immaculate landscaped grounds, gardens and waterways.

Places of interest nearby: Birmingham's city attractions and Warwick's imposing castle. Stratford upon Avon is within easy reach. **Directions: From M40 follow signs to Henley-in-Arden, taking the A4189 to Claverdon/Warwick.**

In association
with MasterCard

BERYL

WELLS, SOMERSET BA5 3JP
TEL: 01749 678738 FAX: 01749 670508

OWNERS: Eddie and Holly Nowell

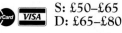

S: £50–£65
D: £65–£80

This nineteenth century Gothic mansion is tastefully furnished with antiques. It also offers hospitality of the highest order.

The host is a famous antique dealer, with a long established shop in Wells, his gardening talents are reflected in the 13 acres of parkland which he has restored with great skill.

His wife is a charming and talented hostess, evident in the attention paid to detail, and an excellent cook. Dinner is served by arrangement in the elegant dining room, with a set menu and house wines, pre-dinner and after-dinner drinks are available. It is possible to have small conferences or private celebrations. The en suite bedrooms have interesting views, with all the requisites for modern comfort.

Places of interest nearby: Wells Cathedral (1 mile), The Roman Baths at Bath, Glastonbury Abbey, Longleat House, Stourhead, Farleigh Castle, Theatres in Bath and Bristol and many more fascinating places. For more active guests there is marvellous golf, fishing, riding, excellent walking and nearby leisure centre. **Directions: Leave Wells on Radstock Road B3139. Opposite B.P. garage turn left into Hawkers Lane, Beryl is signed at top with a leafy 500yd drive to the main gate.**

WELLS

GLENCOT HOUSE

GLENCOT LANE, WOOKEY HOLE, NR WELLS, SOMERSET BA5 1BH
TEL: 01749 677160 FAX: 01749 670210

OWNER: Jenny Attia

| 13 rms | 13 ens | | SMALL HOTEL |

MasterCard VISA

S: £57.50
D: £80–£98

Idyllically situated in 18 acres of sheltered gardens and parkland with river frontage, Glencot House is an imposing Grade II listed Victorian mansion built in grand Jacobean style. It has been sensitively renovated to its former glory to provide comfortable country house accommodation and a homely atmosphere.

This elegantly furnished hotel has countless beautiful features: carved ceilings, walnut panelling, mullioned windows, massive fireplaces, antiques and sumptuous chandeliers. The bedrooms are decorated and furnished with period pieces. All have full en-suite facilities and splendid views. Many have four-poster or half tester beds.

Guests can enjoy pleasant walks in the garden, trout fishing in the river, snooker, table tennis, a sauna or a dip in the jet-stream pool. The small, intimate bar has a balcony overlooking the grounds and diverse and delicious fare is served in the restaurant, enriched by beautiful glassware, silver and china.

Places of interest nearby: The caves at Wookey Hole, the cathedral town of Wells, the houses and gardens of Longleat, Stourhead and Montacute, Glastonbury, Bath, the Mendip Hills and the Cheddar Gorge. **Directions: From the M4, exit at junction 18. Take the A46 to Bath and then follow the signs to Wells and Wookey Hole. From the M5. exit at junction 22. Join the A38 and then the A371 towards Wells and Wookey Hole.**

DUNSLEY HALL

DUNSLEY, WHITBY, NORTH YORKSHIRE YO21 3TL
TEL: 01947 893437 FAX: 01947 893505

OWNERS: Bill and Carol Ward

S: £55–£59
D: £89–£130

Stately Dunsley Hall stands in 4 acres of landscaped gardens in North Yorkshire National Park and has survived almost unaltered since being built at the turn of the century. The oak panelling and some of the original carpets and furnishings are still in fine condition.

Each of the 17 en suite bedrooms is individually furnished and some have views to the sea which is only a few minutes walk away. Two of the bedrooms have four-poster beds.

Guests can relax over a drink in the Library Bar whose restful features include mellowed oak panelling, a handsome carved fireplace and stained glass windows or in the Pyemans Bar. Each evening in the attractive Terrace Dining Room with its picture window view over the garden or the Oak Room a table d'hote dinner is served from a menu that changes nightly.

For exercise and health there is a fully equipped fitness room, a sauna and large indoor swimming pool. Outside is a hard tennis court, a 9-hole putting green and a croquet lawn. Dogs are allowed by arrangement only.

Places of interest nearby: Castle Howard, Robin Hood's Bay, the Pickering Steam Railway and the birthplace of Captain Cook. Reduced green fees at Whitby Golf Course.
Directions: From the A171 Whitby-Teeside road, turn right at signpost for Newholme, three miles north of Whitby. Dunsley is the first turning on the left. Dunsley Hall is one mile further on the right.

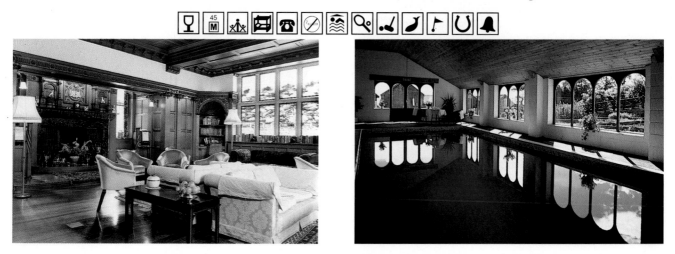

In association
with MasterCard

BEECHLEAS

17 POOLE ROAD, WIMBORNE MINSTER, DORSET BH21 1QA
TEL: 01202 841684 FAX: 01202 849344

OWNER: Josephine McQuillan

9 rms | 9 ens | SMALL HOTEL

S: £65–£85
D: £78–£98

Beechleas is a delightful Georgian Grade II listed town house hotel. It has been carefully restored and offers guests comfortable accommodation in beautifully furnished quality en suite bedrooms.

The hotel's own charming restaurant, which overlooks a pretty walled garden, is bright and airy in the summer and warmed by cosy log fires in the winter. The carefully prepared menu is changed daily and offers dishes using natural produce wherever possible along with the finest fresh ingredients available from the local market.

Sailing trips are available from Poole Harbour, where guests may choose to go fishing. They can play golf on one of the many local courses. It takes just five minutes to walk into the centre of Wimborne, a historic market town with an interesting twintower church built on the site of its old Saxon Abbey during the 12th and 13th centuries.

The hotel, which is closed from 24 December to the end of January, has been awarded two red Stars by the AA and two Rosettes for its restaurant along with a Blue Ribbon from the RAC.

Places of interest nearby: There are many National Trust properties within easy reach, including Kingston Lacy House, Badbury Rings and Corfe Castle. Bournemouth and Poole are a 20 minute drive away. **Directions: From London take M3, M27, A31 and then B3073 to Wimborne.**

In association with MasterCard

HOLBROOK HOUSE HOTEL

WINCANTON, SOMERSET BA9 8BS
TEL: 01963 32377 FAX: 01963 32681

OWNER: Holbrook House Ltd
GENERAL MANAGER: Giovanni Testagrossa MHCIMA
CHEF: Daren Godfrey

S: from £50
D: from £75

The history of Holbrook dates back to Saxon times, with the earliest records of a property on the site having been drawn up during the reign of Edward III. Today's house lies two miles west of Wincanton at the edge of the low hills that fringe the Blackmore Vale.

The accommodation includes comfortable and well-equipped bedrooms and beautifully proportioned reception rooms creating perfect surroundings in which to relax and unwind. A superb selection of sumptuous dishes is served in the Gallery Restaurant. Head Chef Daren Godfrey uses the fresh meat from animals reared traditionally without growth promoters or hormone replacements, venison and game selected from local shoots on estates and from fish which is delivered fresh each day. The hotel's swimming pool, open May to September is set in the peaceful surroundings of the old orchard, while its grounds also offer facilities to enjoy a game of croquet, squash or tennis. Other activities within easy access include riding, golf, skiing on a dry ski slope and wonderful country walks.

Places of interest nearby: The Fleet Air Arm Museum and the great houses and gardens of Montacute, Longleat and Stourhead. **Directions: Leave the A303 at Wincanton slip Road and join the A371 towards Castle Cary at the first roundabout. Over three more roundabouts and the hotel driveway is on the right immediately after the third.**

For hotel location, see maps on pages 266-272

In association with MasterCard

THE COUNTRY HOUSE AT WINCHELSEA

HASTINGS ROAD, WINCHELSEA, EAST SUSSEX TN36 4AD
TEL: 01797 226669

OWNER: Mary Carmichael

| 3 rms | 3 ens |

S: from £46
D: from £64

With spectacular views toward the ancient hill town of Winchelsea and completely surrounded by National Trust countryside, this traditional Sussex farmhouse commands a unique position. It is a listed building of great character and charm standing in its own two acres of lovely walled garden.

The individually styled bedrooms offer guests wonderful garden and country views with en suite facilities, colour T.V., direct-dial telephone and complimentary beverage trays.

A traditional hearty breakfast is of course included, but for the more health conscious there is always fresh fruit, low fat cereals or maybe a little poached fish!

A pre-ordered light Supper or Dinner is available from Monday to Saturday, and your host will be pleased to discuss the daily changing menu. Aperitifs can be enjoyed in the lounge bar, and a few well-chosen wines are offered to compliment your meal.

Nothing is too much trouble for your caring hostess at this delightful house to ensure a most relaxing and memorable stay.

Places of interest nearby: The medieval towns of Rye and Winchelsea, National Trust properties and gardens, coastal or Romney Marsh walks. **Directions: Set back from the A259 on the Hastings side of Winchelsea and approximately seven minutes from Rye by car.**

BRAEMOUNT HOUSE HOTEL

SUNNY BANK ROAD, WINDERMERE, CUMBRIA LA23 2EN
TEL: 015394 45967 FAX: 015394 45967

OWNERS: Ian and Anne Hill

5 rms	5 ens		SMALL HOTEL

 S: £35–£40
D: £45–£70

Braemount House is a delightful country house strictly non-smoking in the heart of the Lake District, just minutes from Lake Windermere. The owners, Ian and Anne Hill, guarantee you a warm welcome, and the general ambience is one of comfort and tranquillity.The bedrooms are all en suite and are individually furnished.

Noted for their characteristically imaginative cuisine, the Hills pride themselves on their catering. Ian is a born chef and he creates a full breakfast that includes locally made sausages and a variety of other tempting dishes that lift the morning meal out of the ordinary and give a great start to the day.

Places of interest nearby: Ten minutes walk away lies Lake Windermere itself where guests can enjoy a whole range of water sports or boat trips, and there are many interesting walks closeby for the energetic fell-walker. At Grasmere there is the William Wordsworth Museum, Dove Cottage, where he lived and Hill Top Farm, the house of Beatrix Potter is not far away. **Directions: From junction 36 on the M6 take the A591 to Windermere. Turn left following the one way system signposted Bowness, 100 yards past the clock tower, turn left into Queen's Drive, then first right into Sunny Bank Road. The hotel is 50 yards on the left.**

FAYRER GARDEN HOUSE HOTEL

LYTH VALLEY ROAD, BOWNESS-ON-WINDERMERE, CUMBRIA LA23 3JP
TEL: 015394 88195 FAX: 015394 45986

OWNERS: Iain and Jackie Garside

18 rms	18 ens	SMALL HOTEL

S: £55–£85
D: £89–£180
(including dinner)

Overlooking Lake Windermere in spacious gardens and grounds this lovely Victorian House is a very comfortable hotel where guests enjoy the spectacular views over the water, a real welcome and marvellous value for money.

The delightful lounges and bar and the superb air conditioned restaurant all enjoy Lake views. There is an excellent table d'hôte menu in the award winning restaurant changing daily using local produce where possible, fish game and poultry and also a small à la carte choice. The wine list is excellent and very reasonably priced.

Many of the attractive bedrooms face the Lake, some having 4 poster beds and whirlpool baths en suite, there are also ground floor rooms suitable for the elderly or infirm.

The nearby Parklands Leisure Complex has an indoor pool, sauna, steam room, badminton, snooker and squash complimentary to hotel residents. Special breaks available. **Places of interest nearby:** The Windermere Steamboat Museum, Boating from Bowness Pier and golf at Windermere Golf Club and The Beatrix Potter Attraction close by. **Directions: Junction 36 off the M6, A590 past Kendal. Take B5284 at the next roundabout, turn left at the end and the hotel is 350 yards on the right.**

QUARRY GARTH COUNTRY HOUSE HOTEL AND RESTAURANT

WINDERMERE, CUMBRIA LA23 1L7
TEL: 015394 88282 FAX: 015394 46584

OWNER: Ken MacLean
MANAGER: John Mathers
CHEF: Brian Parsons

S: £50–£60
D: £70–£110

This mellow Edwardian house enjoys an idyllic setting in eight acres of peaceful woodland gardens near Lake Windermere. Its new owner, Ken MacLean, and his staff invite guests to come and sample Quarry Garth's high standards of comfort and hospitality.

The individually designed bedrooms are all en suite some with four-poster or king-size beds. A new à la carte restaurant Le Louvre has been added to complement the existing table d'hôte restaurant. Le Louvre overlooks the landscaped gardens and serves the finest Anglo-French cuisine. It is open for lunch and dinner, with the option of dining on the terrace in summer. The elegant but unpretentious lounge is dotted with fresh flowers, books,

magazines and a variety of local guide books.

Secluded some 50 yards from the main hotel stands the Quarry Lodge, containing three en suite bedrooms on the ground floor (2 with spa baths) and a large lounge dining room on the first floor.

A woodland trail within the grounds offers a relaxing 15 minute walk among rich wildlife. A sauna and spa bathroom is available for use by guests.

Places of interest nearby: The beautiful lakes, the homes of Wordsworth and Beatrix Potter and many historic home and gardens. **Directions: From exit 36 of M6, take A590 for 3 miles then A591 to Windermere. Continue on A591 for 2 miles and the entrance is on the right.**

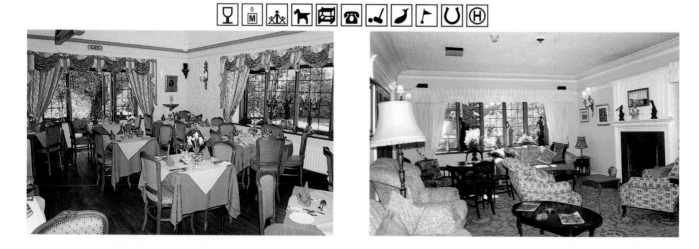

In association with MasterCard

WOOD HALL HOTEL COUNTRY CLUB

SHOTTISHAM, WOODBRIDGE, SUFFOLK IP12 3EG
TEL: 01394 411283 FAX: 01394 410007

OWNERS: Harvey and Carole Storch

12 rms | 12 ens | SMALL HOTEL

S: £75
D: £75–£95
Suite: £105

Three miles from Woodbridge, on the Deben estuary, this Elizabethan manor house has been transformed into a secluded and luxurious hotel. A walled garden and lake are just part of the magnificent grounds surrounding Wood Hall – which is approached by a long tree lined drive.

The historic background is evident, the reception rooms having fine panelled walls, ornate ceilings and big, open fireplaces, extremely welcoming on dull afternoons

The bedrooms are romantic, each with its own colour scheme reflected in lovely fabrics. Antiques vie with modern comforts, and the bathrooms are wonderfully equipped.

Guests enjoy cocktails at the bar and a choice of three restaurants with appetising menus that include exotic and traditional dishes, grills and local fish. The wine list is excellent and reasonably priced. Additionally there is a magnificent banqueting suite, ideal for conferences and seminars, with appropriate equipment available.

Places of interest nearby: Residents have complimentary membership of the Wood Hall Country Club, which has squash, tennis, croquet, a heated outdoor pool, sauna and solarium. Local attractions include ten golf courses, good sailing off the Suffolk Coast at Woodbridge, fishing and shooting, bird sanctuaries, Aldeburgh Music Festival. **Directions: A12 towards Lowestoft, then A1152 through Melton, next roundabout B1083 towards Bawdsey, after 3 miles hotel is on right.**

In association with MasterCard

THE PARSONAGE COUNTRY HOUSE HOTEL

ESCRICK, YORK, NORTH YORKSHIRE YO4 6LE
TEL: 01904 728111 FAX: 01904 728151

OWNERS: Paul and Karan Ridley
MANAGER: Paul Ransome

17 rms | 17 ens | SMALL HOTEL

S: £70–£98
D: £105–£130

Surrounded by wide expanses of lawn, formal gardens and wild woodland, The Parsonage Country House Hotel provides an oasis of comfort and tranquillity. In the nearby breathtakingly beautiful hills and valleys are hidden ancient hamlets and villages still immersed in the old way of life.

The Parsonage has been passed down through various noble families and baronies from Count Alan of Brittany in the early 11th century, to the de Lascelles, the Knyvetts, Thompsons, Lawleys and finally the Forbes Adams retaining all of its charm and many original features.

Each bedroom has been furnished with comfort and luxury in mind and features a full range of modern facilities. Two of the larger rooms contain magnificent four poster beds. The two new conference suites in the coach house make an ideal venue for executive meetings or conferences.

A highly appetising selection of Anglo-French dishes is created by the chef, who uses only the freshest, high quality local ingredients. A varied and carefully selected wine list is available to complement any meal.

Places of interest nearby: The Parsonage is a perfect base from which to visit York and Harrogate, the estates of Castle Howard, the three Cistercian Abbeys, the Yorkshire coastline or the Yorkshire Dales. **Directions: Escrick is on the A19 a few miles south of York.**

HOPE HOUSE

HIGH STREET, YOXFORD, SAXMUNDHAM, SUFFOLK IP17 3HP
TEL: 01728 668281 FAX: 01728 668281 E-MAIL: HopeHouseYoxfordUK@compuserve.com

OWNERS: Michael Block and Roger Mildren

S: £35–£50
D: £70–£90

A Queen Anne style house with recorded 14th century origins situated in a village described as "The Garden of Suffolk" because of its lush setting between stretches of parkland. Built in 1665, Hope House has undergone extensive renovation and been refurbished to the highest standards while respecting all original features.

It is furnished with antiques and modern, comfortable pieces where appropriate. The principal public rooms have handmade carpets and matching upholstery. Rich drapes, paintings and prints enhance the house's natural welcoming atmosphere. The delightfully comfortable and attractive bedrooms contain ingenious bathrooms which the owners have cleverly managed to incorporate without interfering with the rooms' historic styles and proportions.

Easily accesible and with a host of sporting activities available nearby, elegant Hope House and its romantic walled garden are in the heart of an environment where visitors can truly relax.

Places of interest nearby: Yoxford is ideally situated for touring the Suffolk coast and visiting Southwold, RSPB Minsmere, Aldeburgh, Framlingham Castle, Leiston Abbey and Helmingham Hall. **Directions: Yoxford is just off the A12 between Woodbridge and Lowestoft.**

Johansens Recommended Country Houses in
Wales

Snowdonia, Nant Gwynant

Magnificent scenery, a rich variety of natural, cultural and modern leisure attractions, and the very best accommodation awaits the Johansens visitor to Wales.

Wales, like Caesar's Gaul, can be divided into three parts – South Wales, Mid Wales and North Wales. These parts are determined by physical geography, mountain groups which break up the country east-west and are fissured by narrow valleys. These lock a large part of the population into small settlements – not dissimilar from those others built around markets and staging posts along the drovers routes – fostering a strong sense of community. The Celtic folk that the Romans encountered were a civilised and artistic people whose sense of design and skills in oratory were greatly admired. These Celtic origins are still apparent today in the language that is spoken by 250,000 – understood by many more – and to be seen everywhere in Wales.

South Wales' industrial past is now enshrined in museums – like Big Pit, the Rhondda Heritage Park and the Industrial and Maritime Museum in Cardiff Bay. For the industrial valleys have been greened again and now house commuter villages for people who work in the new high-tech and service industries along the M4 and the Heads of the Valleys Roads. The old ports that declined with coal and steel are being revived as marinas, with an imaginative mix of commercial and social development.

Nowhere is this more so than in Cardiff Bay,

the former dockland of the capital city. Here a modern maritime city is being catered to compare with any in the world – the centre piece of which is a barrage from Queen Alexandra Dock to Penarth. But the city already has so much to commend it – more parkland per head of population than any other city in the UK and a graceful civic centre modelled on Lutyens' plans for New Delhi.

Swansea is a modern city which over the last 25 years has regenerated a lunar landscape left by 200 years of metal processing in the Lower Swansea Valley into a great green lung in which are set a mixture of commercial and leisure developments. It has also created an attractive marina from its disused dockland. And on its western door-step it has an Area of Outstanding Natural Beauty, the Gower Peninsula.

Carmarthen and Pembrokeshire have lovely beaches, cosy coves, lush pastures and plump hills into which are set golf courses to please the eye and to challenge the handicap. The area boasts fantastic fishing, wonderful walks and watersports galore – and two fantastic parks at Pembrey and Oakwood offering a wide range of attractions and amusements.

Mid Wales is a marvellous land beyond

those blue remembered hills – a rolling, round green country with a silver filigree of rivers and lakes. Buttressed to the north by Cader Idris and to the south by the Brecon Beacons, this lovely hilly region is threaded by rivers and streams and old drovers roads that simply invite exploration – whether on foot, horseback or mountain bike. The land looks and leans towards the west, to the 75 miles long crescent of Cardigan Bay with its magnificent Heritage Coast studded with small ports.

North Wales has mountains offering bracing walks or pre-Everest training, a coast that holds charms for the sailor, the water-sports enthusiast or the sunbather. It has rivers, lakes and forest in which walkers, anglers, mountain-bikers and wild water canoeists can lose themselves and each other. It has castles galore – fine examples built by Welsh lords and by Edward I.

But Wales' greatest asset is its people and the welcome they give the friendly visitor – Croeso I Cymru, Welcome to Wales.

For more information about Wales, please contact:–

Wales Tourist Board
Brunel House
2 Fitzalan Road
Cardiff
Wales CF2 1UY
Tel: 01222 475226

In association with MasterCard

PLAS PENHELIG COUNTRY HOUSE HOTEL AND RESTAURANT

ABERDOVEY, GWYNEDD LL35 0NA
TEL: 01654 767676 FAX: 01654 767783

OWNERS: The Richardson Family

11 rms 11 ens

S: £45.50
D: £80-£90

A wooded driveway leads the way to Plas Penhelig, a splendid Edwardian country house set in 7 acres of secluded grounds and offering wonderful views across the tranquil Dovey estuary. Guests are given the warmest welcome from the resident owner and his dedicated staff who work hard to create a homely atmosphere.

The hotel lounges, complete with card tables, reading lamps and glowing log fires, provide a restful setting in which to enjoy morning coffee or afternoon tea. Then, when the pure Welsh air has taken effect, a good night's sleep is ensured in the comfortable bedrooms.

Crisp table linen, gleaming cutlery and elegant floral decorations set the scene for an excellent meal in the hotel's restaurant. Fresh fruit, seasonal vegetables and salads are among the home grown fare, complementing freshly supplied local meat, game and fish to create an excellent range of dishes. Lighter meals and snacks can be enjoyed in the cocktail bar or on the terrace.

While a walk in the award-winning landscaped gardens will prove hard to resist, a putting green and croquet lawn are available for the more energetic.

Places of interest nearby: The lovely sandy beaches of Cardigan Bay, Snowdonia National Park, craft centres and the Centre for Alternative Technology are all within easy reach. **Directions: On the A493 Machynlleth to Tywyn road in Aberdovey.**

ABERGAVENNY (Glangrwyney)

GLANGRWYNEY COURT

GLANGRWYNEY, NR CRICKHOWELL, POWYS NP8 1ES
TEL: 01873 811288 FAX: 01873 810317

OWNERS: Warwick and Christina Jackson

S: £35–£40
D: £65–£75

This graceful Georgian mansion is set in four acres of secluded mature gardens on the Monmouthshire–Powys borders. There is a walled garden and in summer visitors can sit in perfect peace enjoying the views of the rolling hills. The house is furnished with antiques, fine porcelain and paintings. The delightful drawing room and dining room are exclusive to guests. The music room has a grand piano and other instruments. Guests are ensured of a warm welcome.

Hospitality offered includes a traditional breakfast and, by prior discussion, a delicious four-course dinner based on the seasonal fresh produce available.

All the bedrooms have been individually decorated and furnished and the Romantic West Room is especially popular with honeymooners. Four rooms are en suite – The Master rooom has a steam shower and luxuriously deep bath. The twin room has its own private Jacuzzi.

Places of interest nearby: In summer, guests play croquet, tennis and boules or relax in the garden. If agreed beforehand, dogs are welcome. Golf, pony trekking, and fishing are nearby, also the Brecon Beacons National Park for walkers. Hereford Cathedral and the market towns of Abergavenny and Crickhowell are close by, as are the spectacular Talybont and Gwryne Fawr Reservoirs. **Directions: The Court is signed from Crickhowell on the A40 between Brecon and Abergavenny.**

LLANWENARTH HOUSE

GOVILON, ABERGAVENNY, GWENT NP7 9SF
TEL: 01873 830289 FAX: 01873 832199

OWNERS: Bruce and Amanda Weatherill

In association
with MasterCard

| 4 rms | 4 ens | |

S: £50–£62
D: £70–£80

Llanwenarth House overlooks the Vale of Usk and stands in its own beautiful grounds within the Brecon Beacons National Park. It was built from local rose-grey limestone in the 16th century by the Morgan family, ancestors of Sir Henry Morgan, privateer and Lieutenant Governor of Jamaica. Careful restoration has ensured that the house has retained all of its character, while bringing it up to the highest level of comfort. Guests are personally looked after by the family, who offer comfortable accommodation in period furnished rooms. Many of the elegant spacious bedrooms offer lovely views of the grounds and surrounding countryside. Fine cuisine is prepared by Amanda, a Cordon Bleu cook who makes full use of local game, fish, home-produced meat, poultry and organically grown fruit and vegetables from their own kitchen garden. Dinner is served by candlelight in the beautiful Georgian dining room. Credit Cards not accepted.

Sporting activities in the vicinity include trout and salmon fishing on the River Usk, walking, pony trekking, climbing, rough shooting and golf.

Places of interest nearby: Chepstow and Raglan Castles, and Tintern Abbey. **Directions: From the roundabout one mile east of Abergavenny follow the A465 towards Merthyr Tydfil for three miles to the next roundabout. Take first exit to Govilon and the ¹/₂ mile driveway is 150 yards along on the righthand side.**

ABERGAVENNY (Llanfihangel Crucorney)

PENYCLAWDD COURT

LLANFIHANGEL CRUCORNEY, ABERGAVENNY, GWENT NP7 7LB
TEL: 01873 890719 FAX: 01873 890848

OWNERS: Julia Horton Evans and Ken Peacock
CHEF: Julia Horton Evans

S: £45
D: £74

Winner of Johansens 1996 Most Excellent Country House Award, Penyclawdd Court is a Grade II Star Listed Tudor Manor House, situated at the foot of Bryn Arw mountain in the Brecon Beacons National Park. The authentic restoration of the house has been recognised by an accolade from H.R.H. the Prince of Wales. In the grounds is a Norman motte and bailey – a scheduled ancient monument. There is also a traditional herb garden and a walled knot garden. The Court has its own free-range hens and a flock of prize-winning pedigree Jacob sheep.

Featured regularly in magazines and on T.V. and Radio, the house is furnished with antiques and there are huge stone fireplaces, flagstone floors and exposed beams. Because of its age, there are many steps, stairs and sloping floors to negotiate, which sadly means that the house is not best suited to everybody.

Four-course dinners can be provided by prior arrangement using home produced or local ingredients. Groups can enjoy researched 15th to 17th Century feasts. **Places of interest nearby:** Situated as it is in a National Park, the surrounding area offers some wonderful walks. Pony-trekking and golf are available locally. **Directions:** Penyclawdd Court is ¹/₂ mile off **A465 Abergavenny –Hereford road signposted Pantygelli.**

In association
with MasterCard

TAN-Y-FOEL

CAPEL GARMON, NR BETWS-Y-COED, ABERCONWY LL26 0RE
TEL: 01690 710507 FAX: 01690 710681

OWNERS: Peter and Janet Pitman

7 rms   7 ens

S: £65–£90
D: £95–£150

This exquisite house, recently described as "a jewel box of colour", has won many accolades as an outstanding small country hotel, a fine example of country elegance at its best.

Set in breathtaking surroundings, commanding magnificent views of the verdant Conwy Valley and the rugged peaks of Snowdonia.

Once inside Tan-y-Foel a "no smoking" policy prevails, there are seven extremely comfortable bedrooms, each have their own individual style with warm colours and rich decorations, thoughtful small touches add to their charm and the bathrooms are delightful.

This is also celebrated for its impeccable cuisine, wild salmon, samphire, lamb and game are some of the ingredients used. The wine list is equally distinguished with over 90 excellent choices.

Peter and Janet give a personal welcome which perfectly complements the nature of their fine house, it is no surprise the two day "Special Offer Breaks" are so popular.

Places of interest nearby: Great Little Trains of Wales, Bodnant Gardens, Conwy Castle and Snowdonia.
Directions: From Chester, A55 to Llandudno, the A470 towards Betws-y-Coed. Two miles outside Llanrwst fork left towards Capel Garmon-Nebo. Tan-y-Foel is just over a mile up the hill on the left-hand side.

OLD GWERNYFED COUNTRY MANOR

FELINDRE, THREE COCKS, BRECON, POWYS LD3 0SU
TEL: 01497 847376

OWNERS: Roger and Dawn Beetham

S: £39–£45
D: £65–£98

Old Gwernyfed is a historian's delight – its passage through the ages has been carefully documented and its antiquated features well preserved. Set in 13 acres in the foothills of the Black Mountains, it was built circa 1600 as a manor house of great importance in its day.

Over the years, Roger and Dawn Beetham have lavished much attention on the building to restore it to its former glory. They have made no attempt to disguise the age of the building, preferring to enhance its original characteristics.

One of the lounges, which is oak panelled from floor to ceiling, is overlooked by the splendid balustraded minstrels gallery. Most of the bedrooms enjoy outstanding views and there is a good choice of four-poster, half-tester and canopied beds. Traffic noise is non-existent.

The dining room is dominated by its cavernous 12 foot fireplace, only rediscovered in recent years. A small table d'hôte menu is changed daily and all dishes are cooked freshly using produce from the garden or local suppliers. Closed mid-December to mid-March.

Places of interest nearby: Hay-on-Wye and the market town of Brecon. Local activities include canoeing, sailing, pony-trekking and gliding. **Directions: From Brecon turn off A438 after the Three Cocks Hotel. Take every turning to right for 1³/₄ miles. Go through Felindre and Old Gwernyfed is 200 yards on right.**

In association
with MasterCard

TY'N RHOS COUNTRY HOUSE

SEION LLANDDEINIOLEN, CAERNARFON, GWYNEDD LL55 3AE
TEL: 01248 670489 FAX: 01248 670079

OWNERS: Lynda and Nigel Kettle

10 rms	10 ens			SMALL HOTEL

S: £45–£55
D: £60–£85

Ty'n Rhos is not the typical country house hotel. This immaculate small hotel of 10 bedrooms is based on a farmhouse which has been extended and improved to provide the highest standards of accommodation and food. Guests enjoy the peaceful surroundings of green fields with wonderful open views across to nearby Caernarfon, the Menai Strait and Anglesey.

Award-winning Ty'n Rhos is the creation of Lynda and Nigel Kettle. They originally intended to run Ty'n Rhos as a full-time farm. Although a 72 acre farm still, the emphasis is firmly on looking after their guests. Ty'n Rhos's appeal is now based on a unique blend of personal service, the highest professional standards and exceptional value for money.

The beautifully appointed bedrooms, all fully en suite, have all the comforts of a stylish hotel. But perhaps the most important single element in Ty'n Rhos's success is the food which is based on the finest, fresh local ingredients. It was awarded the coveted title of Taste of Wales Restaurant of the Year 1996. It's a refreshing change to stay at this small hotel with a big reputation for its food, quality and value for money, superbly located between Snowdonia and the sea within easy touring distance of all of North Wales. **Directions: Situated in the hamlet of Seion off the B4366 and B4547. Reached from the East by A5 or A55.**

THE PEMBROKESHIRE RETREAT

RHOSYGILWEN MANSION, CILGERRAN, NR CARDIGAN, DYFED SA43 2TW
TEL: 01239 841387

OWNERS: Mr and Mrs Glen Peters
MANAGER: Mr R Wilson
CHEF: Richard Wilson

10 rms | 8 ens

S: £50
D: £90
(including dinner)

A long, wide, curving drive brings visitors to the arched entrance of imposing Rhosygilwen Mansion, surrounded by 55 acres of grounds with an arboretum, orchard and wooded walks. Dating from 1850, this listed, grey-stoned building has been carefully restored to maintain period integrity and houses The Retreat, a place of reflection and diversion and for those seeking to blend activity with relaxation, The coast of Pembrokeshire is a wonderful place for sighting dolphins and seals.

Rhosygilwen is a family home, totally non-smoking, aiming to offer hospitality and attention at a level that many formal hotels cannot achieve. Spacious rooms include a large panelled drawing room, library and conservatory. Eight of the 10 bedrooms are en suite and all have modern comforts and views over the surrounding farmland and Preseli hills. Dining is from a set menu or by arrangement to meet any special requirements. Tennis, croquet and cricket nets are within the grounds and angling, sailing, canoeing, shooting and riding can be arranged.

Places of interest nearby: Cardigan with its three-arched bridge over the River Teifi, the sands and harbour at Newquay and the scenic Pembrokeshire Coastal Path.
Directions: From the A487 Aberystwyth to Fishguard road take the A478 from Cardigan and after about two miles turn left to Cilgerran at Rhoshill.

BERTHLWYD HALL HOTEL

LLECHWEDD, NR CONWY, GWYNEDD LL32 8DQ
TEL: 01492 592409 FAX: 01492 572290

OWNERS: Brian and Joanna Griffin

| 9 rms | 9 ens | SMALL HOTEL |

S: from £58
D: from £78

Only one and a half miles from historic Conwy, on the edge of the Snowdonia national park, in sight of its famous castle, is Berthlwyd Hall Hotel, a charming Victorian and much loved landmark of the Conwy Valley. Many of the Victorian characteristics have been preserved, such as the splendid oak panelling in the entrance hall, a wide staircase sweeping up to an impressive galleried landing, elaborately carved fireplaces and stained-glass windows. The hotel has been furnished with an attention to detail giving the impression of a luxurious private house in the grand style. Each of the nine en suite bedrooms has been individually styled and comfortably appointed. Recent refurbishments include a snooker room and a function conference room seating up to 20 persons plus a Victorian kitchen where 2 day cookery demonstrations take place.

Resident proprietors Brian and Joanna Griffin spent some years in the Périgord region of south-west France, renowned for its gastronomic heritage and the inspiration for their restaurant, 'Truffles', acclaimed as one of the finest restaurants in North Wales.

Places of interest nearby: Snowdonia, the Welsh coast, Anglesey and Bodnant Gardens. **Directions: A55 into Conwy town, round one way system turning left after Lancaster Square into Sychant Pass Road, after 1 mile look for hotel sign on left. Turn left and continue for ½ mile. The Hall is approached through a small private chalet park.**

THE OLD RECTORY

LLANRWST ROAD, LLANSANFFRAID GLAN CONWY, COLWYN BAY, CONWY LL28 5LF
TEL: 01492 580611 FAX: 01492 584555

OWNERS: Michael and Wendy Vaughan

6 rms | 6 ens

S: £79–£99
D: £99–£129

Enjoy dramatic Snowdonian vistas, breathtaking sunsets and views of floodlit Conwy Castle from this idyllic country house set in large gardens overlooking Conwy Bird Reserve. Awarded 2 AA Red Stars for outstanding levels of comfort, service and hospitality and 3 Rosettes for food.

Wendy's cooking has consistently featured in Egon Ronay and all other good food guides. Her gourmet four-course dinners combine a lightness of touch and delicacy of flavour with artistic presentation. Welsh mountain lamb, locally reared Welsh black beef and fish landed at Conwy are on her menu. An award-winning wine list complements her fine cuisine. Most diets are catered for.

Antiques and Victorian watercolours decorate the interiors. The luxury en suite bedrooms have draped beds, bathrobes, ironing centres, fresh fruit and flowers.

Michael is happy to share his knowledge of Welsh history, language and culture and always has time to assist in planning touring routes. Relax in the garden and watch the River Conwy ebb and flow and you will see why this elegant Georgian home is a 'beautiful haven of peace'.

Places of interest nearby: Bodnant Gardens, Historic Conwy, Victorian Llandudno Spa, Betws-Y-Coed, Snowdonia. Walk the Roman road to Aber Falls, Chester, Caernarfon and Angelsey 40 mins. **Directions: On the A470, ¹/₂ mile south of the A55 junction, two miles from Llandudno Junction Station.**

DOLGELLAU (Ganllwyd)

DOLMELYNLLYN HALL

GANLLWYD, DOLGELLAU, GWYNEDD LL40 2HP
TEL: 01341 440273 FAX: 01341 440640

OWNERS: Jon Barkwith and Joanna Reddicliffe
CHEF: Joanna Reddicliffe

S: £45–£55
D: £75–£105

The approach to Dolmelynllyn Hall, which is entirely non-smoking, set in the amazing scenery of south Snowdonia, leads through a winding, beech-lined drive that brings guests to the doorway. A house has stood on the site since the 1500s, extended in the 18th and 19th centuries. Bedrooms are individually decorated and comfortably furnished. Joanna Reddicliffe, the daughter of the house, prepares a daily changing four-course menu with choices in each course including vegetarian dishes.

There is a conservatory bar, and a large sitting room with full-length windows overlooking the valley. Dogs are allowed in two of the bedrooms only.

The hotel is surrounded by three acres of formal gardens, bounded by a swiftly running stream which flows into a small lake. Guests can take advantage of the hotel's free fishing on 10 miles of river and three local lakes.

Places of interest nearby: Adjoining the grounds are 1,200 acres of mountains, meadow and forest, where it is possible to walk all day without seeing a car or crossing a road. Castles, slate caverns, waterfalls and a gold mine can all be visitied nearby, but the theme here is relaxation amid wonderful surroundings, comfort and only the gentlest of activities. **Directions: Dolmelynllyn Hall is off the main A470 Dolgellau– Llandudno road, just north of Dolgellau. Dinner, bed and breakfast, combined rates and short breaks are available.**

ABER ARTRO HALL

LLANBEDR, GWYNEDD, NORTH WALES LL45 2PA
TEL: 01341 241374 FAX: 01341 241547

OWNERS: Mark and Karen Evans

3 rms | 2 ens

D: £40–£80
Suite: £80–£100

The splendour of the Snowdonia National Park forms the backdrop for this handsome, grey stone Jacobean mansion tucked away between the the picturesque Cwm Bychan valley and the beautiful beach fringed coastline of North Wales. It has a colourful and romantic history, having connections with a former Prince of Wales and the composer Rachmaninov. Aber Artro Hall stands majestically in 32 acres of grounds that include terraced gardens and woodlands alongside the banks of the salmon and sea trout-laden Rivers Artro and Nantol on which the hall has fishing rights. As well as magnificent original features, this former country gentleman's retreat offers guests a full range of modern facilities, including period style, en suite bedrooms with scenic views, a fully-equipped work-out studio, tennis court, badminton and snooker room as well as the more relaxing surrounding of an elegant drawing room and comfortable oak-panelled main hall with massive open fireplace.

Places of nearby: Attractions include the Italianate village of Portmeiron, Edward I's splendid 13th century castle at Harlech, Barmouth, Porthmadoc, Shell Island, Snowdonia, and former slate and gold mines. **Directions: Aber Artro Hall is 1½ miles off the A496 Harlech to Barmouth road. At Llanbedr take the road signposted Cwm Nantcol/Cwy Bychan and fork right 1½ miles up lane following Gardens sign.**

WATERWYNCH HOUSE HOTEL

WATERWYNCH BAY, TENBY, PEMBROKESHIRE, DYFED SA70 8JT
TEL: 01834 842464 FAX: 01834 845076

OWNERS: Bette and Geoff Hampton

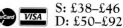
S: £38–£46
D: £50–£92

Waterwynch House is a uniquely secluded retreat nestling in a pretty little cove on the beautiful shores of Carmathen Bay. Surrounded by the Pembrokeshire Coastal National Park and 27 acres of its own woodland and gardens, it is a quiet, intimate hotel with an enviable reputation for friendly hospitality and personal service.

Dating from 1820 when it was built as a family home for Tenby based artist Charles Norris, the hotel retains its peaceful charm of the past. It is an ideal base from which to enjoy coastal walks, the wildlife and superb scenery, or just to relax on the private beach.

The 16 tastefully furnished and decorated bedrooms offer every modern comfort. Some have balconies and sea views, others overlook the gardens. An ample selection of table d'hôte and à la carte menus caters for the most discerning connoisseur in the dining room with its panoramic view over the bay. As well as some unusual speciality dishes there are a good selection of fish courses. **Places of interest nearby:** Superb walking along the adjacent Pembrokeshire coastal path, bird-watching, painting, fishing, golf and croquet, bowls and putting. **Directions: Off the A478 Kilgetty to Tenby road. Signposted on the left half a mile after the New Hedges roundabout.**

PARVA FARMHOUSE AND RESTAURANT

TINTERN, CHEPSTOW, GWENT NP6 6SQ
TEL: 01291 689411 FAX: 01291 689557

OWNERS: Dereck and Vickie Stubbs
CHEF: Dereck Stubbs

9 rms 9 ens

S: £44–£64
D: £64–£80

Surrounded by the glorious, wooded hillsides of the beautiful lower Wye Valley and just a mile from 12th century Tintern Abbey, one of the finest relics of Britain's monastic age, Parva Farmhouse is a homely haven where visitors can relax and forget the pressures of their daily world. For country lovers there is no more ideal spot. The salmon and trout teeming River Wye flows just 50 yards from the hotel's small, flower filled garden, there is an abundance of wildlife and hundreds of tempting walks.

Built during the 17th century, Parva provides today every comfort. The bedrooms are well furnished and most have pretty views across the River Wye. The beamed lounge with its log-burning fireplace, "Honesty Bar" and deep Chesterfield sofas and chairs is the perfect place to relax and chat over the day's happenings.

The crowning glory of Parva is the excellent food (AA rosette), home-cooked by chef-patron Dereck Stubbs and served in the Inglenook Restaurant before a 14-foot beamed fireplace. Golf, shooting and riding are close by and there is horse racing at Chepstow.

Places of interest nearby: Tintern Abbey, castles at Abergavenny and Chepstow, Offa's Dyke, the Royal Forest of Dean, many old ruins and ancient monuments.
Directions: From the M48, exit at junction 2 and join the A466 towards Monmouth. The hotel is on the north edge of Tintern Village.

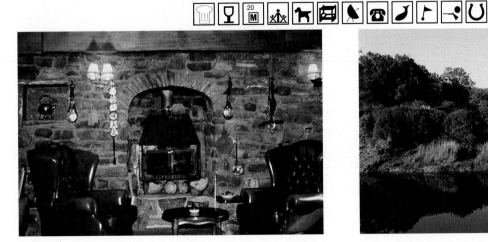

HIGHLAND.
An almost feminine charm and character all of its own. Light and aromatic, the Gentle Spirit is rich in body with a soft heather honey finish.

ISLE OF SKYE.
Assertive but not heavy. Fully flavoured with a pungent, peaty ruggedness. It explodes on the palate and lingers on. Well balanced. A sweetish seaweedy aroma.

SPEYSIDE.
Finely balanced with a dry, rather delicate aroma, good firm body and a smoky finish. A pleasantly austere malt of great distinction with a character all its own.

WEST HIGHLAND.
Oban is the West Highland malt. A singular, rich and complex malt with the merest suggestion of peat in the aroma, slightly smoky with a long smooth finish.

ISLE OF ISLAY.
Seaweed, peat, smoke and earth are all elements of the assertive Islay character. Pungent, an intensely dry 16 year old malt with a firm robust body and powerful aroma.

LOWLAND.
Typically soft, restrained and with a touch of sweetness. An exceptionally pale smooth malt which, experts agree, reaches perfection at 10 years maturity.

DALWHINNIE	TALISKER	CRAGGANMORE	OBAN	LAGAVULIN	GLENKINCHIE
15 YEARS OLD	10 YEARS OLD	12 YEARS OLD	14 YEARS OLD	16 YEARS OLD	10 YEARS OLD
HIGHLAND	SKYE	SPEYSIDE	WEST HIGHLAND	ISLAY	LOWLAND

Les grands crus de Scotland.

In the great wine-growing regions, there are certain growths from a single estate that are inevitably superior.

For the Scots, there are the single malts. Subtle variations in water, weather, peat and the distilling process itself lend each single malt its singular character.

Each Malt is an authentic, traditional malt with its own identity, inherent in both taste and aroma.

The Classic Malts are the finest examples of the main malt producing regions. To savour them, one by one, is a rare journey of discovery.

SIX OF SCOTLAND'S FINEST MALT WHISKIES

Isle of Skye

Johansens Recommended Country Houses in
Scotland

Myths and mountains, lochs and legends – Scotland's stunning scenic splendour acts as a magnet for visitors from all over the globe. Superb as it is, Scotland's charismatic charm is more than just visual.

Rich in history and heritage this ancient nation can trace its origins back over 14 centuries when the 'Scots' tribe from Ireland who had carved out their new Kingdom of Dalriada from land held by the Picts in the 5th Century, eventually gave their name to the united nation of Picts and Scots - Scotland.

Prehistoric sites can be found in almost every corner of Scotland, including the outer islands (Orkney has a particularly rich concentration of bronze age ruins), and ancient standing stones have long been a fascination for curious visitors.

Several new archaeological attractions have opened recently, including Kilmartin House in Argyll. Close to Dunadd, the ancient capital of Dalriada, - the birthplace of Scotland, Kilmartin House brings 6000 years of history to life with imaginative audio visual displays, exhibitions and a range of prehistoric artefacts from Argyll, the original 'coastline of the Gael' (Earraghaidheal in Gaelic).

Across the country in Grampian region, Archeolink at Oyne, around 25 miles north of Aberdeen, is a £4 million interpretative centre which looks set to become a major visitor attraction for the north east. Situated in 40 acres around Berry Hill, an iron age enclosure, the Centre applies state-of-the-art technology to Aberdeenshire's wealth of Stone Circles, Symbol Stones and ancient hill forts.

Far from being stuck in the past, Scotland boasts cosmopolitan cities throbbing with life and vitality. Vibrant arts and culture, magnificent architecture, superb shopping and exciting night-life are all there to be enjoyed.

Getting around is easy with a modern transport infrastructure and communications befitting a nation whose sons invented the telephone, television and tarmacadam! Indeed, air, rail and ferry links are on the increase and competitive economy fares have encouraged many new visitors, but don't worry, beyond the city boundaries space, peace and tranquillity are still the order of the day and you don't have to go far off the beaten track to find solitude and wilderness.

The glorious natural environment remains one of Scotland's most attractive features offering endless options for sports, including walking, cycling, sailing, riding and climbing.

The home of golf and the Highland games, Scotland is an outdoor enthusiast's dreamland. But you don't have to be active to appreciate this wealth of natural brilliance.

Travelling by car is simple and enjoyable; and where but Scotland would you find main roads bordering world-famous beauty spots, such as Loch Lomond and Loch Ness?

You can take your car by ferry to most of Scotland's numerous islands and a new Irish ferry service to Campbeltown has opened up the Kintyre Peninsula - an area of outstanding natural beauty.

Kintyre's coastline, characteristically for Scotland's west coast, is riveted with ruined ramparts and crowned with castellations. The stone walls bear witness to Argyll's bloody past, for this area has seen numerous battles, often between rival clans, with a massacre at Dunaverty Castle on a scale more heinous than Glencoe.

For all their feuding, the clans gave Scotland some of its most recognisable icons. Kilts, bagpipes, Highland Games and dancing - all survived and flourished despite the ban imposed following the Jacobite defeat at Culloden in 1746. Scotland's relationship with England these days is more cordial. The historic 'Stone of Destiny' - the stone which pillowed Jacob's head as he dreamed his dream, later became the property of the migrating Celtic tribe who eventually settled in Scotland in AD498 - was stolen from Scone by Edward I of England in 1296.

Seven hundred years later the Government of Great Britain returned this ceremonial seat for the inauguration of Scots' Kings to Scotland and it can now be seen on display in Edinburgh Castle.

The lavish history and heritage of the oldest Kingdom in Europe is matched by its majestic landscapes and superlative scenery. Friendly and welcoming, the Scots are proud of their country and you'll find them eager to share its many delights and attractions.

For more information on Scotland, please contact:-

The Scottish Tourist Board
23 Ravleston Terrace
Edinburgh
EH4 3EU
Tel: 0131 332 2433

In association
with MasterCard

BALGONIE COUNTRY HOUSE

BRAEMAR PLACE, BALLATER, ROYAL DEESIDE, ABERDEENSHIRE AB35 5NQ
TEL: 013397 55482 FAX: 013397 55482

OWNERS: John and Priscilla Finnie

9 rms	9 ens			S: £59
				D: £99

In the heart of one of Scotland's most unspoilt areas, on the outskirts of the village of Ballater, lies Balgonie House. Winner of the 1997 Johansens Country House Award for Excellence. This Edwardian-style building is set within four acres of mature gardens and commands wonderful views over the local golf course towards the hills of Glen Muick beyond. Balgonie's nine bedrooms are each named after a fishing pool on the River Dee. They are individually decorated and furnished and most offer lovely outlooks from their windows. Amenities include private bathrooms, colour television and direct-dial telephones. At the heart of the hotel is the dining room, offering superb Scottish menus: including fresh salmon from the Dee, succulent local game, high quality Aberdeen Angus beef and seafood from the coastal fishing ports and vintage wine chosen from an excellent list. Balgonie has won the coveted Taste of Scotland Prestige Award for its cuisine, also 2 AA Red Star and 2 Rosettes.

Places of interest nearby: The village of Ballater, a five minute walk away, is a thriving community. As suppliers to the Queen, many of its shops sport Royal Warrant shields. This is an ideal centre for golf, hillwalking, sightseeing and touring. Balmoral Castle is within easy reach, as are both the Malt Whisky Trail and Castle Trail.

Directions: Upon entering Ballater from Braemar on the A93, Balgonie House is signposted on the right.

BLAIRLOGIE HOUSE

BLAIRLOGIE BY STIRLING FK9 5QE
TEL: 01259 761441

OWNER: Dorothy Collie

| 7 rms | 7 ens |

S: £52.50
D: £72–£82

In the heart of Scotland, located in a region steeped in history, lies Blairlogie House. This elegant Victorian Country House nestles under the slopes of the Ochil Hills and is set in 11 acres of lovely landscaped woodland. The individually decorated and furnished bedrooms provide every modern comfort and convenience.

In the intimate atmosphere of the dining room, a delicious menu is presented. Featured among the many tempting dishes on offer are gastronomic delights such as fillet of salmon with fresh herb butter; whole trout with parsley and garlic butter; grilled sirloin steak with a malt and wild mushroom sauce; and seared aubergine with pesto, tomato and mozzarella. An excellent selection of both desserts and wine is available to complement any meal.

Numbered among the host of activities available for the sporting enthusiast are fishing in loch and river, game shooting, golf at St Andrews and Gleneagles, ice-skating and swimming.

Places of interest nearby: Rob Roy's grave at Balquidder, the Palace of Linlithgow and the Adam showpiece at Hopetoun House are all within 30 minutes drive of the house. Bannockburn and Sheriffmuir are just 10 minutes away, and Edinburgh, Stirling, Perth and Dunfermline are within easy reach. **Directions: At the roundabout after the Stirling exit of the M8 or M9, take the A91 St Andrews Road for 6 miles. Blairlogie House is on the left.**

AUCHENSKEOCH LODGE

BY DALBEATTIE, KIRKCUDBRIGHTSHIRE DG5 4PG
TEL/FAX: 01387 780277

OWNERS: Christopher and Mary Broom-Smith

S: £38
D: £60

Auchenskeoch Lodge stands in 20 acres of unspoiled grounds just five miles from historic Dalbeattie and the Solway Firth, a fast running tidal inlet biting deep into tree-covered and heathered hills.

Compact Stewartry towns with their rows of 18th-century streets, ruined castles, mysterious earthworks and stone piles of prehistory stud the beautiful, surrounding Galloway countryside

Formerly a Victorian shooting lodge, Auchenskeoch's individual charm is enhanced by highly polished antique furniture, open log fires and an interesting collection of paintings and books.

The bedrooms are spacious and comfortably furnished.

Each has an en suite bath or shower room and one is on the ground floor and suitable for disabled guests.

Meals are served at one long oak table. The set four-course dinners make full use of local produce, whenever possible from the hotel's garden which also features a croquet lawn and a small fishing loch. Special spring and autumn break rates are available.

Places of interest nearby: Among the local attractions are Castle Douglas, New Abbey, Glen Trool and Kirkcudbright. **Directions: From Dumfries take the A711 towards Dalbeattie. Just before entering the town turn left onto the B793, signposted to Caulkerbush. Auchenskeoch is approximately seven miles further on.**

In association with MasterCard

BROOMLANDS HOUSE

HAUGH ROAD, DALBEATTIE, DUMFRIES AND GALLOWAY DG5 4AR
TEL: 01556 611463 FAX: 01556 611462

OWNERS: Mushira and James Maddison

3 rms | 3 ens

D: £44
D: £64 – including 4 course dinner

Broomlands House stands impressively granite solid as befits the criteria laid down by the local quarry owner who built it in 1903. Situated a few miles from Dalbeattie, this glistening, grey-stone country house probably represents the finest of its type in South West Scotland.

All around are Stewartry towns with rows of attractive 18th century streets and coastal walks, mysterious earthworks and stone piles of prehistory.

Good food and homely comfort are the ingredients provided under the personal supervision of owners James and Mushira Maddison from the moment visitors step through the welcoming, arched doorway. The interior is furnished to provide elegant comfort and the three en suite bedrooms are spacious and well equipped.

The à la carte menu is offered using local produce extensively and Mushira produces excellent cuisine in the charming dining room which overlooks the garden and patio. Deep, soft sofas and chairs fronting an open fire and marble fountain in the lounge create delightful surroundings for pre or post dinner relaxation.

Places of interest nearby: Choose from any of 23 golf course, 23 gardens, forests, lakes, Castles or museums and historic Dumfries where Robert Burns lived from 1791 until his death 1796. **Directions: Dalbeattie is 14 miles south west of Dumfries and approached via A711. The house is located on B794**

KINKELL HOUSE

EASTER KINKELL, BY DINGWALL, ROSS-SHIRE IV7 8HY
TEL: 01349 861270 FAX: 01349 865902

OWNERS: Steve and Marsha Fraser
CHEF: Marsha Fraser

7 rms | 7 ens | SMALL HOTEL

S: £40–£55
D: £70–£80

Proprietors Steve and Marsha Fraser delight in providing distinctive Highlands hospitality at Kinkell House, a splendid 19th century farmhouse tastefully restored with antiques and traditional furnishings on the beautiful Black Isle. Situated just a few miles north of Inverness the hotel is an ideal central point from which to explore the magnificent surrounding countryside with its historic castles, whisky distilleries, mountains, lochs and lakes.

The spacious, centrally-heated bedrooms are all en suite. Each is provided with a television, telephone and complimentary tea and coffee facilities with home made shortbread. The award-winning restaurant has panoramic views of 3,433ft-high Ben Wyvis, the Cromarty Firth and the mountains of Western Ross. A daily changing menu personally supervised by Marsha Fraser uses the best local produce.

For the sporting enthusiast there is fishing on the Conan and Beauly rivers, shooting, stalking, climbing, golf and riding. Visits to Skye and Ullapool can be arranged.
Places of interest nearby: Cromarty's fine beaches at the north-east tip of Black Isle, the historic county town of Inverness and Loch Ness, 18th century Fort George and the ruins of Urquhart Castle. Ross. **Directions: Kinkell House is approximately 10 miles north of Inverness, on the B9169 one mile west of the A9 and one mile east of the A835.**

In association with MasterCard

POLMAILY HOUSE HOTEL

DRUMNADROCHIT, LOCH NESS, INVERNESS-SHIRE IV3 6XT
TEL: 01456 450343 FAX: 01456 450813

OWNERS: John and Sonia Whittington-Davies

S: £45–£55
D: £90–£105
Suite: £84–£122

The mysterious Loch Ness lies just below this stylish Edwardian house from which there are views of the slopes of Glen Urquhart and the peaks of Glen Afric. Soaring eagles, deer, wild cat and salmon abound and guests enjoy the 18 acres of garden, woodland and trout pond

A family run hotel making other families especially welcome and the safe facilities for youngsters help parents relax and appreciate their surroundings. With an indoor and outdoor play area and separate children's dinner, Polmaily House is unique in country house facilities for families.

The owners are proud of their kitchen, and guests can start the day with a full Highland breakfast. Dinner, served in the spacious and elegant dining room, reflects the local game, beef, fish and garden produce stocking the larder. Carefully chosen wines are reasonably priced.

The delightful bedrooms are all en suite, with one ground floor room ideal for elderly and disabled guests. The family rooms have videos!

Places of interest nearby: On the estate there are ponies, a hard tennis court, heated indoor swimming pool, sauna, solarium, gym and a croquet lawn. Nearby there is superb golf, skiing, fishing with tuition available, and stalking. **Directions: By car from Inverness, follow the A82 signposted to Fort William, after 16 miles at Drumnadrochit turn onto A831 signposted to Glen Affric and the hotel is on this road after two miles.**

In association
with MasterCard

No 22 Murrayfield Gardens

22 MURRAYFIELD GARDENS, EDINBURGH, LOTHIAN EH12 6DF
TEL: 0131 337 3569 FAX: 0131 337 3803 E-MAIL: NO22FORBANDB@DIAL.PIPEX.COM

OWNERS: Tim and Christine MacDowel

S: £40–£45
D: £70–£80

This large Victorian town house is situated in one of Edinburgh's most prestigious residential areas. Surrounded by its own delightful gardens, featuring attractive ornamental trees and shrubs, it provides panoramic views of the distant hills. Owners Tim and Christine MacDowel have taken great care to create a delightfully relaxed and friendly atmosphere for their guests.

The attractive accommodation at first floor level comprises three distinctly individual rooms; two double and one twin. Each is furnished traditionally, but has an individuality in style and decor. There is a spacious and comfortable drawing room and, for breakfast, a delightful sun-drenched dining room overlooking the gardens.

Although this is primarily a bed and breakfast establishment, dinner can be provided if 24 hours notice is given. Private driveway and street parking in an unrestricted area is available.

The house is well located for Edinburgh Airport, The Forth Road Bridge and the motorway network.

Places of interest nearby: No 22 Murrayfield Gardens is well placed for guests wishing to explore the various attractions of Edinburgh, including its Castle, the National Gallery, Palace of Holyrood House and a host of historic houses. The Highlands are within one hour's drive. **Directions: No 22 is 1 mile due west of Princes Street, just off Corstorphine Road.**

CHAPEL HOUSE

KETTLEBRIDGE, NR CUPAR, FIFE KY15 7TU
TEL: 01337 831790 FAX: 01337 831790

OWNERS: The Stewart Family

4 rms   4 ens

MasterCard VISA from £60

Chapel House occupies an elevated position in beautiful countryside overlooking the Howe of Fife. The original Georgian house was built of sandstone in 1737 and substantially extended in 1910, considerably increasing the number of rooms and enhancing their proportions. As a result the house now has four beautiful reception rooms elegantly furbished in great style and comfort. The drawing room has huge bay windows, Victorian pillars and a grand piano. It gives directly onto an oak panelled billiard room which retains its original carved inglenook fireplace.

The guest bedrooms are all spacious and private with stunning views over the hills. All have en suite bathrooms that retain their original cast iron Victorian fittings. Some rooms have four poster beds. There are ten acres of grounds, including a grass tennis court, a croquet lawn and several acres of established woodland, with a trout pool and burn.

Guests can enjoy menus based on fresh local produce, prepared with flair and imagination. Alternatively there are many fine local restaurants.

Places of interest nearby: Falkland Palace, Scone Palace and distilleries nearby. St Andrews golf course is just one of many championship golf courses within a 30 minute drive. Other sporting activities can be easily arranged, including fishing, deer stalking, shooting and off road driving. **Directions: From M90 junction 3, take A92 to Muirhead roundabout and keep right to Kettlebridge.**

CULCREUCH CASTLE HOTEL

FINTRY, STIRLINGSHIRE G63 0LW
TEL: 01360 860555; FAX: 01360 860556

OWNER: Andrew Haslam

S: £55–£80
D: £80–£130

Less than 20 miles from the bustle of Glasgow, Culcreuch Castle stands among the moors, lochs, glens and pinewooded wilds of Stirlingshire, close to Loch Lomond. Built in 1296, this grand ancestral seat of the once-feared Galbraith clan today overlooks 1,600 acres of superb parkland between the Campsie Fells and the Fintry Hills.

The owners, the Haslams, have renovated Culcreuch as a first-class country hotel while preserving its august past in antiques, oil paintings and old, worn steps. All eight bedrooms are en suite, some with four-poster beds. Their names – The Napier Suite, The Keep Room, or The Speirs' Room – help piece together the Castle's history.

Stay a night in the Chinese Bird Room, with its 18th century hand-painted wallpaper. After dark the Phantom Piper sometimes roams and plays. Dinner prepared by award winning chef William Finneaty is served by candlelight in the panelled dining room; a four-course meal prepared from fresh, local produce costs £23.50, and there is a cellar of fine wines. Self-catering accommodation is also available.

Places of interest nearby: Fishing, walking in the Endrick Valley, visiting Loch Lomond, the village of Fintry, and Stirling, to the east. Glasgow and Edinburgh airports are a 55 minute drive. **Directions: Exit M9 junction 10. A84 east towards Stirling. First right, first right and then join A811. Go 10 miles west to junction with B822 at Kippen. Turn left, go via Kippen to Fintry.**

ASHBURN HOUSE

5 ACHINTORE ROAD, FORT WILLIAM, INVERNESS-SHIRE PH33 6RQ
TEL: 01397 706000 FAX: 01397 706000

OWNERS: Sandra and Allan Henderson
CHEF: Sandra Henderson

 7 rms 7 ens

S: £30-£35
D: £60-£70

Ashburn House lies on the very edge of Fort William, deep in the heart of the Highlands at the foot of mighty Ben Nevis. The soaring, 4,406 feet-high mass dominates the south-east end of the Great Glen where wild rivers are hustled seawards by tumbling waterfalls.

This lovely Victorian hotel on the shore of Loch Linnhe has been sympathetically restored to retain its traditional features. These include high corniced ceilings and a magnificent barley twist staircase. There are stunning views from the conservatory lounge westward across the loch to the Ardgour Hills. All seven bedrooms are en suite and offer every modern comfort.

Ashburn House serves a truly authentic Highland breakfast to satisfy the heartiest appetite. Dinner is not provided but there are a variety of good restaurants and dining establishments within the vicinity. Among local activities are golf, fishing, climbing, sailing, touring the towns and islands or taking a trip on the steam trains. **Places of interest nearby:** Inverlochy Castle, Mallaig, Loch Ness and Ben Nevis whose summit can be reached via a five mile long path from Achintee Farm. **Directions: Approaching Fort William from the south on the A82 Ashburn is 300 yards after entering the 30 mph zone, on the right.**

In association
with MasterCard

CHAPELTOUN HOUSE HOTEL

IRVINE ROAD, NR STEWARTON, AYRSHIRE KA3 3ED
TEL: 01560 482696 FAX: 01560 485100 E-MAIL: chapeltounhouse@compuserve.com

OWNERS: The Dobson Family
HOST: Simon Dobson

8 rms 8 ens

S: £79–£95
D: £119–£145

In its exceptional setting, Chapeltoun House offers all the luxury of an Edwardian private house whose caring staff respond to the needs of every guest. The house is a peaceful haven with its log fires and comfortable furnishings, and is set amidst 20 acres of woodland and gardens in the heart of Ayrshire's celebrated golfing country.

Oak panelling and log fires are the setting for "Scottish Chef of the Year 1997", David Auchie's award winning cuisine.

Located close to both Glasgow and Prestwick Airports, Chapeltoun must appeal to all travellers and serious golfers who are accustomed to enjoying the finest quality of hospitality and first-class golf courses.

Places of interest nearby: Attractions within easy reach include Culzean Castle at Maybole, Dean Castle and Kilmarnock, Ayr Races, Burns Cottage and Museum. The Scottish Maritime Musem at Irvine, the Burrel collection and Glasgow city centre are all within half an hour's driving. Ferries take visitors to the beautiful islands of Arran, Cumbrae and Bute. **Directions: By road from Glasgow – from the Fenwick exit on the A77 (m77/A77 Glasgow to Kilmarnock road) take B778 to Stewarton Cross. Turn left and continue under the railway viaduct, then take second right on to B769 towards Irvine for 2 miles. Chapeltoun House is signposted on right. Glasgow airport is 30 minutes away, Prestwick Airport 20 minutes.**

ARDCONNEL HOUSE

WOODLANDS TERRACE, GRANTOWN-ON-SPEY, MORAYSHIRE, PH26 3JU
TEL/FAX: 01479 872104

OWNERS: Barbara and Michel Bouchard
CHEF: Michel Bouchard

6 rms	6 ens

D: £50–£65

Ardconnel House is a splendid example of Victorian architecture at its best – built in 1890 it is surrounded by well-kept gardens and has an aura of old world charm and courtesy. It is in a peaceful residential part of Grantown-on-Spey, close to the river, and has magnificent views of pine trees, lochs and hills.

The guest rooms are a joy to behold – period furniture, lovely fabrics and elegantly decorated. The bathrooms are well designed.

The sitting room is wonderfully relaxing at the end of a long day – it has a big fire in winter, comfortable large chairs and a restful ambience. Speyside malt whiskies taste well here! The handsome dining room is perfect for lingering over superb food – local game and Speyside salmon often feature in the short menu. The selection of wines is reasonably priced.

The Bouchards are extremely hospitable, but the hotel has two restrictions: no smoking and the minimum age for children is ten years.

Places of interest nearby: Loch Ness, Balmoral, Braemar, Aviemore, Ben Nevis and the Cairngorms. Sports include golf, fishing, bowls, tennis, sailing; ski-ing and curling in winter. Whisky distilleries, potteries, woollen mills, castles and gardens are nearby. **Directions: Leave A9 at Carrbridge, taking A938. Ardconnel House is on the left approaching the town.**

THE OLD MANSE OF MARNOCH

BRIDGE OF MARNOCH, BY HUNTLY, ABERDEENSHIRE AB54 5RS
TEL: 01466 780873 FAX: 01466 780873

OWNERS: Patrick and Keren Carter
CHEF: Keren Carter

S: £60
D: £94

Dating back to the late 1700s, The Old Manse of Marnoch is set in four acres of mature gardens on the banks of the River Deveron. Designed to create a unique and welcoming atmosphere for guests, this stylish country house is ideal for those seeking peace and quiet in an idyllic setting. The luxurious en suite bedrooms are superbly appointed, tastefully decorated and furnished with antiques. The lounge and dining room echo their striking and individual decor.

Generous Scottish breakfasts and award-winning food are notable features of this delightful establishment. The kitchen garden provides the fresh vegetables and fruit which contribute to the mouth-watering cuisine, with other ingredients supplied locally. Vegetarian and special diets can be catered for without fuss. Along with the better known clarets, Burgundies and Rhône wines, there is a selection of unusual wines to tempt more adventurous palates and to complement the imaginative dishes.

Every country sport is available locally and golfers can choose between parkland or links courses. Spectacular coastal scenery and sandy beaches are within easy reach and the area offers a wealth of lovely walks.

Places of interest nearby: Huntly Castle, Elgin Cathedral and the major cultural centres of Aberdeen and Inverness.
Directions: The Old Manse is on the B9117 less than a mile off the main A97 Huntly to Banff.

CULDUTHEL LODGE

14 CULDUTHEL ROAD, INVERNESS, INVERNESS-SHIRE IV2 4AG
TEL/FAX: 01463 240089

OWNERS: David and Marion Bonsor

| 12 rms | 12 ens | SMALL HOTEL |

S: £45
D: £75–£90

This beautifully appointed hotel, just a few minutes walk from the town centre, is a Grade II Georgian residence set in its own grounds and offering splendid views of the River Ness and surrounding countryside. Great emphasis is placed on providing good food, comfort and a quiet, friendly atmosphere.

On arrival in their rooms, guests are greeted with fresh fruit, flowers and a small decanter of sherry. Each bedroom is individually decorated and furnished to a high standard of comfort and provides every modern amenity including a CD/cassette player.

Delicious, freshly prepared food is presented by a table d'hôte menu which offers choices at each course, including Scottish fare and local produce. A carefully selected range of wines is available to complement the appetising and nourishing meals.

Places of interest nearby: Inverness is a good base for guests wishing to tour the Highlands and the north and west coasts. The Isle of Skye, Royal Deeside and the splendours of the Spey Valley are within a day's travel.

Directions: Take the B851 out of Inverness. Culduthel Road is a continuation of Castle Street and the Lodge is less than half a mile from the city centre on the right.

ARDVOURLIE CASTLE

AIRD AMHULAIDH, ISLE OF HARRIS, WESTERN ISLES HS3 3AB
TEL: 01859 502307 FAX: 01859 502348

OWNER: Derek Martin

S: £70–£80
D: £140–£160
(including dinner)

Despite its name, this was a hunting lodge built in 1863 by the Earl of Dunmore now restored recently to its full glory. Some rooms have gas and oil lamps, and fire-grates from the original period: mahogany-panelled baths with brass fittings add to the luxurious setting. With just four guest rooms, visitors are guaranteed a warm welcome and personal service from brother and sister team Derek and Pamela Martin. Each room has a private bathroom.

The castle stands on the shores of Loch Seaforth: further on are the sandy beaches of the west coast and the rocky wilderness of South Harris. Otters and seals frequent the bay and golden eagles can be seen over the hills.

The menu at Ardvourlie is based upon local produce wherever possible, including salmon, trout, island lamb, Scottish cheeses and Stornaway oatcakes. Vegetarian meals are available by arrangement. The food is Taste of Scotland Michelin and Good Hotel Guide recommended. Ardvourlie Castle has a residents' licence and a self-service bar.

Places of interest nearby: Hill-walking (it is advisable to bring suitable clothing), beaches of the West Coast, Callanish Stones, Rodel Church. Salmon and trout fishing on Harris. **Directions: The castle stands on the shores of Loch Seaforth 24 miles from Stornoway and 10 miles from Tarbert.**

KILLIECHRONAN

KILLIECHRONAN, ISLE OF MULL, ARGYLL PA72 6JU
TEL: 01680 300403 FAX: 01680 300463

OWNERS: Mr and Mrs John Leroy
MANAGERS: Margaret and Patrick Freytag

| 6 rms | 6 ens | |

S: £73–£87
D: £61–£76
(including dinner)

An original Highland lodge, built in 1846, now a superb country house hotel, ideally located at the head of Loch na Keal. The owners already have an established reputation in Scotland with The Manor House Hotel at Oban and The Lake Hotel at Port of Menteith.

This, their third hotel, is their own family home and contains a magnificent collection of antiques and pictures. Most of the rooms face south, overlooking the sheltered grounds, part of the 5,000 acre estate.

Bringing the chef from the Manor House has ensured those high standards in the restaurant, awarded 2 AA rosettes that one associates with the Leroy family and there is a fine wine list to complement the menu.

There are just six bedrooms, all en suite, with telephone and other modern comforts.

The area is renowned for its outstanding beauty. Visit Fingal's Cave, the white beach at Calgary, Duart Castle, the herring village of Tobermory and Torosay set in Italianate gardens. There is fishing, sailing, golf, pony treking and a fairly easy walk to the summit of Ben More. **Directions: Mull is reached by the ferry from Oban (40 minute crossing) or Lochalin. Take A849 to Salen. Left on B8035. House on right 2 miles after.**

ARDSHEAL HOUSE

KENTALLEN OF APPIN, ARGYLL PA38 4BX
TEL: 01631 740227 FAX 01631 740342

OWNERS: Neil and Philippa Sutherland

S: £37
D: £74

A long private drive winds alongside lovely Loch Linnhe and through ancient woodland to this magnificent 18th century granite and stone manor which stands high on a natural promontory of pink marble with magnificent views over the loch and the mountains of Morvern. The scenery is breathtaking even for the West Highlands.

Set in 800 acres of hills, woods, gardens and shore front, Ardsheal House has a charming country house ambience and a friendly welcome is extended to all visitors by the resident owners.

The reception hall is particularly attractive, with warm polished oak panelling, an imposing open fire and a unique barrel window. Family antiques and bright fabrics are to be found in all the individually furnished bedrooms.

Philippa Sutherland serves memorable, daily changing four-course dinners in the attractive dining room. Vegetables, herbs and fruit from the garden and home-made jellies, jams and preserves form the basis for her innovative set meals.

Places of interest nearby: Islands, castles, lochs and glens, Oban's Cathedral of the Isles and ruined 13th century castle. **Directions: Ardsheal House is on the A828 five miles south of the Ballachulish Bridge between Glencoe and Appin on the way to Oban. From Glasgow and Edinburgh, follow the signs to Crianlarich and take the A82 north to Ballachulish.**

THE KILLIECRANKIE HOTEL

KILLIECRANKIE, BY PITLOCHRY, PERTHSHIRE PH16 5LG
TEL: 01796 473220 FAX: 01796 472451

OWNERS: Colin and Carole Anderson

S: £57–£80
D: £114–£160
(including dinner)

The Killiecrankie Hotel is peacefully situated in four acres of landscaped gardens overlooking the Pass of Killiecrankie and River Garry. It was here, in 1689, that the Jacobites clashed with William of Orange's men in a battle to gain supremacy over the crowns of England and Scotland – an event which illustrates the area's rich heritage.

Guests will find a friendly welcome and a relaxed, informal style. There are ten charming bedrooms, including one ground floor suite. All are very comfortably furnished and decorated to a high standard. There is a cosy residents' sitting room with a patio in the garden in fine weather.

With two AA Rosettes, the Dining Room has a very good reputation. Fresh ingredients indigenous to Scotland are used and presented with flair and imagination. Menus offer a good, balanced choice: start perhaps with Grilled Isle of Gigha Goats Cheese with Asparagus Salad or Ballottine of Duck, before going to a main course of Chargrilled Monkfish with Basil and Pinenut Pesto or Braised Fillet of Pork in an Ale and Caraway Sauce with Herb Dumplings. In the bar, a superb range of bar meals is served at lunch and supper time. Closed one week in December, all of January and February. 3 night breaks at Christmas/New Year – also in Spring and Autumn.

Places of interest nearby: Blair Castle, Pitlochry Festival Theatre – golfing, fishing, shooting and hill-walking.
Directions: Turn off the main A9 at sign for Killiecrankie.

THE KINLOCHBERVIE HOTEL

KINLOCHBERVIE, BY LAIRG, SUTHERLAND IV27 4RP
TEL: 01971 521275 FAX: 01971 521438

OWNERS: Stewart and Val McHattie
MANAGERS: Jill and Linda McHattie
CHEF: Ross McKay

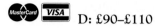 D: £90–£110

The Kinlochbervie Hotel stands amongst the awesome beauty of the Atlantic coastline just below Cape Wrath, once the turning point for marauding Viking longships. It overlooks the little fishing port and lochs and offers magnificent views over the open sea whose depths and roaring waves attract divers and surfers from miles around.

The Kinlochbervie incorporates all that that visitors would expect from a quality three-star hotel. The lounges and bars are comfortably relaxing, the bedrooms warm and cosy and the restaurant imparts exactly the right atmosphere in which to savour the Scottish delights of the Kinlochbervie's kitchens and cellars. In addition to local lamb and venison, delicious fish figures prominently on the menus, as the daily arrival of deep-sea trawlers to the local market ensures a plentiful supply of shellfish, monkfish, turbot and sole. Excellent wines complement the fine cooking. Ornithologists and naturalists will revel in the abundance of wildlife, golfers will find a challenge on the the most northerly course in Britain, just a short drive away. Fly and sea fishing can be arranged.

Places of interest nearby: Europe's highest waterfall at Kylesku, Handa Island bird sanctuary, Cape Wrath and the sandy stretches of Oldshoremore, Polin and Sheigra. **Directions: Take the A836 and then the A838 north west from Laire. At Rhiconich, turn left onto the B801 which runs alongside Loch Inchard to Kinlochbervie.**

In association with MasterCard

KINROSS (Cleish)

NIVINGSTONE COUNTRY HOUSE

CLEISH, NR KINROSS, KINROSS-SHIRE, KY13 7LS
TEL: 01577 850216 FAX: 01577 850238 E-MAIL: 100414,1237@compuserve.com

OWNER: Allan Deeson
CHEF: Tom McConnell

S: £82–£120
D: £104.50–£137.50

Peacefully set in 12 acres of landscaped gardens at the foot of the Cleish Hills, this comfortable old country house and its celebrated restaurant offer the warmest of welcomes. Standing more or less half-way between Edinburgh and Perth the original 1725 building has benefited from several architectural additions and it is now further enlarged and refurbished with all the characteristics of an up-to-date hotel.

Nivington House, personally managed by Peter and Agnes Aretez, is particularly well known for its fine food, prepared from traditional Scottish produce such as Perthshire venison and locally caught salmon. The restaurant has regularly been commended in leading guides and deservedly it has "Taste of Scotland" status and an AA rosette. The menus are changed daily. The attractive en suite bedrooms are decorated in soft, subtle colours, with Laura Ashley fabrics and wallpapers. In the grounds there is a putting green and practice net for keen golfers. Sporting facilities within easy reach include the famous golf courses at St Andrews, Murrayshall and countless others of lesser renown.

Places of interest nearby: Loch Leven is popular for trout fishing and there are boat trips to Loch Leven Castle. **Directions: From M90 take exit 5 onto B9097 towards Crook of Devon. Cleish is 2 miles from motorway. Price guide: Single £75–£100; double/twin £95–£125.**

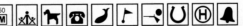

In association
with MasterCard

WELL VIEW HOTEL

BALLPLAY ROAD, MOFFAT, DUMFRIESSHIRE DG10 9JU
TEL: 01683 220184 FAX: 01683 220088

OWNERS: John and Janet Schuckardt

| 6 rms | 6 ens |

S: £40–£48
D: £58–£84

This delightful Victorian house on the edge of Moffat has been in excellent hands for the last ten years – the host being elected to the Academy of Wine Service and the hostess a member of the Craft Guild of Chefs, giving master classes on special occasions.

Guests enjoy an apéritif and canapé in the elegant lounge while studying the menu, or, after dinner, relax with homemade sweets accompanying the coffee – and, may be, an excellent malt whisky. Dinner in the charming, non-smoking, dining room, is six courses – including a sorbet – cooked with great flair and beautifully presented. Vegetarian dishes are available by prior request. The Cellar holds many fine wines from all parts of the world.

The bedrooms are all en suite and extremely comfortable, reflecting the high standards of hospitality throughout the hotel.

Places of interest nearby: Moffat is surrounded by mountains: Glasgow is reached over Beattock Summit, Edinburgh over the Devil's Beef Tub. St Mary's Loch and the Border Abbeys are also within driving distance.
Directions: Moffat is three miles from the M74/A74 trunk road between Carlisle and Glasgow. Pass the centre of the town on A708 (Selkirk) and turn left at crossroads into Ballplay Road. The hotel is a short distance on the right.

In association with MasterCard

BOATH HOUSE

AULDEARN, NAIRN, INVERNESS IV12 5TE
TEL: 01667 454896 FAX: 01667 455469

OWNERS: Don and Wendy Mathieson
CHEF: Charles Lockley

6 rms | 6 ens

S: £55–£85
D: £65–£110

This classic Georgian country mansion, set in 20 acres of grounds, has been described as the most beautiful Regency house in Scotland. It was built in 1825 for the Dunbar family, replacing 'the great stone house' mentioned in a court circular from Mary Queen of Scots' time.

Over the years the house passed through various hands and fell into disrepair. In the early 1990s, it was bought by the present owners and sympathetically restored to recreate its original splendour. The six en suite bedrooms, which have all been decorated according to individual themes, are spacious and well furnished. The reception rooms match their high standard of comfort.

The restaurant offers excellent views over the lake and menus which are chosen daily, dependent on fresh produce available from the kitchen garden and local suppliers. An excellent choice of both traditional and modern starters and main courses is followed by mouth-watering, diet defying delights desserts such as caramel and passion fruit brûlée; meringue served with a honey, whisky and toasted oatmeal ice cream and fresh raspberries; and chocolate and prune parfait served with blackcurrent and red wine coulis.

Places of interest nearby: Cawdor Castle, Elgin Cathedral, Culloden Battlefield and Brodie Castle.
Directions: Well sign posted off the A96 Aberdeen to Inverness Road at Auldrean, 2 miles east of Nairn.

DUNGALLAN HOUSE HOTEL

GALLANACH ROAD, OBAN, ARGYLL PA34 4PD
TEL: 01631 563799 FAX: 01631 566711

OWNERS: George and Janice Stewart

| 12 rms | 10 ens | | SMALL HOTEL |

S: £35–£45
D: £35–£45

Peacefully set in five acres of gardens and lawns and with sloping woodland front and rear this impressive old Victorian house offers the warmest of welcomes. Although just a 15 minutes walk away from the bustling main centre of Oban, Dungallan has a restful country atmosphere and enjoys magnificent panoramic views over Oban Bay to the Island of Mull, Lismore and the spectacular Hills of Morvern.

Built in 1870 by the Campbell family, Dungallan House has undergone a major programme of upgrading to provide full facilities for today's visitor and to enhance the elegance of the building. Most bedrooms have a wonderful outlook and are harmoniously decorated reflecting the high standards of hospitality throughout the hotel.

In the spacious dining room guests can savour superb traditional Scottish meals prepared with the best of local produce by Janice Stewart who, with owner and husband George now runs Dungallan House after building up high reputations during 13 years at Arisaig Hotel, along the coast. A carefully chosen wine list complements the menu. Sporting activities locally include fishing, sailing and golf. **Places of interest nearby:** Oban is Scotland's main ferry port for the Western Isles and the many day trips are a splendid way of discovering this beautiful area. **Directions: The Hotel is on the southern outskirts of Oban beyond the ferry terminal and then follow signs for Gallanach.**

THE MANOR HOUSE HOTEL

GALLANACH ROAD, OBAN, ARGYLL PA34 4LS
TEL: 01631 562087 FAX: 01631 563053

OWNERS: Mr and Mrs John Leroy

11 rms | 11 ens | SMALL HOTEL

S: £62–£87
D: £46–£76
(including dinner)

Late Georgian in style, The Manor House was built in 1780 as the principal residence of the Duke of Argyll's Oban estate. Today it is a hotel where great care has been taken to preserve the elegance of its bygone days. The Manor House occupies a prime position overlooking Oban Bay, the islands and the mountains of Movern and Mull.

In the dining room guests can enjoy a fine blend of Scottish and French cooking, with the emphasis on local seafood and game in season. The table d'hôte menus take pride of place and are changed daily to offer a choice of starters, intermediate fish course or soup, home-made sorbet, choice of main courses, choice of puddings, and to round off, coffee and mints. The restaurant menu is partnered by a cellar of wines and selection of malt whiskies.

The bedrooms have twin or double beds, all with en suite bathrooms, TV and tea-making facilities. The Manor House Hotel is quietly located on the outskirts of Oban, yet within easy walking distance of the town. Special mini-breaks are available for stays of two nights or more. Closed Sunday night until Tuesday afternoon from November to February. Special Christmas and Hogmanay breaks available.

Places of interest nearby: Oban is Scotland's main ferry port for trips to the Western Isles and the many day tours are a splendid way of discovering this beautiful area.
Directions: The Manor House Hotel is situated on the western outskirts of Oban beyond the ferry boat pier.

In association
with MasterCard

MELDRUM HOUSE

OLDMELDRUM, ABERDEENSHIRE AB51 0AE
TEL: 01651 872294 FAX: 01651 872464

OWNERS: Douglas and Eileen Pearson
CHEF: Mark Will

| 9 rms | 9 ens |

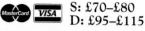

S: £70–£80
D: £95–£115

Solid and baronial with magnificent conically-roofed towers and tall, intricate chimneys, Meldrum House stands majestically on a grassy crest surrounded by 15 acres of landscaped parklands and beautiful countryside. Built in the 13th century this fine building is steeped in Scottish history and offers visitors a rare opportunity to enjoy the style and elegance of a bygone era combined with all the modern comforts of a first-class hotel.

Proprietors Douglas and Eileen Pearson are proud of their tradition of country house hospitality and have complemented the house's magnificent interior with many fine antiques, objets d'art and ancestral portraits.

The individually designed bedrooms are spacious and have full en suite facilities. Unpretentious and relaxing, the large public rooms have open fires. There is also a large, ornate open fire in the enchanting restaurant where excellent traditional Scottish cuisine is served. A championship golf course will soon be created in the hotel's grounds, which also includes a trout-stocked lake.

Places of interest nearby: Fifteenth century Fyvie Castle, Haddo House, the Maiden Stone at Inverurie, a Christian monument bearing carvings of Pictish symbols and a Celtic cross, Pitmedden Gardens whisky trail and Castle Trail.
Directions: Oldmeldrum is on the **A947, 18 miles north of Aberdeen. 13 miles from Dyce Airport.**

DUPPLIN CASTLE

DUPPLIN ESTATE, BY PERTH, PERTHSHIRE PH2 0PY
TEL: 01738 623224 FAX: 01738 444140

OWNERS: Derek and Angela Straker

4 rms	4 ens					S: £65
						D: £110

Dupplin, a rare mid-20th century Scottish Mansion, stands in 30 acres of private parkland, with sweeping lawns and mature woodlands. The original edifice was razed to the ground by fire and its 19th century successor was replaced by the current building, completed in 1969, to the design of one of Scotland's leading architects, Schomber Scott. The Castle has now been upgraded to the comfort and luxury expected of today's discerning guests.

The original castle's balustraded terrace and rose garden remain and the impressive landscaping, of some antiquity, offers panoramic views south over the lovely River Earn valley to the hills beyond.

The luxurious bedrooms are individually appointed, with en suite facilities, and the gracious reception rooms are elegantly furnished with fine antiques, paintings and books, creating an atmosphere of a bygone era of tranquillity and elegance.

Dinner (must be booked 24hrs in advance) is served house-party style, with all guests seated round the dining room table. Scottish country house cuisine is complemented by informal but highly efficient and friendly service.

Golf, Salmon fishing, shooting and roe-stalking are available only by prior arrangement.

Places of interest nearby: Scone Palace, Perth, the ancient capital of Scotland. Both Edinburgh and Glasgow are just an hour's drive away. **Directions: Please contact the Castle.**

NEWMILN COUNTRY HOUSE

NEWMILN ESTATE, GUILDTOWN, PERTH, PERTHSHIRE PH2 6AE
TEL: 01738 552364 FAX: 01738 553505

OWNERS: James and Elaine McFarlane
CHEF: J. Paul Burns

S: £70–£130
D: £125–£200

A rich but homely style of hospitality awaits guests at Newmiln Country House. This superb 18th century mansion is set within a 700-acre sporting estate and offers breathtaking views of the surrounding natural woodlands and waterfalls. With its warm and friendly atmosphere, the house is ideal for romantic weekends, family celebrations or a simply peaceful break away.

The beautifully proportioned public rooms, with their cosy log fires and intricate wood panelling, are ideal settings for a quiet read or drink, while the immaculate bedrooms boast the highest standards of comfort.

The talented chef creates sumptuous cuisine featuring the best local produce – prime fillet of Perthshire beef on onion and toasted pine-nut marmalade; pigeon oven roasted, presented with salad leaves and redcurrant jus; and east coast Lobster Thermidor. Immaculately presented dishes are complemented with a fine selection of wines. There is no smoking in the dining room. Awarded 3 AA Rosettes for food and was MaCallam 'Taste of Scotland Country Hotel of the Year Awards 1997' runner up.

Guests can use the tennis court and horses are available on site for experienced riders. For golf St Andrews, Gleneagles and Carnoustie are an easy drive away.

Places of interest nearby: Scone Palace, Blair Castle and Perth Racecourse. **Directions: A93 Blairgowrie road out of Perth. 3 miles after Scone Palace on left.**

DUNFALLANDY HOUSE

LOGIERAIT ROAD, PITLOCHRY, PERTHSHIRE PH16 5NA
TEL: 01796 472648 FAX: 01796 472017

OWNERS: Michael and Jane Bardsley

8 rms | 8 ens

S: £42–£47
D: £60–£70

Dunfallandy House is a secluded Georgian Mansion House built in 1790 and now lovingly restored and converted into a fine small Country House Hotel.

In an elevated position, in three and a half acres of grounds, within the Dunfallandy Estate, surrounded by the splendour of the Tummel Valley it stands above the highland town of Pitlochry. The House retains many historic features, yet it has all been sympathetically modernised to provide year round comfort including central heating.

The bedrooms are designed and furnished to a high standard. All double/twin rooms have en-suite shower/bath, toilet and washbasin. Some have four-poster beds. All are equipped with colour televisions, clock radios, tea and coffee making facilities, hairdryers and trouser presses.

Full Scottish or light continental breakfasts are served in the Georgian dining room, where guests can later enjoy a delicious dinner – vegetarian dishes available. Before or after dining guests can relax in front of the open fire in the Green Room, where they may select a good book and enjoy a fine malt whisky from the oak-panelled bar.

Places of interest nearby: Golf, fishing, shooting and riding. Pitochry Theatre and the famous salmon ladder.

Directions: From Pitlochry take road signposted Pitlochry Festival Theatre, cross river, turn left on road signposted Dunfallandy, hotel is 500 yards on the right.

In association
with MasterCard

DRUIMNEIL

PORT APPIN, ARGYLLSHIRE PA38 4DQ
TEL: 01631 730228

OWNER: Janet Glaisher
CHEF: Janet Glaisher

3 rms | 3 ens

S: £35
D: £60

Twenty miles north of Oban lies Druimneil, a grand mid-Victorian country house overlooking the lovely Sound of Shuna and Loch Linnhe, which stretches inland from the sea towards Loch Lochy. Wildlife is abundant. Rare birds of prey, deer, otters and seals can often be seen.

The hotel is owned and run by Janet Glaisher, who goes out of her way to ensure that guests enjoy their stay. It is excellent in every way and is the ideal base for touring the jagged coastline and surrounding mountain ranges.

In the dining room guests enjoy traditional country house meals with the emphasis on local seafood and fruit from the kitchen garden. The downstairs rooms are spacious and elegant with antique family furniture, fine pictures and porcelain, while the three upstairs en suite bedrooms have all modern comforts. The hotel's boat "Tiddely-Wee" is available for fishing and viewing the nearby seal colony.

Places of interest nearby: Oban's Cathedral of the Isles and ruined 13th century castle. This is Scotland's main ferry port for trips to the Western Isles and the many day tours are a splendid way of discovering this beautiful area. **Directions: Take the A85 and A828 coastal roads north from Oban to Tynribbie. Then turn west for Port Appin.**

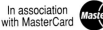
THE LAKE HOTEL

PORT OF MENTEITH, PERTHSHIRE FK8 3RA
TEL: 01877 385258 FAX: 01877 385671

OWNERS: Mr and Mrs John Leroy

16 rms | 16 ens | SMALL HOTEL

S: £62–£98
D: £92–£174
(including dinner)

The Lake Hotel is set in a splendid sheltered position on the banks of the Lake of Menteith in the Trossachs. Its lawn runs down to the edge of the lake, which in winter months often freezes over. When this happens, it is not unusual for locals to bring out their skates for a skim over the ice.

Guests are assured of all the amenities of an STB 4 Crown Highly Commended hotel. A programme of refurbishment has been completed, so the interiors have fresh decoration and furnishings. All bedrooms have en suite facilities and the details that will make your stay comfortable. There is an elegant lounge and a large conservatory from which the vista of lake and mountains is stunning.

The à la carte and table d'hôte menus present a varied choice of imaginatively prepared dishes. The table d'hôte menus are particularly good value: start with chicken & herb terrine with sun dried tomato dressing, followed by sorbet, then after a main course of grilled halibut with spinach, saffron potatoes and an orange & aniseed sauce, enjoy a Drambuie parfait with raspberry coulis before your coffee and home-made petits fours. Special rates are available for mini-breaks of two nights or more.

Places of interest nearby: Inchmahome Priory – haven for both Mary, Queen of Scots and Robert the Bruce – Loch Lomond and Stirling Castle. **Directions: Situated on the A81 road, south of Callander and east of Aberfoyle, on the northern banks of the Lake of Menteith.**

STRATHTUMMEL (By Pitlochry)

QUEEN'S VIEW HOTEL

In association
with MasterCard

STRATHTUMMEL, BY PITLOCHRY, PERTHSHIRE PH16 5NR
TEL: 01796 473291 FAX: 01796 473515 E-MAIL: queensviewhotel@compuserve.com

OWNERS: Richard and Norma Tomlinson
CHEF: Norma Tomlinson

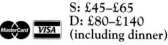

S: £45–£65
D: £80–£140
(including dinner)

Queen's View Hotel stands high and majestically overlooking the shimmering waters of Loch Tummel, close to the little town of Pitlochry and just a few miles from the ancient city of Perth. All around are the splendours of the Tummel Valley and the good things that Scotland has to offer. Despite its stunning location, the hotel has been a well kept secret for many years. Owners Richard and Norma Tomlinson have now sympathetically renovated it to provide relaxing comfort and modern facilities.

The bedrooms, including a family suite, are furnished to a high standard and have magnificent views over the loch 150 feet below. All but one of the bedrooms are en suite.

There is an attractive and well furnished lounge, a comfortable bar where you can enjoy a fine malt whisky and out of the ordinary lunchtime food and there is also a very pleasant restaurant with a growing reputation for its innovative and tasty cuisine. Many theatre goers like to take two courses before the performance returning for a drink or coffee and pudding afterwards. The hotel is closed from mid January to early March.

Places of interest nearby: Pitlochy has its own theatre. Fishing within the grounds. Golf, riding and curling can be arranged. Blair Castle, Bruar Falls, Scone Palace and Balmoral are close. **Directions: A9 to Pitlochry then B8079 north. Turn left onto B8019 for Tummel Bridge and the hotel is three miles miles further on.**

BORGIE LODGE HOTEL

SKERRAY, BY TONGUE, SUTHERLAND KW14 7TH
TEL: 01641 521332 FAX: 01641 521332

OWNERS: Peter and Jacqui MacGregor

6 rms | 5 ens | SMALL HOTEL

 S: £50
D: £80

In a secluded glen on the banks of the River Borgie in North Sutherland lies a perfect Highland retreat – Borgie Lodge. This country house is a haven for anyone seeking peace and tranquillity or looking to enjoy pursuits such as walking and fishing in stunning surroundings.

Traditionally furnished with tartan carpets and sporting prints, the Lodge is warmed by crackling log fires which help create a cosy atmosphere in which to unwind. Warm hospitality is combined with simple comforts to guarantee a memorable stay. In the evenings guests gather in the Naver Lounge for a pre-dinner dram before choosing dishes from their hostess's daily changing menu. Jacqui's cuisine features Caithness beef and lamb, Sutherland venison and fresh fish and seafood from the North Sea, complemented by vegetables from her kitchen garden.

Fishing enthusiasts can make the most of the Lodge's salmon fishing rights on the Rivers Borgie and Halladale or use its boats for catching wild brown trout on the hotel's 20 hill lochs. The area is also a hillwalker's paradise, with Ben Hope, Ben Loyal and Ben Kilbreck all within 30 minutes drive.

Places of interest nearby: Borgie Falls and Torrisdale beach. There are also craft shops and museums to explore.
Directions: From Tongue take the A836 East for 7 miles and then turn left at Torrisdale Road. The hotel is ½ mile on the right.

HILDON LTD.
Hildon House, Broughton, Hampshire SO20 8DG
01794-301 747, Fax 01794-301 718

Johansens Recommended Country Houses in
Ireland

Connemara landscape
Co Galway

Celtic treasures and legends, medieval architecture, racecourses and golf courses, great art collections and a richness of literature are all to be found amongst the green landscapes of Ireland.

While Ireland's number of annual visitors has been breaking its own newly-created record each year in the present decade making it the fastest growing tourism destination in Europe, it is the performance of Irish golf which stands out as the greatest success story of all. Golf has become the Republic's flagship product among a multiplicity of attractions and leisure pursuits which now account for a yearly visitor number which considerably exceeds that of the resident population.

The great historic golf courses of Ireland are well known internationally, Portmarnock, Royal Dublin, Ballybunion and Waterville being formidable among them as links challenges of world standard, while the parkland contrast is confidently provided on the verdant fairways of such as Woodbrook, Mullingar or Headford. In Ireland it is virtually impossible to be more than 20 miles away from a golf course, and every town or village of more than a thousand souls has a course of its very own. The 1990's have seen the development of even more new courses to cater for increasing international demand, and several world status professionals have brought their individual design talents to their construction.

It is the hidden gems, however, when stumbled upon which regularly compel their discoverers to speak of them in whispers, and the scenic, rugged countryside along the Atlantic seaboard provides Ireland's greatest source of such lesser-known treasures. Six of these courses have now come together to form a unique western golfing challenge group known as West Coast Links. Set in the purity of an unspoiled environment and amid the distinct Celtic culture and natural warmth of the rural community, their aim is to ensure that the visitor's golfing holiday will be both invigorating and memorable.

Much of Ireland's history is preserved in the architecture and ancient monuments of many of the towns and villages around the country and an association, Heritage Towns of Ireland, can assist the visitor in achieving the most comprehensive experience during a visit.

In addition to the many beautiful forest parks, Ireland has three internationally recognised national parks. Killarney National Park is perhaps the best known with Muckross House and Gardens as the centrepiece of this magnificent lakeside park. Connemara National Park in Letterfrack is set amid the wild rugged beauty so typical of the West of Ireland, and Glenveagh National Park in County Donegal has a beautiful castle and gardens.

The ancient history of Northern Ireland is comparable to that of the Greeks and Egyptians with the old tales of derring do, bravery and romance of the ancient Celts brought back to life at museums and centres including the Navan Centre of Armagh and the Tower Museum of Derry City.

Visitors to Ireland who make the journey north are inevitably surprised by "how different it is", or "how tidy it is", or "how rural it is". And this is what they enjoy.

Northern Ireland has made a name for itself as a place where welcomes are genuine and the land unspoilt. The last great outdoors playground for western Europe, this part of the island of Ireland remains top favourite among those in the know.

Wild salmon and trout anglers are tempted here by some of the world's best rivers. The Foyle system stands out as one of the best but the Bann, Bush, Erne and Melvin are other rivers and lakes teeming with indigenous sonnghan and dollaghan trout.

Similarly, golfers from the four corners return year after year to the freedom of the great links courses of the north coast. Both Royal Portrush and Royal County Down feature time after time in the world's top ten list of courses which is an indication of the quality available here.

And walkers, ramblers, watersports enthusiasts and other outdoor lovers know Northern Ireland's secret charms and are attracted back again and again.

But it's not all blustery outdoors. With the warmth of the fire in an Ulster bar surrounded by music and friends you will wish never to have to leave. The top class restaurants will seduce you as they have top food connoisseurs from around the world.

The fun of a good night's entertainment with live music, traditional Irish, jazz, rock or classical will help make any stay very memorable and can be enjoyed in most parts of the north.

Ultimately, you'll find an ancient culture here which was already 2,000 years old when St Patrick arrived from Britain 1,500 years ago.

Northern Ireland is special. Once visitors make their way here, they are sure to find what they are looking for – even if they didn't know what they were looking for in the first place!

Heritage Towns of Ireland
City Hall
Main Street
Cashel
Co Tipperary
Tel: 00 353 62 62068

West Coast Links
Teach Sonas
Rinville West
Oranmore
Co Galway
Ireland
Tel: 00 353 91 794500

For more information about Ireland and Northern Ireland please contact:

The Irish Tourist Board
Bord Failte
Baggot Street Bridge
Dublin 2
Tel: 00 353 1 676 5871

Northern Ireland Tourist Board
St Anne's Court
59 North Street
Belfast BT1 1NB
Tel: 01232 246609

GLASSDRUMMAN LODGE COUNTRY HOUSE & RESTAURANT

85 MILL ROAD, ANNALONG, CO DOWN, N. IRELAND BT34 4RH
TEL: 013967 68451 FAX: 013967 67041

OWNERS: Graeme and Joan Hall
MANAGER: Joan Hall

10 rms | 10 ens | SMALL HOTEL

MasterCard VISA

S: £75–£95
D: £95–£125
Suite: £125–£135

A warm and friendly Irish welcome awaits arrivals as they enter Glassdrumman Lodge, situated in Co Down's dramatically beautiful landscape where "the Mountains of Mourne sweep down to the sea". This majestic range of mountains, rich in history and legend, is one of Ireland's most picturesque areas.

The philosophy of owners Graeme and Joan Hall is "simple excellence". Their ten en suite bedrooms are tastefully furnished, have all modern comforts, 24-hour room service – some bedrooms have panoramic views while others look out over the hills and mountains. Dinner is an occasion, with guests sitting round a 20-foot long pine table or at their own private table, to be served with highly acclaimed cuisine produced from a variety of local produce, much of which is grown on the lodge farm.

Walking in the Mourne Mountains is a popular pastime and horseriding and trekking are close by the lodge. Good beaches, sailing, fishing, tennis and the world famous Royal County Down golf course are within easy reach.

Places of interest nearby: Silent Valley, Spelga Dam, Tollymore Forest and the seaside town of Newcastle.

Directions: From Dublin take the N1 to Newry and then the A2 coast road for 25 miles towards Annalong. Turn left at Halfway House into Mill Road. From Belfast and Lisburn take the A24 to Newcastle and join the A2 south for approximately seven miles to Annalong.

30 M | ☎ | ⌀ | ⌐ | U | H

ARD-NA-SIDHE

CARAGH LAKE, CO KERRY, IRELAND
TEL: 00 353 66 69105 FAX: 00 353 66 68282

OWNERS: Killarney Hotels Ltd.

19 rms | 19 ens

S: £70–£110
D: £125–£146

This romantic Victorian former country house was built in 1880 by an English lady who called it the 'House of Fairies'. Surrounded by a magnificent park, it is situated at Caragh Lake, 17 miles from Killarney. The house is furnished with valuable antiques and still retains the atmosphere of a private residence. Its tastefully decorated and furnished bedrooms, along with the comfortable reception rooms, offer guests luxurious surroundings in which to relax and unwind. Simple but delicious cuisine is served in the elegant restaurant. A sample menu might include cockle and mussel broth with pesto, followed by grilled sirloin steak with onion and mustard crust, buttered carrots and leeks and rosemary potatoes. For sweet try the peach and mint ragout with lemon sorbet, baby pineapple with strawberry ice and fresh fruits, or cheese selection. The hotel has twice won first prize in the National Gardens Competition. This is an idyllic setting in which to read, paint, walk and explore. Boating and fishing are available on Caragh Lake and the facilities of sister hotels The Europe and Dunloe Castle in Killarney can be used by Ard Na Sidhe guests. Some of Ireland's most beautiful golf courses are just a few minutes away by car.

Places of interest nearby: The picturesque town of Killarney, surrounded by lakes and mountains, just a few miles from the Atlantic coast. **Directions: West of Killorglin off N70 on the side of Caragh Lake.**

In association with MasterCard

CARAGH LODGE

CARAGH LAKE, CO KERRY
TEL: 00 353 66 69115 FAX: 00 353 66 69316 E-MAIL: caraghl@IOL.IE

OWNERS: Mary Gaunt
CHEF: Mary Gaunt

S: IR£66
D: IR£99–IR£132
Suite: IR£198

15 rms | 15 ens

The breathtaking slopes of Ireland's highest mountain range, McGillycuddy Reeks, rise majestically above this elegant Victorian hotel whose award winning gardens run gently down to the shore of Caragh Lake. Less than a mile from the spectacular Ring of Kerry, Caragh Lodge offers an unsurpassed blend of luxury, heritage, tranquillity, hospitality and service. It is excellent in every way and an ideal base for the sightseeing, golfing and fishing enthusiast.

All the en suite bedrooms are decorated with period furnishings and antiques, with the converted garden rooms looking over magnificent displays of magnolias, camelias, rhododendrons, azaleas and rare sub-tropical shrubs. The exquisite dining room overlooks the lake and Mary Gaunt personally prepares menus of the finest Irish food, including freshly caught salmon, succulent Kerry lamb, garden grown vegetables and homebaked breads. Open 24 Apr – 18 Oct '98.

Caragh Lodge's gardens conceal an all-weather tennis court and sauna chalet. Salmon and trout swim in the lake and two boats are available for angling guests. Ghillies or permits for fishing in the two local rivers can be arranged. There are also local golf courses.

Places of interest nearby: The Ring of Kerry, Dingle Peninsula, Gap of Dunloe, Killarney and Tralee.
Directions: From Killorglin travel on N70 towards Glenbeigh and take second road signposted for Caragh Lake. At lake turn left, Caragh Lodge is on your right.

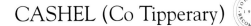

CASHEL PALACE HOTEL

MAIN STREET, CASHEL, CO TIPPERARY
TEL: 00 353 62 62707 FAX: 00 353 62 61521 E-MAIL: cphotel@ibm.net

OWNERS: Silkestan Ltd
MANAGER: Anna Stakelum

13 rms | 13 ens

S: IR£95–IR£105
D: IR£130–IR£155
Suite: IR£175–IR£210

This magnificent and luxurious 18th century hotel stands in the shadow of the famous Rock of Cashel at the heart of a heritage town surrounded by a wealth of historical sites. Built in 1730 as a palace for Archbishop Theophilus Bolton it is a jewel of late Queen Anne and early Georgian style. Described as "A place of notable hospitality" in Loveday's Tour of 1732, the Cashel Palace Hotel's beauty is complemented by 22 acres of walled gardens which include a private walk to the Rock of Cashel and two mulberry trees planted in 1702 to commemorate the coronation of Queen Anne.

The hotel has been lovingly restored with great attention given to preserving its character and integrity.

Spacious bedrooms echo the style and elegance of the 18th century and are individually furnished to the highest standards. The tradition of fine food continues in the relaxed ambience of the Bishops Buttery which specialises in lighter modern Irish cuisine with classical influences.

Local leisure activities include pony trekking, horse riding, golf, tennis, trout and salmon fishing.

Places of interest nearby: Cashel is an ideal base from which to tour Munster and the South East and is within easy reach of Cahir Castle, the Devil's Bit Mountain and Holy Cross. **Directions: Cashel is on the junction of the N8 and N74.**

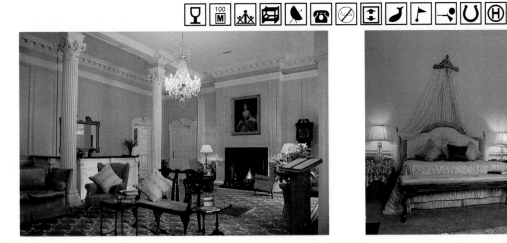

ABERDEEN LODGE

53-55 PARK AVENUE, OFF AILESBURY ROAD, DUBLIN 4
TEL: 00 353 1 2838155 FAX: 00 353 1 2837877 E-MAIL: aberdeen@iol.ie

OWNER: Pat Halpin

S: IR£60–IR£90
D: IR£80–IR£120
Suite: IR£95–IR£145

17 rms 17 ens

This symbol of classical Edwardian architecture has a prime site in a serene tree-lined avenue in what is often called Dublin's Embassy Belt. Set in its own large formal gardens, Aberdeen Lodge provides high quality accommodation, comfort and service accompanied by all the modern luxuries which visitors to a flourishing capital city would expect today.

Every room is an elegant reminder of Edwardian grace and Pat Halpin and his family's renowned hotel experience is evident in the detail of decor and operation. They pride themselves on being able to ensure that the needs of guests are met quickly and efficiently.

Each of the tastefully furnished bedrooms is en suite and designed in complete harmony with the house. The spacious suites feature a Jacuzzi and period style furniture.

The award winning intimate Breakfast Room is complemented by a special menu served between 11am and 10pm, accompanied by a good selection of fine wines from around the world.

Places of interest nearby: The hotel makes an ideal base from which to explore Dublin and enjoy shopping in the famous Grafton Street. As well as many first-class golf courses there is horse racing and two major marinas along the coast. Lansdowne Road rugby ground is a short walk.
Directions: Off Ailesbury Road, Aberdeen Lodge is 7 minutes from the city centre by D.A.R.T. bus.

HALPINS HOTEL AND VITTLE'S RESTAURANT

ERIN STREET, KILKEE, CO CLARE
TEL: 00 353 65 56032 FAX: 00 353 65 56317 E-MAIL: halpins@iol.ie

OWNER: Pat Halpin
MANAGER: Ann Keane
CHEF: Ethel O'Donnell

S: IR£35–IR£50
D: IR£65–IR£90

The welcome that awaits guests to Halpins Hotel is in the best traditions of Irish hospitality. Built in 1880, this charming hotel with a unique "shop-style" entrance is situated in a terrace at the heart of a popular resort facing a one mile long semi-circular sweep of sand. Surrounded by fine cliff scenery and reputed to be the safest bathing place in Ireland, Kilkee has attracted distinguished visitors from all over Europe for almost two centuries, among them literary figures such as Alfred Tennyson and Charlotte Brontë. Egon Ronay Commended and RAC Highly Acclaimed.

The Halpin family has owned and run the hotel for 15 years and are proud of its reputation for its friendly style and excellent standards. There are 12 prettily decorated en suite bedrooms, all of which are individually furnished.

The bar and lounge are famous for their old world atmosphere, complemented by quality food and fine wines of the world. The hotel restaurant Vittle's is one of the best in town. Chef Ethel O'Donnell produces wonderful modern Irish cuisine to suit all tastes.

Places of interest nearby: Kilkee Golf Club. The famous cliffs of Moher and Ailwee Caves, Doonbeg castle, Scattery Island's 6th century monastic settlement, Loop Head and the lunar-type landscape of the Burren.
Directions: Kilkee is situated on the N67 road from Galway, just 50 minutes from Shannon airport.

In association
with MasterCard

EARLS COURT HOUSE

WOODLAWN JUNCTION, MUCKROSS ROAD, KILLARNEY, CO KERRY
TEL: 00 353 64 34009 FAX: 00 353 64 34366

OWNERS: Ray and Emer Moynihan

| 11 rms | 11 ens | |

S: IR£40–IR£60
D: IR£60–IR£80

Earls Court House stands elevated and shadowed by tall, whispering trees just a five minutes walk from the bustling town centre of Killarney. It is in the heart of beautiful Co Kerry, surrounded by the 25,000 acres of Killarney National Park with its lakes, mountains and magnificent gardens where giant rhododendrons and tropical plants grow in abundance. Owners Ray and Emer Moynihan pride themselves that the hotel is a haven of tranquillity where relaxation comes naturally and service and hospitality is of the highest standards.

Earls Court is a purpose built, spacious hotel in the country house tradition. Fine antiques, prints and fabrics adorn the rooms throughout. Magnificent carved beds complement the charming, en suite bedrooms which are furnished with all modern amenities. Most of the bedrooms have private balconies with views over the open spaces of Muckross Park.

The hotel is an ideal base from which to tour Kerry, to explore Killarney National Park, or play south west Ireland's premier golf courses. Pony trekking, salmon and trout fishing can be arranged. Dinner is not available, but there are many good restaurants close by. The hotel is closed from November 5 to February 28.

Places of interest nearby: Killarney National Park.
Directions: Earls Court House is close to the centre of Killarney, just off the N71 Muckross Road.

CASTLE GROVE COUNTRY HOUSE

RAMELTON ROAD, LETTERKENNY, CO DONEGAL
TEL: 00 353 74 51118 FAX: 00 353 74 51384

OWNER: Mary J. Sweeny

12 rms   12 ens

S: IR£45–£50
D: IR£60–IR£90
Suite: IR130–IR160

This elegant Georgian House, reached by a mile long avenue through parkland, is in a sheltered position with a spectacular view of Lough Swilly.

True Irish hospitality is offered at this family-owned country residence with its gracious reception rooms and the charming drawing room looking out on the extensive grounds. There is a separate television room.

The dining room is very popular with the people who live in the neighbourhood, so reservations are necessary. The succulent dishes offered on the extensive menu reflecting the marvellous local produce – especially the fish – are served in great style accompanied by wines from a list of the highest calibre. Small corporate lunches are a speciality.

The bedrooms are spacious, all recently refurbished and equipped with modern necessities.

Donegal is famous for its white sand beaches and clean seas. The scenery is superb along the coast roads and in the mountains. Glenveagh National Park is fascinating, with its castle and famous gardens. One can meet Derek Hill at his fine Art Gallery at Churchill. Activities nearby include golf, fishing (lake, river and deep sea). Rough and walked up shoots are available throughout the season. Riding can be arranged on request. **Directions: Castle Grove is three miles from Letterkenny, off the R245.**

In association
with MasterCard

PORTAFERRY HOTEL

THE STRAND, PORTAFERRY, CO DOWN BT22 1PE
TEL: 012477 28231 FAX: 012477 28999 E-MAIL: portfery@iol.ie

OWNERS: John and Marie Herlihy

| 12 rms | 12 ens | SMALL HOTEL |

S: £55
D: £90

The welcome that awaits guests to Portaferry Hotel is in the best traditions of Irish hospitality. The original terrace of houses which now forms the Portaferry dates back to the mid-18th century. Recent extensions have been carried out with great care to preserve the unique character of this charming waterside hostelry.

The hotel's superbly appointed bedrooms are individually styled and many have attractive views of Strangford Lough. A good range of facilities is available to ensure maximum comfort and convenience.

Diners in the AA 2 rosettes award-winning restaurant can enjoy an abundance of freshly caught prawns, turbot, brill, sole, scallops, lobster and mussels. The hotel enjoys an international reputation for its seafood, which is landed daily. Also available is the best Ulster beef, Mourne lamb and game from neighbouring estates.

Places of interest nearby: Within easy reach are the National Trust properties of Mount Stewart and Castleward; Castle Espie; Exploris; Greyabbey Village with its numerous antique shops; the heritage town of Downpatrick; and the world renowned Royal County Down golf course. **Directions: From Belfast (A20) via Newtownards and Kircubbin. From Newry (A25) via Downpatrick and Strangford and a short ferry crossing.**

In association
with MasterCard

COOPERSHILL HOUSE

RIVERSTOWN, CO SLIGO
TEL: 00 353 71 65108 FAX: 00 353 71 65466 TELEX: 40301

OWNERS: Brian and Lindy O'Hara

8 rms | 7 ens

S: IR£55–IR£60
D: IR£90–IR£100

Winner of Johansens 1995 Country House Award, Coopershill is a fine example of a Georgian family mansion. Home to seven generations of the O'Hara family since 1774, it combines the spaciousness and elegance of an earlier age with modern comforts. Public rooms are furnished in period style with gilt-framed portraits, hunting trophies and antiques. Five of the bedrooms have four-poster or canopy beds and all have private bathrooms.

Dinner is served by candle-light in the elegant dining room, where good cooking is complemented by a wide choice of wines. Open log fires and personal attention from owners Brian and Lindy O'Hara help to create the warm atmosphere and hospitality that typify Coopershill. Out of season the house is open to parties of 8 to 16 people at a special rate. Tariffs are reduced if guests stay for three consecutive nights or more.

The River Arrow winds through the 500-acre estate and boating, trout and coarse fishing are available. Shooting is not permitted, leaving the abundant wildlife undisturbed. There is an excellent hard tennis court and also a croquet lawn. There are marvellous mountain and lakeside walks to enjoy in the area. Closed 1st November to mid-March.
Places of interest nearby: Sligo and Yeats country.
Directions: Leave N4 Sligo–Dublin road at Drumfin follow signs for Coopershill. One mile on, turn left.

LISS ARD LAKE LODGE

SKIBBEREEN, CO CORK
TEL: 00 353 28 40000 FAX: 00 353 28 40001 E-MAIL: Lissardlalohotel@tinet.ie

DIRECTORS: Claudia Meister and Gisa Deilman

| 10 rms | 10 ens | ⚘ | SMALL HOTEL |

S: IR£90–IR£165
D: IR£90–IR£220

This recently renovated hotel set in the tranquil and beautiful West Cork countryside was originally the summer home of a wealthy Victorian landowner.

Refined and minimalistic furnishings are to be found in the excellent bedrooms, each of which is equipped with a TV, video, stereo and PC and Fax points.

A generous and balanced breakfast is available until noon, so there is no rush for late risers! The hotel's restaurant serves light, imaginative, international cuisine, with local meat, fish and vegetables carefully prepared to suit all tastes. An excellent wine list is available.

Guests are invited to stroll through the surrounding Liss Ard Gardens, a unique project which creates ten contemporary landscaped "garden-rooms" out of a 50-acre park. Sample the delights of a Woodland Walk, Wild Flower Meadow or Irish Sky Garden. Other leisure activities available close by include golf, cycling, fishing in the hotel's own lake, sailing and scuba-diving.

Places of interest nearby: Cape Clear, Baltimore, Castletownsend, Mizen Head and Fastnet. **Directions: In Skibbereen, follow the one way system for 400 metres and turn left at roundabout onto L60, direction Castletownsend (Liss Ard signpost 5km). After 3½kms you will see Lake Abisdealy on your right. Turn right after lake, direction Tragumna, (Liss Ard signpost 1½km) and follow this road to the Lodge.**

MARKREE CASTLE

COLLOONEY, COUNTY SLIGO, IRELAND
TEL: 00 353 71 67800 FAX: 00 353 71 67840 E-MAIL: markree@iol.ie

OWNER: Charles Cooper

14 rms 14 ens

S: IR£62.50
D: IR£105
De luxe: IR£115

Regarded as one of Ireland's major architectural masterpieces, Markree Castle is Sligo's oldest inhabited castle. It has been the home of the Cooper family since 1640, but over the years the house has undergone a number of transformations. Today, the castle retains its family atmosphere and the character of the old building, while providing every modern comfort.

The interior boasts a spectacular oak staircase. This is overlooked by a stained glass window, purportedly tracing the Cooper family tree back to the time of King John of England. There are a variety of notable reception rooms, in addition to the interconnecting dining rooms which feature Louis-Philippe style plasterwork created by Italian craftsmen in 1845. An imaginative menu is provided

The bedrooms vary in character and style, but all offer views over the gardens or surrounding countryside.

Markree is in the heart of "Yeats Country", with magnificent scenery all around. The Rosses Point golf course and the Strandhill course are within a few miles. Trout and salmon fishing can be arranged nearby.

Places of interest nearby: Carrowmore, which has Europe's largest and oldest collection of megalithic remains; Lissadell House; Yeats's grave at Drumcliffe; and the town of Donegal. **Directions: Nine miles from Sligo airport, 125 from Dublin via N4. Collooney is just south of Sligo town.**

THE OLD RECTORY

WICKLOW TOWN, CO WICKLOW, IRELAND
TEL: 00 353 404 67048 FAX: 00 353 404 69181 E-MAIL: oldrec@indigo.ie

OWNERS: Paul and Linda Saunders

5 rms | 5 ens

S: IR£75
D: IR£100

The Old Rectory is situated in secluded gardens on the edge of the harbour town of Wicklow in County Wicklow, "the Garden of Ireland". A peaceful Victorian house, personally run by Paul and Linda Saunders, it combines charming country house accommodation with an elegant gourmet restaurant. The house is freshly decorated throughout and furnished with style. A small Fitness Suite includes aerobic equipment and a relaxing sauna. Individually designed bedrooms offer en suite bathrooms and lots of little extras to make you feel welcome. This special ambience has made it a winner of the coveted AA "Inspector's Selected" award for Ireland. The restaurant is exceptional and featured on TV's *"Gourmet Ireland"* and *"Summer Holiday"* series. Set gourmet and à la carte menus use fresh sea food, local and organic produce enhanced with herbs and edible flowers. Vegetarians welcome. In May/June 10-course "floral dinners" are a highlight of the Wicklow Gardens Festival. The Old Rectory also offers a choice of breakfasts which have won the National Breakfast award for Ireland.

Places of interest nearby: Glendalough and the Wicklow Mountains National Park, Powerscourt Gardens, Mount Usher Gardens, Russborough House, "Ballykissangel", 20 golf courses including Druids Glen (Irish Open July 1996–98). **Directions: 30m south of Dublin on N11, then 1m south of Rathnew on R750. Entrance has stone walls.**

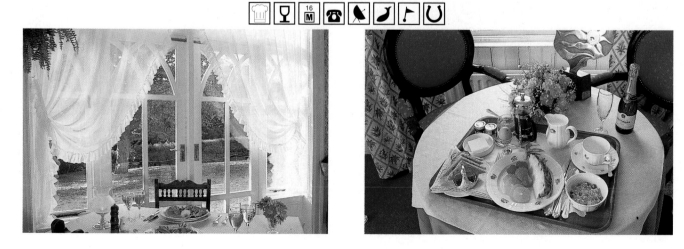

SMOKING DAMAGES THE HEALTH
OF THOSE AROUND YOU

Chief Medical Officers' Warning

'THE VALUE OF LIFE CAN BE MEASURED BY HOW MANY TIMES YOUR SOUL HAS BEEN DEEPLY STIRRED.'

Soichiro Honda

Soichiro Honda was the inspiration behind what is now the world's largest engine manufacturer. His concern for man and the environment led us to build not only the world's most fuel-efficient car (9426 mpg) but also the winner of the Darwin to Adelaide race for solar-powered vehicles. His search for excellence gave rise to us winning 6 consecutive Formula 1 constructor's championships. It also led to the all-aluminium NSX, a car capable of 168mph and in which, at 70mph with the roof off, you don't need to raise your voice. Soichiro Honda, a softly spoken man, would have approved. For more information on our current range of cars, call **0345 159 159.**

HONDA

First man, then machine

St Ouen's Bay Jersey

Johansens Recommended Country Houses in
Channel Islands

With a wealth of wonderful scenery, magnificent coastlines, historic buildings, natural and man-made attractions plus mouthwatering local produce, the Channel Islands provide a memorable destination that's distinctly different.

ALL OF THE JOHANSENS RECOMMENDED ESTABLISHMENTS IN THE CHANNEL ISLANDS ARE ABLE TO MAKE FAVOURABLE TRAVEL ARRANGEMENTS FOR YOU.

Jersey and Guernsey offer VAT free shopping, the official language is English, passports are not required and both islands can be reached by sea from Poole or any one of about 30 airports in Britain and Europe.

And don't forget the other islands. Herm has dazzling beaches, Sark lives in a rural timewarp without traffic and Alderney's cobbled streets, pretty cottages and Victorian forts are another world again.

JERSEY

The largest and most southerly of the Channel Islands, Jersey measures only nine miles by five and is just fourteen miles from the French coast. The island slopes from north to south, creating dramatic differences between the high cliffs of the north and broad sandy bays of the south.

Jersey was originally part of Normandy. When William the Conqueror invaded England, it came under English rule until 1204, when King John lost Normandy to France.

The Islanders were given a choice – stay with Normandy or remain loyal to the English Crown. They chose England and gained rights and privileges which to this day are subject not to the British Parliament, but only to the reigning monarch.

The French influence is still strong however, and visitors are often surprised to find the names of streets and villages in French. The granite architecture of the farms and manor houses has a Continental feel too, and in rural areas, you may still hear farmworkers speaking in the local 'patois' or dialect.

Food is also something for which Jersey is renowned. It has an excellent choice of restaurants serving everything from simple family meals to gourmet dishes. Shellfish and fresh fish are the specialities of the Island and

lobster, crab, seafood platter, bass and Jersey plaice feature on many menus. The annual Good Food Festival, held in early summer, is a must for food lovers.

History enthusiasts can trace the Island's development from prehistory to the present day through a variety of different sites. The Channel Islands were the only part of the British Isles to be occupied by the Germans during World War II and there are reminders all over Jersey.

For a small island, Jersey boasts more than its fair share of fascinating museums where the emphasis is very definitely 'hands on' history. Jersey Museum in St Helier; The Hamptonne Country Life Museum; and the new Maritime Museum which opened in July 1997.

You're never far from Jersey's spectacular coastline – all 50 miles of it – but the interior of the Island is worth exploring too. The largely rural landscape is criss-crossed by a network of narrow country roads, some of which have recently been designated as 'Green Lanes', where priority is given to walkers, cyclists and horseriders.

But the cultural attractions of Jersey can never eclipse the Island's natural beauty. Every bend in the lane, every turn in the coast path reveals a new view to be savoured and enjoyed.

GUERNSEY

Guernsey, somewhat smaller than its sister island, supports a successful, self-sufficient economy which mixes finance, horticulture and, of course, tourism – all within a total area of 25 square miles. Its charming little capital, St Peter Port, rises in tiers above the quaysides of the busy harbour where the colourful banners of yachts of all nations flutter in the sunshine. Needless to say, delicious seafood features prominently on the menus, though all tastes are catered for by the chefs of many nationalities who have settled in the island.

Guernsey offers enormous variety within its

relatively small size. The south coast comprises high cliffs, covered, in springtime, with a profusion of colourful flowers, at the foot of which nestle beautiful little sandy coves.

A network of cliff paths provides splendid walking all the way from St Peter Port to Pleinmont Point in the far south west corner of the island. These paths stretch for a total distance of some 25 miles, one spectacular seaview succeeding the other all the way. Inland, high-banked country lanes lead past old granite farmhouses and tiny fields, where the local breed of cows, famed for their superb cream, contentedly graze.

The west and north coasts comprise a series of sweeping sandy beaches where rocky outcrops are dotted with little pools, teaming with sea life, which provide hours of fascination for youngsters.

Guernsey's heritage provides a fascinating choice of subjects to study during a holiday. The island is girded with fortifications dating back to prehistoric times, and of paramount interest is Castle Cornet, dating from the 13th to 17th centuries, which dominates the harbour of St Peter Port and contains imaginatively conceived maritime and other museums. Other fortifications include 18th century coastal defence towers and the many substantial bunkers, tunnels and towers constructed by the occupying German forces during the second World War, a number of which have now been skilfully refurbished.

And it is this feeling of bygone ages which, coupled with the highest modern standards, prove so great an attraction to visitors to the island.

For further information, please contact:

Jersey Tourism
38 Dover Street, London, W1X 3RB
Tel: 0171 493 5278

Guernsey Tourist Board
PO Box 23, St Peter Port, Guernsey, GY1 3AN
Tel: 01481 723557 (24 hrs); 01481 723552

In association
with MasterCard **MasterCard**

BELLA LUCE HOTEL & RESTAURANT

LA FOSSE, ST MARTIN, GUERNSEY, CHANNEL ISLANDS GY4 6EB
TEL: 01481 38764 FAX: 01481 39561

OWNER: Richard Cann
MANAGER: John Cockcroft

| 28 rms | 28 ens | | SMALL HOTEL |

MasterCard VISA AMERICAN EXPRESS

S: From £35
D: From £70

The Bella Luce is one of Guernsey's original Norman manor houses. Set in splendid grounds on the most select side of the island, this perfectly preserved house includes extensions built in the 14th century. Happily the utmost care has been taken to maintain its period character during upgrading, so today's hotel offers excellent accommodation with every modern amenity.

Drinks are served throughout the day in the hotel's lounge bar, which dates back to the 11th century and is the oldest part of the building. Here, under the fine oak beamed ceiling, guests can enjoy a lunch and savour the cheerful and serene old world.

A varied table d'hôte menu, offering a wide range of English and Continental dishes, is provided in the restaurant which enjoys an excellent reputation throughout the island. A comprehensive à la carte menu featuring fresh seafood specialities is also available.

In a sun-trapped corner of the gardens there is a swimming pool surrounded by sun-beds and providing a perfect location for relaxation. Refreshments are served throughout the day and there is a sauna/solarium room nearby.

Places of interest nearby: Within easy reach of the three most beautiful south coast bays of Moulin Huet, Petit Port and Saints. Marine trips operate daily in season to Herm, Sark, Jersey and the nearby coast of France. **Directions: 5 minutes from the airport and St Peter Port.**

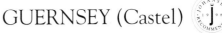

GUERNSEY (Castel)

HOTEL HOUGUE DU POMMIER

HOUGUE DU POMMIER ROAD, GUERNSEY, CHANNEL ISLANDS GY5 7FQ
TEL: 01481 56531 FAX: 01481 56260

OWNERS: Michael and Anne Swan
MANAGER: Stephen Bone
CHEF: Andrew Till

| 44 rms | 44 ens | SMALL HOTEL |

MasterCard VISA AMERICAN EXPRESS

S: from £28
D: from £56

Once an early 18th century farmhouse, Hougue du Pommier retains much of the charm and character of those former days. Standing in 10 acres of beautifully cultivated grounds on the west coast, this enchanting hotel gives easy access to any part of the island and is only 10 minutes walk from the superb sandy beaches of Grandes Rocques and Cobo. Owners Michael and Anne Swan and manager Stephen Bone have created a happy, relaxed and welcoming atmosphere, offering visitors excellent value for money. All en suite bedrooms are comfortable and the nine deluxe rooms offer improved facilities including mini-bars, trouser press, and hair dryers. The dining room, occupies the original farmhouse and has six linked rooms; there is an excellent daily menu as well as a first class à la carte menu. The Tudor Bar is popular with locals for both lunch and dinner and during the summer lunches are served in the pretty tea garden. The new conservatory lounge overlooks the tea garden and is very comfortable – whatever the weather. To the rear of the hotel is a 10 hole pitch and putt and 9 hole putting green. The heated outdoor swimming pool is open from Easter to September. The hotel's courtesy coach will take guests to St Peter Port (from April to October) and the less energetic can use the Guernsey Indoor Bowling Stadium which is situated 100 metres from the hotel. **Directions:** Off the main coast road east of Cobo Bay on the west side of the island.

In association
with MasterCard

La Favorita Hotel

FERMAIN BAY, GUERNSEY, CHANNEL ISLANDS GY4 6SD
TEL: 01481 35666 FAX: 01481 35413

OWNERS: Simon and Helen Wood

37 rms 37 ens SMALL HOTEL

S: from £41
D: from £76

Once a fine private country house, La Favorita retains all the charm and character of those former days. The hotel is comfortable and fully licensed. Set in its own grounds, a few minutes walk from Guernsey's famous Fermain Bay, it enjoys spectacular views over the sea towards Jersey.

The bedrooms are comfortable and provide every modern amenity, including colour TV, radio, and refreshment tray. Guernsey's mild climate means that it has much to offer out of season and the hotel also has a full range of facilities to satisfy the extra needs of spring, autumn and winter guests, including the indoor pool.

La Favorita has an excellent reputation for traditional English cooking and island seafood specialities. The restaurant is strictly no smoking. A coffee shop serves a wide range of lunch dishes and bar suppers for those who enjoy a more informal meal.

St Peter Port is within easy walking distance, whether taking the woodland walk which follows the coastline or the more direct route past Victor Hugo's house.

Places of interest nearby: The coast of Guernsey and all the island's attractions. Boat trips to Jersey, Alderney, Herm and Sark can easily be arranged. **Directions: Fermain Bay is 10 minutes from the airport and five minutes from St Peter Port on the east coast of Guernsey.**

HOTEL LA TOUR

RUE DE CROQUET, ST AUBIN, JERSEY JE3 8BR
TEL: 01534 43770 FAX: 01534 47143

OWNERS: Samantha and Victor Gomes
CHEF: Victor Gomes

26 rms | 26 ens

S: £23–£40.50
D: £23–£40.50
(price per person)

Samantha and Victor Gomes are continually seeking to improve their quiet little High Street hotel with special trimmings and extra personal touches and have now introduced a lovely, compact landscaped garden for guests to relax in on sunny days and balmy evenings. La Tour stands alongside elegant houses built for merchants who traded when St Aubin was Jersey's main port. The hotel has character, style and commanding views over the town's historic harbour and fort.

There is a variety of bedroom styles. Each room is extremely comfortable and has everything a visitor would expect. The Tower Suite has a terrace from which guests can sit and enjoy magnificent views of St Aubin's Bay.

Chef-patron Victor prides himself on the award winning meals he provides for discerning diners in the intimate restaurant. The use of fresh Jersey produce complements a good selection of fine wines.

Activities available nearby are swimming, sea fishing, sailing, water sports, walking and golf at two 18-hole courses.

Places of interest nearby: St Helier, three miles away, the central fish and vegetable markets, Jersey Museum and all the island's attractions. **Directions: Heading towards St Aubin from the Beaumont roundabout, take the second right turn signed La Haule. Then take the left fork into Rue de Croquet. The hotel is on the right.**

Halliday Meecham

ARCHITECTS • INTERIOR DESIGNERS

JOHANSENS PREFERRED ARCHITECTURAL ADVISOR PARTNER

A complete architectural and interior design service for hoteliers and restauranteurs supported by a truly personal and professional practice founded in 1908.

We take great care in the design and management of contracts for the repair, refurbishment, extension and interior design of contemporary, period and listed buildings, and in the design of new uses for old buildings.

Our experience extends to hotels, restaurants and bars, swimming and leisure facilities, conference and seminar venues.

We work nationally and are interested in projects of all sizes. The hallmark of our work is an attractive project finished on time, within cost and without disruption.

Why not have an exploratory discussion to see how we can help you achieve your objectives?

RECIPIENTS OF OVER TWENTY AWARDS IN THE LAST TEN YEARS

0161 661 5566

Peter House, St. Peter's Square

Oxford Street

Manchester M1 5AN

Johansens Recommended Inns With Restaurants in Great Britain

ENGLAND

Amberley,Near Arundel – The Boathouse Brasserie, Houghton Bridge, Amberley, BN18 9LR. Tel: 01798 831059

Ambleside (Great Langdale) – The New Dungeon Ghyll Hotel, Great Langdale, Ambleside, LA22 9JY. Tel: 015394 37213

Appleby-In-Westmorland – The Royal Oak Inn, Bongate, Appleby-In-Westmorland, CA16 6UN. Tel: 017683 51463

Ashbourne (Hognaston) – Red Lion Inn, Main Street, Hognaston, Ashbourne, DE6 1PR. Tel: 01335 370396

Askrigg (Wensleydale) – The Kings Arms Hotel And Restaurant, Market Place, Askrigg-In-Wensleydale, Askrigg-In-Wensleydale, DL8 3HQ. Tel: 01969 650258

Badby Nr Daventry – The Windmill At Badby, Main Street, Badby, NN11 6AN. Tel: 01327 702363

Bassenthwaite Lake – The Pheasant Inn, Bassenthwaite Lake, CA13 9YE. Tel: 017687 76234

Beckington Nr Bath – The Woolpack Inn, Beckington, BA3 6SP. Tel: 01373 831244

Belford – The Blue Bell Hotel, Market Place, Belford, NE70 7NE. Tel: 01668 213543

Blakeney – White Horse Hotel, 4 High Street, Blakeney, Holt, NR25 7AL. Tel: 01263 740574

Boroughbridge – The Crown Hotel, Horsefair, Boroughbridge, YO5 9LB. Tel: 01423 322328

Bourton-On-The-Water – The Old Manse, Victoria Street, Bourton-On-The-Water, GL54 2BX. Tel: 01451 820082

Bridport (West Bexington) – The Manor Hotel, West Bexington, Dorchester, DT2 9DF. Tel: 01308 897616

Brixham (Churston Ferrers) – Ye Olde Churston Court Inn, Churston Ferrers, TQ5 0JE. Tel: 01803 842186

Broadway – The Broadway Hotel, The Green, Broadway, WR12 7AA. Tel: 01386 852401

Burford – The Lamb Inn, Sheep Street, Burford, OX18 4LR. Tel: 01993 823155

Burford – Cotswold Gateway Hotel, Cheltenham Road, Burford, OX18 4HX. Tel: 01993 822695

Burnham Market – The Hoste Arms Hotel, The Green, Burnham Market, PE31 8HD. Tel: 01328 738777

Burnley (Fence) – Fence Gate Inn, Wheatley Lane Road, Fence, BB12 9EE. Tel: 01282 618101

Burnsall (Skipton) – The Red Lion, By the bridge at Burnsall, BD23 6BU. Tel: 01756 720204

Burton Upon Trent (Branston) – The Old Vicarage Restaurant, Main Street, Branston, Burton Upon Trent, DE14 3EX. Tel: 01283 533222

Burton Upon Trent (Sudbury) – Boar's Head Hotel, Lichfield Road, Sudbury, DE6 5GX. Tel: 01283 820344

Calver,Nr Bakewell – The Chequers Inn, Froggatt Edge, S30 1ZB. Tel: 01433 630231

Camborne – Tyacks Hotel, 27 Commercial Street, Camborne, TR14 8LD. Tel: 01209 612424

Cambridge – Panos Hotel & Restaurant, 154-156 Hills Road, Cambridge, CB2 2PB. Tel: 01223 212958

Carlisle (Talkin Tarn) – The Tarn End House Hotel, Talkin Tarn, Brampton, CA8 1LS. Tel: 016977 2340

Castle Ashby – The Falcon Hotel, Castle Ashby, Northampton, NN7 1LF. Tel: 01604 696200

Castle Combe – The Castle Inn, Castle Combe, SN14 7HN. Tel: 01249 783030

Castle Donington – Donington Manor Hotel, High Street, Castle Donington, DE74 2PP. Tel: 01332 810253

Cheltenham (Birdlip) – Kingshead House Restaurant, Birdlip, GL4 8JH. Tel: 01452 862299

Chester (Tarporley) – Wild Boar Hotel & Restaurant, Whitchurch Road, Near Beeston, Tarporley, CW6 9NW. Tel: 01829 260309

Chester (Tarporley) – The Swan Hotel, 50 High Street, Tarporley, CW6 0AG. Tel: 01829 733838

Chipping Campden (Broad Campden) – The Noel Arms, High Street, Chipping Campden, GL55 6AT. Tel: 01386 840317

Cirencester (Coln St-Aldwyns) – The New Inn, Coln St-Aldwyns, GL7 5AN. Tel: 01285 750651

Cirencester (Meysey Hampton) – The Masons Arms, Meysey Hampton, GL7 5JT. Tel: 01285 850164

Clavering (Stansted) – The Cricketers, Clavering, CB11 4QT. Tel: 01799 550442

Cleobury Mortimer – The Redfern Hotel, Cleobury Mortimer, DY14 8AA. Tel: 01299 270 395

Cleobury Mortimer – The Crown At Hopton, Hopton Wafers, Cleobury Mortimer, DY14 0NB. Tel: 01299 270372

Clovelly – New Inn Hotel, High Street, Clovelly, EX39 5TQ. Tel: 01237 431303

Colchester – The Red Lion Hotel, High Street, Colchester, CO1 1DJ. Tel: 01206 577986

Crowborough – Winston Manor, Beacon Road, Crowborough, TN6 1AD. Tel: 01892 652772

Dartmouth – The Victoria Hotel, Victoria Road, Dartmouth, TQ6 9RT. Tel: 01803 832572

Dorchester-On-Thames – The George Hotel, High Street, Dorchester-On-Thames, OX10 7HH. Tel: 01865 340404

Dulverton (Exbridge) – The Anchor Country Inn & Hotel, Exbridge, TA22 9AZ. Tel: 01398 323433

East Witton (Wensleydale) – The Blue Lion, East Witton, DL8 4SN. Tel: 01969 624273

East Grinstead (Felbridge) – The Woodcock Inn & Restaurant, Woodcock Hill, Felbridge. Tel: 01342 325859

Eccleshall – The George Hotel, Eccleshall, ST21 6DF. Tel: 01785 850300

Egton – The Wheatsheaf Inn, Egton, YO21 1TZ. Tel: 01947 895271

Eton/Windsor – The Christopher Hotel, High Street, Eton, Windsor, SL4 6AN. Tel: 01753 852359

Evesham (Offenham) – The Riverside Restaurant and Hotel, The Parks, Offenham Road, WR11 5JP. Tel: 01386 446200

Exmoor (Withypool) – The Royal Oak Inn, Withypool, Emoor National Park, TA24 7QP. Tel: 01643 831506/7

Eyam (Foolow) – The Bulls Head Inn, Foolow, Eyam, Hope Valley, S32 5QR. Tel: 01433 630873

Falmouth (Constantine) – Trengilly Wartha Country Inn & Restaurant, Nancenoy, Constantine, Falmouth, TR11 5RP. Tel: 01326 340332

Fordingbridge (New Forest) – The Woodfalls Inn, The Ridge, Woodfalls, Fordingbridge, SP5 2LN. Tel: 01725 513222

Fulbeck (Lincoln) – Hare & Hounds, The Green, Fulbeck, NG32 3SS. Tel: 01400 272090

Goathland – Mallyan Spout Hotel, Goathland, YO22 5AN. Tel: 01947 896486

Godalming – The Inn On The Lake, Ockford Road, Godalming, GU7 1RH. Tel: 01483 415575

Goring-On-Thames – The Leatherne Bottel Riverside Inn & Restaurant, The Bridleway, Goring-On-Thames, RG8 0HS. Tel: 01491 872667

Grimsthorpe (Bourne) – The Black Horse Inn, Grimsthorpe, Bourne, PE10 0LY. Tel: 01778 591247

Grindleford – The Maynard Arms, Main Road, Grindleford, S32 2HE. Tel: 01433 630321

Halifax/Huddersfield – The Rock Inn Hotel, Holywell Green, Halifax, HX4 9BS. Tel: 01422 379721

Handcross (Slaugham) – The Chequers At Slaugham, Slaugham, RH17 6AQ. Tel: 01444 400239/400996

Harrogate (Killinghall) – The Low Hall Hotel, Ripon Road, Killinghall, Harrogate, HG3 2AY. Tel: 01423 508598

Harrogate (Ripley Castle) – The Boar's Head Hotel, Ripley, Harrogate, HG3 3AY. Tel: 01423 771888

Hatherleigh – The George Hotel, Market Street, Hatherleigh, EX20 3JN. Tel: 01837 810454

Hathersage – The Plough Inn, Leadmill Bridge, Hathersage, S30 1BA. Tel: 01433 650319

Haworth – Old White Lion Hotel, Haworth, Keighley, BD22 8DU. Tel: 01535 642313

Hay-On-Wye – Rhydspence Inn, Whitney-On-Wye, HR3 6EU. Tel: 01497 831262

Hayfield (High Peak) – The Waltzing Weasel, New Mills Road, Birch Vale High Peak, Hayfield, SK22 1BT. Tel: 01663 743402

Helmsley – The Feversham Arms Hotel, Helmsley, YO6 5AG. Tel: 01439 770766

Helmsley – The Feathers Hotel, Market Place, Helmsley, YO6 5BH. Tel: 01439 770275

Henley (Ibstone) – The Fox Country Hotel, Ibstone, HP14 3GG. Tel: 01491 638289

Hinkley (Nr Leicester) – Barnacles Restaurant, Watlins Street, LE10 3JA. Tel: 01455 633220

Honiton (Wilmington) – Home Farm Hotel, Wilmington, EX14 9JQ. Tel: 01404 831278

Kirkby Lonsdale – Whoop Hall Inn, Burrow-With-Burrow, Kirkby Lonsdale, LA6 2HP. Tel: 015242 71284

Knutsford – Longview Hotel And Restaurant, 51/55 Manchester Road, Knutsford, WA16 0LX. Tel: 01565 632119

Ledbury – The Feathers Hotel, High Street, Ledbury, HR8 1DS. Tel: 01531 635266

Leek (Blackshaw Moor) – The Three Horseshoes Inn & Restaurant, Buxton Road, Blackshaw Moor, ST13 8TW. Tel: 01538 300296

Leominster (Stoke Prior) – Wheelbarrow Castle, Stoke Prior, Leominster, HR6 0NB. Tel: 01568 612219

Long Melford – The Countrymen, The Green, Long Melford, CO10 9DN. Tel: 01787 312356

Ludlow (Brimfield) – The Roebuck, Brimfield. Tel: 01584 711230

Lynmouth – The Rising Sun, Harbourside, Lynmouth, EX35 6EQ. Tel: 01598 753223

Maidenhead – Boulters Lock Hotel, Boulters Island, Maidenhead, SL6 8PE. Tel: 01628 21291

Maidstone (Ringlestone) – Ringlestone Inn, 'Twixt' Harrietsham and Wormshill, ME17 1NX. Tel: 01622 859900

Maidstone (Warren Street) – The Harrow At Warren Street, Warren Street, ME17 2ED. Tel: 01622 858727

Malmesbury – The Horse And Groom Inn, Charlton, SN16 9DL. Tel: 01666 823904

Mells Nr Bath – The Talbot Inn at Mells, High Street, Mells, BA11 3PN. Tel: 01373 812254

Milton Keynes (Stony Stratford) – The Different Drummer, High Street, Stony Stratford, MK11 1AH. Tel: 01908 564733

Minchinhampton (Hyde) – The Ragged Cot, Hyde, Minchinhampton, GL6 8PE. Tel: 01453 884643/731333

Montacute – The King's Arms Inn & Restaurant, Montacute, TA16 6UU. Tel: 01935 822513

Moretonhampstead – The White Hart Hotel, The Square, Moretonhampstead, TQ13 8NF. Tel: 01647 440406

Newark (Barnby-in-the-Willows) – The Willow Tree, Barnby-in-the-Willows, Newark, NG24 2SA. Tel: 01636 626613

Newbury (Kingsclere) – The Swan Hotel, Swan Street, Kingsclere, RG20 5PP. Tel: 01635 298314

Newby Bridge – The Swan Hotel, Newby Bridge, LA12 8NB. Tel: 015395 31681

Norwich (Rackheath) – The Garden House Hotel, Salhouse Road, Rackheath, Norwich, NR13 6AA. Tel: 01603 720007

Nottingham – Hotel Des Clos, Old Lenton Lane, Nottingham, NG7 2SA. Tel: 01159 866566

Oakham – The Whipper-In Hotel, The Market Place, Oakham, Rutland, LE15 6DT. Tel: 01572 756971

Onneley – The Wheatsheaf Inn At Onneley And La Puerta Del Sol Restaurante Español, Barhill Road, Onneley, CW3 9QF. Tel: 01782 751581

Oxford (Banbury) – Holcombe Hotel, High Street, Deddington, OX15 0SL. Tel: 01869 338274

Oxford (Middleton Stoney) – The Jersey Arms, Middleton Stoney, OX6 8SE. Tel: 01869 343234

Oxford (Minster Lovell) – The Mill & Old Swan, Minster Lovell, OX8 5RN. Tel: 01993 774441

Oxford (Stanton St John) – The Talkhouse, Wheatley Road, Stanton-St-John, OX33 1EX. Tel: 01865 351648

Padstow – The Old Custom House Hotel, South Quay, Padstow, PL28 8ED. Tel: 01841 532359

Pelynt,Nr Looe – Jubilee Inn, Pelynt, PL13 2JZ. Tel: 01503 220312

Petworth (Coultershaw Bridge) – Badgers, Coultershaw Bridge, Petworth, GU28 0JF. Tel: 01798 342651

Petworth (Sutton) – The White Horse Inn, Sutton, RH20 1PS. Tel: 01798 869 221

Pickering – The White Swan, The Market Place, Pickering, YO18 7AA. Tel: 01751 472288

Port Gaverne – The Port Gaverne Hotel, PL29 3SQ. Tel: 01208 880244

Porthleven (Nr Helston) – The Harbour Inn, Commercial Road, Porthleven, TR13 9JD. Tel: 01326 573876

Preston (Goosnargh) – Ye Horn's Inn, Horn's Lane, Goosnargh, PR3 2FJ. Tel: 01772 865230

Reepham (Norwich) – The Old Brewery House Hotel, Market Square, Reepham, Norwich, NR10 4JJ. Tel: 01603 870881

Rugby (Easenhall) – The Golden Lion Inn of Easenhall, Easenall, CV23 0JA. Tel: 01788 832265

Saddleworth (Delph) – The Old Bell Inn Hotel, Huddersfield Road, Delph, Saddleworth, OL3 5EG. Tel: 01457 870130

Settle (Clapham) – The New Inn Hotel, Clapham, LA2 8HH. Tel: 015242 51203

Sevenoaks – The Royal Oak, High Street, Sevenoaks, TN14 5PG. Tel: 01732 451109

Shaftesbury (Motcombe) – The Coppleridge Inn, Motcombe, Shaftesbury, SP7 9HW. Tel: 01747 851980

Sherborne (West Camel) – The Walnut Tree, West Camel, BA22 7QW. Tel: 01935 851292

Shipton-Under-Wychwood – The Shaven Crown Hotel, High Street, Shipton Under Wychwood, OX7 6BA. Tel: 01993 830330

Shipton-Under-Wychwood – The Lamb Inn, Shipton-Under-Wychwood, OX7 6DQ. Tel: 01993 830465

Shrewsbury (Nesscliffe) – The Nesscliffe, Nesscliffe, Shrewsbury, SY4 1DB. Tel: 01743 741430

Southport (Formby) – Tree Tops Country House Restaurant & Motel, Southport Old Road, Formby, L37 0AB. Tel: 01704 879651

St Mawes – The Rising Sun, The Square, St Mawes, TR2 5DJ. Tel: 01326 270233

Stafford (Ingestre) – The Dower House, Ingestre Park, Great Haywood, ST18 0RE. Tel: 01889 270707

Stow-On-The-Wold – The Royalist Hotel, Digbeth Street, Stow-On-The-Wold, GL54 1BN. Tel: 01451 830670

Stow-On-The-Wold (Bledington) – The Kings Head Inn & Restaurant, The Green, Bledington, OX7 6XQ. Tel: 01608 658365

Stow-on-the-Wold (Oddington) – The Horse and Groom, Upper Oddington, Moreton-in-Marsh, GL56 0XH. Tel: 01451 830584

Stratford-upon-Avon – The Coach House Hotel & Cellar Restaurant, 16/17 Warwick Road, Stratford-upon-Avon, CV37 6YW. Tel: 01789 204109 / 299468

Telford (Norton) – The Hundred House Hotel, Bridgnorth Road,Norton, Nr Shifnal, Telford, TF11 9EE. Tel: 01952 730353

Thelbridge – Thelbridge Cross Inn, Thelbridge, EX17 4SQ. Tel: 01884 860316

Thornham – The Lifeboat Inn, Ship Lane, Thornham, PE36 6LT. Tel: 01485 512236

Thorpe Market – Green Farm Restaurant And Hotel, North Walsham Road, Thorpe Market, NR11 8TH. Tel: 01263 833602

Tintagel (Trebarwith Strand) – The Port William, Trebarwith Strand, PL34 0HB. Tel: 01840 770230

Torbryan Nr Totnes – The Old Church House Inn, Torbryan, Ipplepen, TQ12 5UR. Tel: 01803 812372

Torquay (Kingskerswell) – The Barn Owl Inn, Aller Mills, Kingskerswell, TQ12 5AN. Tel: 01803 872130

Totnes (Staverton) – The Sea Trout Inn, Staverton, TQ9 6PA. Tel: 01803 762274

Troutbeck (Near Windermere) – The Mortal Man Hotel, Troutbeck, LA23 1PL. Tel: 015394 33193

Tunbridge Wells – The Royal Wells Inn, Mount Ephraim, Tunbridge Wells, TN4 8BE. Tel: 01892 511188

Upton-Upon-Severn,Nr Malvern – The White Lion Hotel, High Street, Upton-Upon-Severn, WR8 0HJ. Tel: 01684 592551

Weobley – Ye Olde Salutation Inn, Market Pitch, Weobley, HR4 8SJ. Tel: 01544 318443

West Witton (Wensleydale) – The Wensleydale Heifer Inn, West Witton, Wensleydale, DL8 4LS. Tel: 01969 622322

Whitewell – The Inn At Whitewell, Forest Of Bowland, Clitheroe, BB7 3AT. Tel: 01200 448222

Worcester (Knightwick) – The Talbot, Knightwick, Worcester, WR6 5PH. Tel: 01886 821235

Worcester (Severn Stoke) – The Old Schoolhouse, Severn Stoke, Worcester, WR8 9JA. Tel: 01905 371368

Worthing (Bramber) – The Old Tollgate Restaurant And Hotel, The Street, Bramber, Steyning, BN44 3WE. Tel: 01903 879494

Wroxham – The Barton Angler Country Inn, Irstead Road, Neatishead, NR12 8XP. Tel: 01692 630740

Yattendon – The Royal Oak Hotel, Yattendon, Newbury, RG18 0UG. Tel: 01635 201325

York (Easingwold) – The George at Easingwold, Market Place, Easingwold, York, YO6 3AD. Tel: 01347 821698

York (Thorganby) – The Jefferson Arms, Main Street, YO4 6DB. Tel: 01904 448316

WALES

Chepstow – The Castle View Hotel, 16 Bridge Street, Chepstow, NP6 5EZ. Tel: 01291 620349

Llanarmon Dyffryn Ceiriog – The West Arms Hotel, Llanarmon D C, LL20 7LD. Tel: 01691 600665

Llandeilo (Rhosmaen) – The Plough Inn, Rhosmaen, Llandeilo, SA19 6NP. Tel: 01558 823431

Ruthin – Ye Olde Anchor Inn, Rhos Street, Ruthin, LL15 1DX. Tel: 01824 702813

Welshpool – The Royal Oak Hotel & Restaurant, Welshpool, SY7 7DG. Tel: 01938 552217

Welshpool (Berriew) – The Lion Hotel And Restaurant, Berriew, SY21 8PQ. Tel: 01686 640452

SCOTLAND

Banchory (Royal Deeside) – Potarch Hotel, By Banchory, Royal Deeside, AB31 4BD. Tel: 013398 84339

Blair Atholl – The Loft Restaurant, Golf Course Road, Blair Atholl, PH18 5TE. Tel: 01736 481377

Blairgowrie (Glenisla) – The Glenisla Hotel, Kirkton of Glenisla, By Alyth, PH11 8PH. Tel: 01575 582223

Isle Of Skye (Eilean Iarmain) – Hotel Eilean Iarmain or Isle Ornsay Hotel, Sleat, IV43 8QR. Tel: 01471 833332

Isle Of Skye (Uig) – Uig Hotel, Uig, Isle Of Skye, IV51 9YE. Tel: 01470 542205

Moffatt – Annandale Arms Hotel, High Street, Moffatt, DG10 9HF. Tel: 01683 220013

Pitlochry – The Moulin Hotel, Moulin, By Pitlochry, PH16 %EW. Tel: 01796 472196

Powmill (Nr Kinross) – Whinsmuir Country Inn, Powmill, By Dollar, FK14 7NW. Tel: 01577 840595

IRELAND

Crawfordsburn Co Down Northern Ireland – The Old Inn, Crawfordsburn BT19 1JH. Tel: 01247 853255

CHANNEL ISLANDS

Jersey (Gorey) – The Moorings Hotel, Gorey Pier, Jersey, JE3 6EW. Tel: 01534 853633

Jersey (St Brelade) – Sea Crest Hotel and Restaurant, Petit Port, St Brelade, JE3 8HH. Tel: 01534 46353

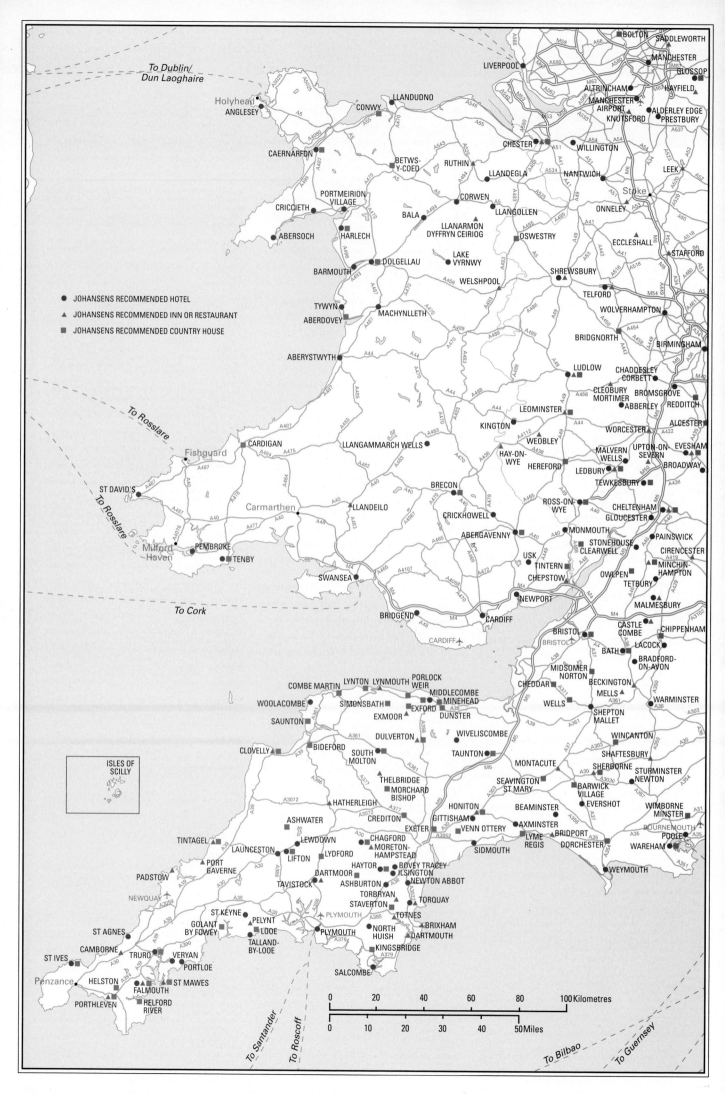

JOHANSENS RECOMMENDED HOTEL
JOHANSENS RECOMMENDED INN OR RESTAURANT
JOHANSENS RECOMMENDED COUNTRY HOUSE

To Dublin/
Dun Laoghaire

To Rosslare

To Rosslare

To Cork

To Santander

To Roscoff

To Bilbao

To Guernsey

ISLES OF
SCILLY

0   20   40   60   80   100 Kilometres
0   10   20   30   40   50 Miles

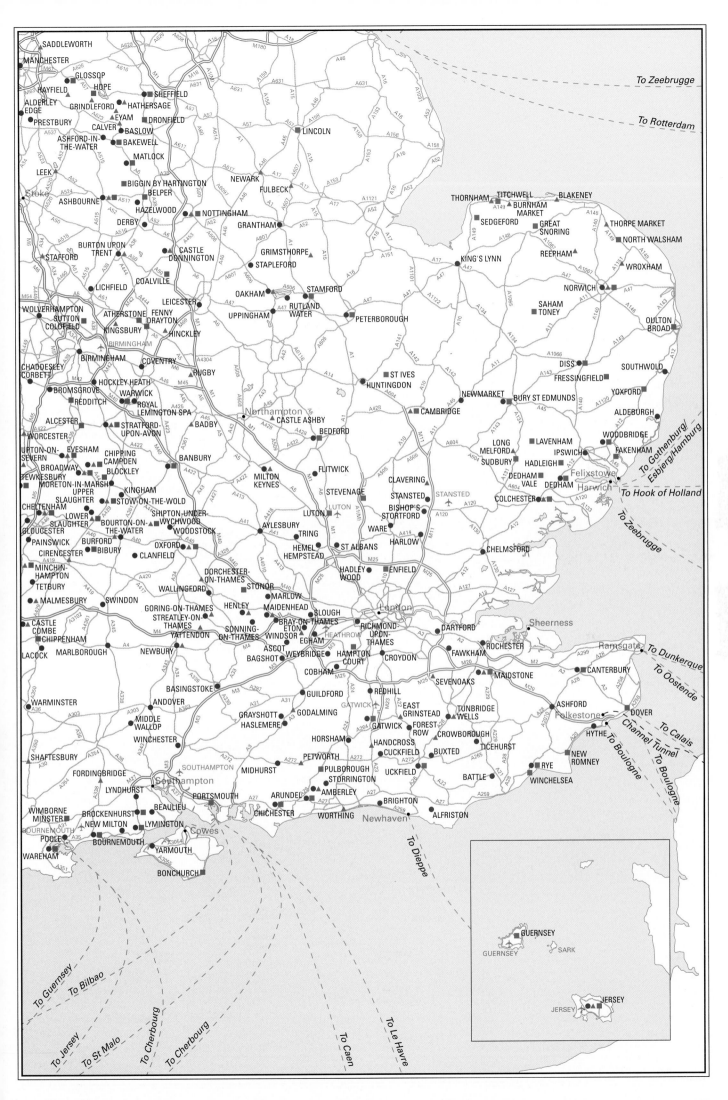

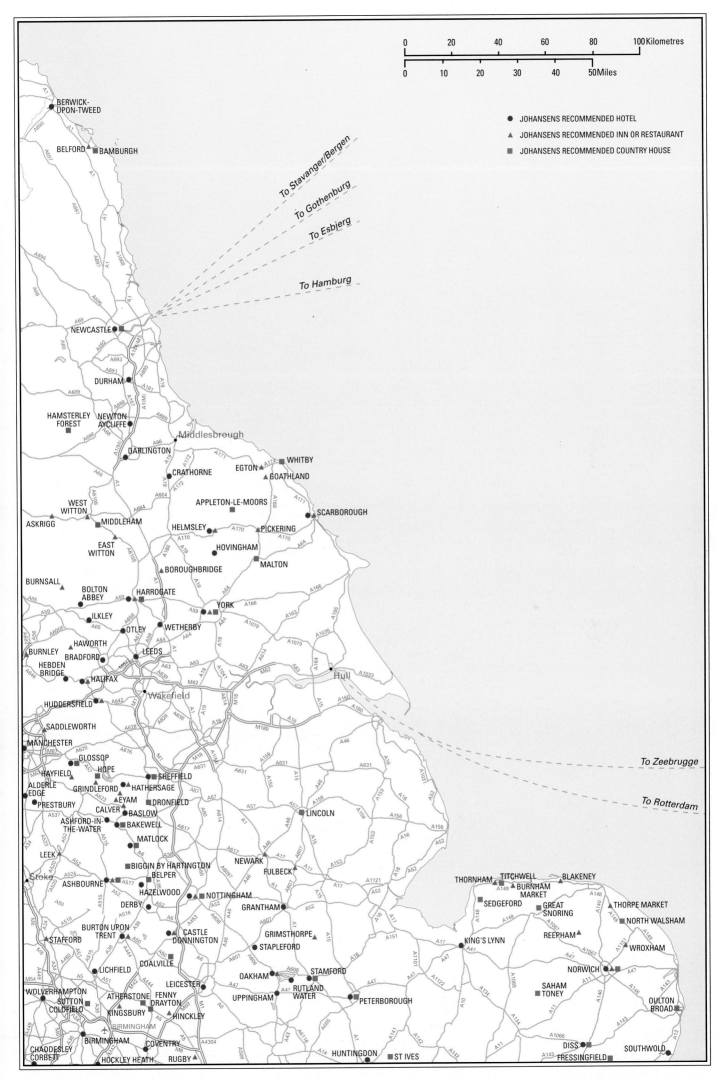

JOHANSENS RECOMMENDED HOTEL
JOHANSENS RECOMMENDED INN OR RESTAURANT
JOHANSENS RECOMMENDED COUNTRY HOUSE

0   20   40   60   80   100 Kilometres
0   10   20   30   40   50 Miles

To Stavanger/Bergen
To Gothenburg
To Esbjerg
To Hamburg
To Zeebrugge
To Rotterdam

BERWICK-UPON-TWEED
BELFORD   BAMBURGH
NEWCASTLE
DURHAM
HAMSTERLEY FOREST   NEWTON AYCLIFFE
Middlesbrough
DARLINGTON
CRATHORNE
EGTON   WHITBY
GOATHLAND
WEST WITTON
APPLETON-LE-MOORS
SCARBOROUGH
ASKRIGG   MIDDLEHAM
HELMSLEY   PICKERING
EAST WITTON
HOVINGHAM
BOROUGHBRIDGE   MALTON
BURNSALL
BOLTON ABBEY   HARROGATE
ILKLEY   YORK
OTLEY   WETHERBY
BURNLEY   HAWORTH
BRADFORD   LEEDS
HEBDEN BRIDGE   HALIFAX   Hull
HUDDERSFIELD   Wakefield
SADDLEWORTH
MANCHESTER
GLOSSOP
HAYFIELD   HOPE
ALDERLE EDGE   GRINDLEFORD   HATHERSAGE   SHEFFIELD
PRESTBURY   EYAM   DRONFIELD
CALVER   BASLOW
ASHFORD-IN-THE-WATER   BAKEWELL   LINCOLN
LEEK   MATLOCK
NEWARK
BIGGIN BY HARTINGTON   BELPER
Stoke   ASHBOURNE   HAZELWOOD   FULBECK
DERBY   NOTTINGHAM   GRANTHAM
BURTON UPON TRENT   GRIMSTHORPE
STAFFORD   CASTLE DONNINGTON   STAPLEFORD
COALVILLE
LICHFIELD   OAKHAM   STAMFORD
WOLVERHAMPTON   LEICESTER
SUTTON COLDFIELD   RUTLAND WATER
ATHERSTONE   FENNY DRAYTON   UPPINGHAM   PETERBOROUGH
KINGSBURY   HINCKLEY
BIRMINGHAM
CHADDESLEY CORBETT   COVENTRY
HOCKLEY HEATH   RUGBY   HUNTINGDON   ST IVES

THORNHAM   TITCHWELL   BLAKENEY
BURNHAM MARKET
SEDGEFORD   GREAT SNORING   THORPE MARKET
NORTH WALSHAM
REEPHAM   WROXHAM
KING'S LYNN   NORWICH
SAHAM TONEY   OULTON BROAD
DISS   SOUTHWOLD
FRESSINGFIELD

© Lovell Johns Ltd, Oxford

269

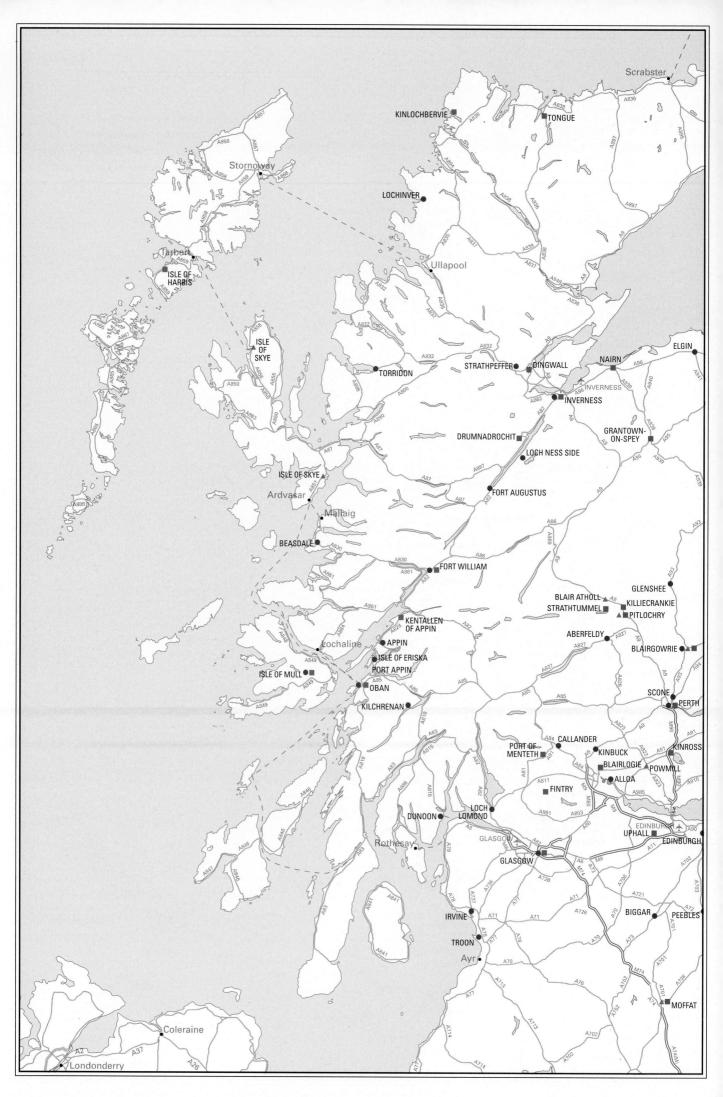

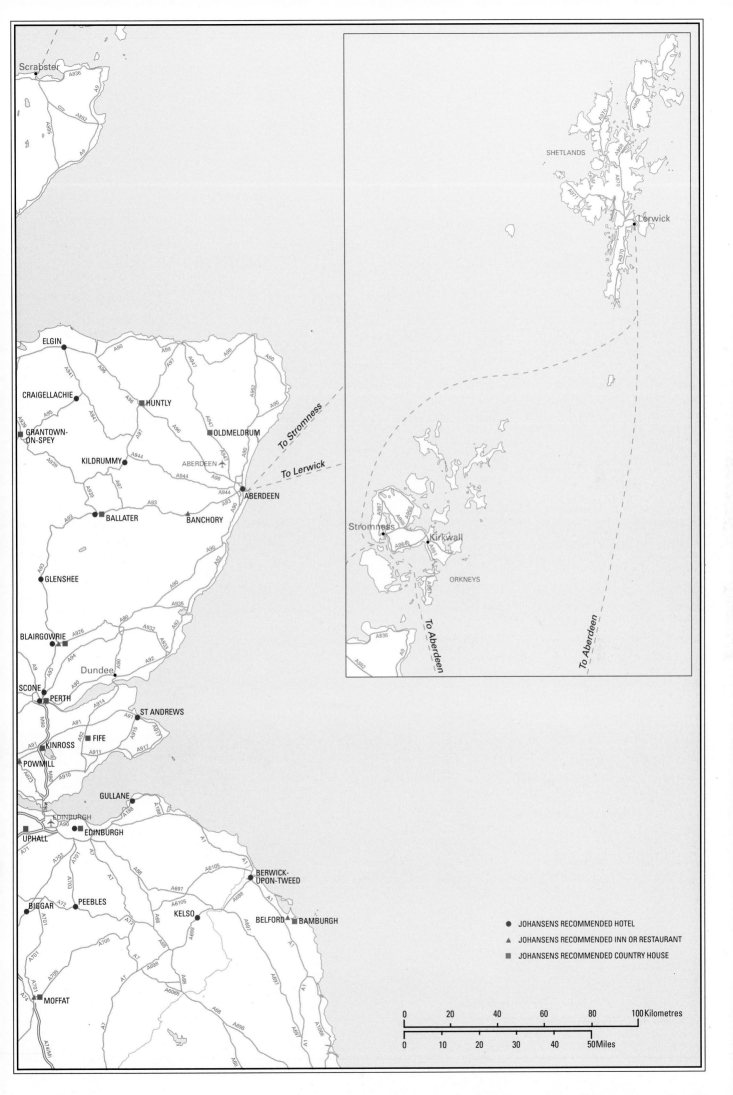

Scrabster

ELGIN

CRAIGELLACHIE

GRANTOWN-
ON-SPEY

HUNTLY

OLDMELDRUM

KILDRUMMY

ABERDEEN

To Stromness

To Lerwick

ABERDEEN

BALLATER

BANCHORY

GLENSHEE

BLAIRGOWRIE

Dundee

SCONE

PERTH

ST ANDREWS

FIFE

KINROSS

POWMILL

GULLANE

EDINBURGH

UPHALL

EDINBURGH

BERWICK-
UPON-TWEED

BIGGAR

PEEBLES

KELSO

BELFORD

BAMBURGH

MOFFAT

SHETLANDS

Lerwick

Stromness

Kirkwall

ORKNEYS

To Aberdeen

To Aberdeen

● JOHANSENS RECOMMENDED HOTEL

▲ JOHANSENS RECOMMENDED INN OR RESTAURANT

■ JOHANSENS RECOMMENDED COUNTRY HOUSE

0   20   40   60   80   100 Kilometres

0   10   20   30   40   50 Miles

JOHANSENS RECOMMENDED HOTEL

JOHANSENS RECOMMENDED INN OR RESTAURANT

JOHANSENS RECOMMENDED COUNTRY HOUSE

| 0 | 20 | 40 | 60 | 80 | 100 Kilometres |

| 0 | 10 | 20 | 30 | 40 | 50 Miles |

Exquisite Toiletries

for Hotels of Distinction

Luxury packaging for that special finishing touch.

Exclusive distributors for:-

Neutrogena

The Crown Perfumery

Customised Collections

Pacific Direct

Johansens Preferred Toiletry Partner

E.Mail Address ~ pacific-direct.demon.co.uk.

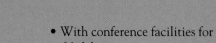

To enable you to use your 1998 Johansens Recommended Country Houses and Small Hotels Guide more effectively, the following four pages of indexes contain a wealth of useful information about the establishments featured in the Guide. As well as listing them alphabetically, by region and by county, the indexes also show which Country Houses and Small Hotels offer certain specialised facilities.

The indexes are listed as follows:

- Alphabetically by region
- By county
- With a swimming pool
- With tennis
- With fishing nearby
- With shooting facilities

- With conference facilities for 30 delegates or more
- Double rooms for £50 or less
- Johansens Preferred Partners
- Country Houses accepting Johansens Privilege Card

1998 Johansens Recommended Country Houses listed alphabetically by region

1998 Johansens Recommended Country Houses by county

Country Houses with shooting nearby

ENGLAND

Play the role of Hotel Inspector

At the back of this book you will see some Guest Survey forms. If you have had an enjoyable stay at one of our recommended country houses and small hotels, or have been in some way disappointed, please complete one of these forms and send it to us FREEPOST.

These reports essentially complement the assessments made by our team of professional inspectors, continually monitoring the standards of hospitality in every establishment in our guides. Guest Survey reports also have an important influence on the selection of nominations for our annual awards for excellence.

'Diversity and excellence for the independent traveller'.

PARTNERS IN INSURANCE

*Lakesure is the Exclusive Partner to
Johansens Recommended Country Houses and offers
SAVINGS ON YOUR PREMIUMS*

*We understand the market and have developed a
number of schemes giving extremely wide cover at a
competitive price and with first class security.*

*We also offer a special basis of quoting each risk using
'OUR UNIQUE NO CLAIMS
BONUS AT INCEPTION'.*

*Call 01702 471135 or 471185 (Phone and fax)
Talk to Bruce Thompson for further details*

WE KNOW OUR BUSINESS

PREFERRED PARTNERS

Preferred partners are those organisations specifically chosen and exclusively recommended by Johansens for the quality and excellence of their products and services for the mutal benefit of Johansens members, readers and independent travellers.

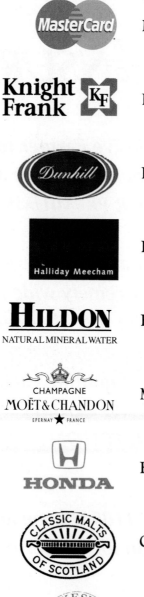

MasterCard International

Knight Frank International

Dunhill Tobacco of London Ltd

Halliday Meecham

Hildon Ltd

Moët & Chandon Champagne

Honda UK Ltd

Classic Malts of Scotland

Lakesure Ltd in association with
Charter Insurance Ltd

Pacific Direct

NPI

Guest Survey Report

Name/location of hotel: _____ Page No: _____

Date of visit: _____

Name & address of guest: _____

_____ Postcode: _____

Please tick one box in each category below:	Excellent	Good	Disappointing	Poor
Bedrooms				
Public Rooms				
Restaurant/Cuisine				
Service				
Welcome/Friendliness				
Value For Money				

PLEASE return your Guest Survey Report form!

Occasionally we may allow other reputable organisations to write with offers which may be of interest.
If you prefer not to here from them, tick this box ☐

To: Johansens, FREEPOST (CB264), 175-179 St John Street, London EC1B 1JQ

✂ ....

Guest Survey Report

Your own Johansens 'inspection' gives reliability to our guides and assists in the selection of Award Nominations

Name/location of hotel: _____ Page No: _____

Date of visit: _____

Name & address of guest: _____

_____ Postcode: _____

Please tick one box in each category below:	Excellent	Good	Disappointing	Poor
Bedrooms				
Public Rooms				
Restaurant/Cuisine				
Service				
Welcome/Friendliness				
Value For Money				

PLEASE return your Guest Survey Report form!

Occasionally we may allow other reputable organisations to write with offers which may be of interest.
If you prefer not to here from them, tick this box ☐

To: Johansens, FREEPOST (CB264), 175-179 St John Street, London EC1B 1JQ

Order Coupon

To order Johansens guides, simply indicate which publications you require by putting the quantity(ies) in the boxes provided. Choose you preferred method of payment and return this coupon (NO STAMP REQUIRED). You may also place your order using FREEPHONE 0800 269397 or by fax on 0171 251 6113.

❏ I enclose a cheque for £_____ payable to Johansens.

❏ I enclose my order on company letterheading, please invoice me. (UK companies only)

❏ Please debit my credit/charge card account (please tick)

❏ MASTERCARD   ❏ VISA   ❏ DINERS   ❏ AMEX   ❏ SWITCH

Switch Issue Number [   ]

Card No [   ][   ][   ][   ]

Signature _____ Expiry Date _____

Name (Mr/Mrs/Miss) _____

Address_____

_____ Postcode _____

(We aim to despatch your order within 10 days, but please allow 28 days for delivery)

Post free to: Johansens, FREEPOST (CB264), 43 Millharbour, London E14 9BR

Occasionally we may allow reputable organisations to write to you with offers which may interest you. If you prefer not to hear from them, tick this box ❏

save £10

	PRICE	QTY	TOTAL
The Collection of 4 Johansens Guides + *Recommended Hotels & Inns – North America FREE* £53.80	£43.80		
The Collection in a Presentation Boxed Set £58.80 + *Recommended Hotels & Inns – N. America FREE*	£48.80		
The 2 CD ROMS £49.90	£39.00		
Recommended Hotels – Great Britain & Ireland 1998	£18.95		
Recommended Country Houses and Small Hotels – GB & Ireland 1998	£10.95		
Recommended Inns with Restaurants – GB & Ireland 1998	£9.95		
Recommended Hotels – Europe 1998	£13.95		
Recommended Hotels – North America 1998	£9.95		
Historic Houses Castles & Gardens, Published and mailed to you in March 1998	£6.95		
CD ROM – Hotels, Country Houses & Inns Great Britain & Ireland 1998 with Historic Houses Castles & Gardens	£29.95		
CD ROM – Recommended Hotels & Inns N. America and Recommended Hotels Europe 1998	£19.95		
1998 Privilege Card – *10% discount, room upgrade when available. VIP Service at participating establishments*		FREE	
The Independent Traveller – *Johansens newsletter including many special offers*		FREE	
Postage & Packing *UK: £4 – or £2 for single orders and CD-Roms Outside UK: Add £5 – or £3 for single orders and CD-Roms*			
	TOTAL	**£**	

CALL THE JOHANSENS CREDIT CARD ORDER SERVICE FREE ☎ **0800 269397**

PRICES VALID UNTIL 31/08/98   2J4

✂ ···

Order Coupon

To order Johansens guides, simply indicate which publications you require by putting the quantity(ies) in the boxes provided. Choose you preferred method of payment and return this coupon (NO STAMP REQUIRED). You may also place your order using FREEPHONE 0800 269397 or by fax on 0171 251 6113.

❏ I enclose a cheque for £_____ payable to Johansens.

❏ I enclose my order on company letterheading, please invoice me. (UK companies only)

❏ Please debit my credit/charge card account (please tick)

❏ MASTERCARD   ❏ VISA   ❏ DINERS   ❏ AMEX   ❏ SWITCH

Switch Issue Number [   ]

Card No [   ][   ][   ][   ]

Signature _____ Expiry Date _____

Name (Mr/Mrs/Miss) _____

Address_____

_____ Postcode _____

(We aim to despatch your order within 10 days, but please allow 28 days for delivery)

Post free to: Johansens, FREEPOST (CB264), 43 Millharbour, London E14 9BR

Occasionally we may allow reputable organisations to write to you with offers which may interest you. If you prefer not to hear from them, tick this box ❏

save £10

	PRICE	QTY	TOTAL
The Collection of 4 Johansens Guides + *Recommended Hotels & Inns – North America FREE* £53.80	£43.80		
The Collection in a Presentation Boxed Set £58.80 + *Recommended Hotels & Inns – N. America FREE*	£48.80		
The 2 CD ROMS £49.90	£39.00		
Recommended Hotels – Great Britain & Ireland 1998	£18.95		
Recommended Country Houses and Small Hotels – GB & Ireland 1998	£10.95		
Recommended Inns with Restaurants – GB & Ireland 1998	£9.95		
Recommended Hotels – Europe 1998	£13.95		
Recommended Hotels – North America 1998	£9.95		
Historic Houses Castles & Gardens, Published and mailed to you in March 1998	£6.95		
CD ROM – Hotels, Country Houses & Inns Great Britain & Ireland 1998 with Historic Houses Castles & Gardens	£29.95		
CD ROM – Recommended Hotels & Inns N. America and Recommended Hotels Europe 1998	£19.95		
1998 Privilege Card – *10% discount, room upgrade when available. VIP Service at participating establishments*		FREE	
The Independent Traveller – *Johansens newsletter including many special offers*		FREE	
Postage & Packing *UK: £4 – or £2 for single orders and CD-Roms Outside UK: Add £5 – or £3 for single orders and CD-Roms*			
	TOTAL	**£**	

CALL THE JOHANSENS CREDIT CARD ORDER SERVICE FREE ☎ **0800 269397**

PRICES VALID UNTIL 31/08/98   2J4

Guest Survey Report

Your own Johansens 'inspection' gives reliability to our guides and assists in the selection of Award Nominations

Name/location of hotel: _____   Page No: _____

Date of visit: _____

Name & address of guest: _____

_____   Postcode: _____

Please tick one box in each category below:	Excellent	Good	Disappointing	Poor
Bedrooms				
Public Rooms				
Restaurant/Cuisine				
Service				
Welcome/Friendliness				
Value For Money				

**PLEASE
return your
Guest Survey
Report form!**

Occasionally we may allow other reputable organisations to write with offers which may be of interest.
If you prefer not to here from them, tick this box ☐

To: Johansens, FREEPOST (CB264), 175-179 St John Street, London EC1B 1JQ

✂ ··

Guest Survey Report

Your own Johansens 'inspection' gives reliability to our guides and assists in the selection of Award Nominations

Name/location of hotel: _____   Page No: _____

Date of visit: _____

Name & address of guest: _____

_____   Postcode: _____

Please tick one box in each category below:	Excellent	Good	Disappointing	Poor
Bedrooms				
Public Rooms				
Restaurant/Cuisine				
Service				
Welcome/Friendliness				
Value For Money				

**PLEASE
return your
Guest Survey
Report form!**

Occasionally we may allow other reputable organisations to write with offers which may be of interest.
If you prefer not to here from them, tick this box ☐

To: Johansens, FREEPOST (CB264), 175-179 St John Street, London EC1B 1JQ

Order Coupon

To order Johansens guides, simply indicate which publications you require by putting the quantity(ies) in the boxes provided. Choose you preferred method of payment and return this coupon (NO STAMP REQUIRED). You may also place your order using FREEPHONE 0800 269397 or by fax on 0171 251 6113.

save £10

❏ I enclose a cheque for £_____ payable to Johansens.

❏ I enclose my order on company letterheading, please invoice me. (UK companies only)

❏ Please debit my credit/charge card account (please tick)

❏ MASTERCARD   ❏ VISA   ❏ DINERS   ❏ AMEX   ❏ SWITCH

Switch Issue Number ☐

Card No ☐ ☐ ☐ ☐

Signature _____ Expiry Date _____

Name (Mr/Mrs/Miss) _____

Address_____

_____ Postcode _____

(We aim to despatch your order within 10 days, but please allow 28 days for delivery)

Post free to: Johansens, FREEPOST (CB264), 43 Millharbour, London E14 9BR

Occasionally we may allow reputable organisations to write to you with offers which may interest you. If you prefer not to hear from them, tick this box ❏

	PRICE	QTY	TOTAL
The Collection of 4 Johansens Guides + Recommended Hotels & Inns – North America FREE £53.80	£43.80		
The Collection in a Presentation Boxed Set £58.80 + Recommended Hotels & Inns – N. America FREE	£48.80		
The 2 CD ROMS £49.90	£39.00		
Recommended Hotels – Great Britain & Ireland 1998	£18.95		
Recommended Country Houses and Small Hotels – GB & Ireland 1998	£10.95		
Recommended Inns with Restaurants – GB & Ireland 1998	£9.95		
Recommended Hotels – Europe 1998	£13.95		
Recommended Hotels – North America 1998	£9.95		
Historic Houses Castles & Gardens, Published and mailed to you in March 1998	£6.95		
CD ROM – Hotels, Country Houses & Inns Great Britain & Ireland 1998 with Historic Houses Castles & Gardens	£29.95		
CD ROM – Recommended Hotels & Inns N. America and Recommended Hotels Europe 1998	£19.95		
1998 Privilege Card – 10% discount, room upgrade when available. VIP Service at participating establishments		FREE	
The Independent Traveller – Johansens newsletter including many special offers		FREE	
Postage & Packing UK: £4 – or £2 for single orders and CD-Roms Outside UK: Add £5 – or £3 for single orders and CD-Roms			
	TOTAL £		

CALL THE JOHANSENS CREDIT CARD ORDER SERVICE FREE ☎ 0800 269397

PRICES VALID UNTIL 31/08/98   2J4

Order Coupon

To order Johansens guides, simply indicate which publications you require by putting the quantity(ies) in the boxes provided. Choose you preferred method of payment and return this coupon (NO STAMP REQUIRED). You may also place your order using FREEPHONE 0800 269397 or by fax on 0171 251 6113.

save £10

❏ I enclose a cheque for £_____ payable to Johansens.

❏ I enclose my order on company letterheading, please invoice me. (UK companies only)

❏ Please debit my credit/charge card account (please tick)

❏ MASTERCARD   ❏ VISA   ❏ DINERS   ❏ AMEX   ❏ SWITCH

Switch Issue Number ☐

Card No ☐ ☐ ☐ ☐

Signature _____ Expiry Date _____

Name (Mr/Mrs/Miss) _____

Address_____

_____ Postcode _____

(We aim to despatch your order within 10 days, but please allow 28 days for delivery)

Post free to: Johansens, FREEPOST (CB264), 43 Millharbour, London E14 9BR

Occasionally we may allow reputable organisations to write to you with offers which may interest you. If you prefer not to hear from them, tick this box ❏

	PRICE	QTY	TOTAL
The Collection of 4 Johansens Guides + Recommended Hotels & Inns – North America FREE £53.80	£43.80		
The Collection in a Presentation Boxed Set £58.80 + Recommended Hotels & Inns – N. America FREE	£48.80		
The 2 CD ROMS £49.90	£39.00		
Recommended Hotels – Great Britain & Ireland 1998	£18.95		
Recommended Country Houses and Small Hotels – GB & Ireland 1998	£10.95		
Recommended Inns with Restaurants – GB & Ireland 1998	£9.95		
Recommended Hotels – Europe 1998	£13.95		
Recommended Hotels – North America 1998	£9.95		
Historic Houses Castles & Gardens, Published and mailed to you in March 1998	£6.95		
CD ROM – Hotels, Country Houses & Inns Great Britain & Ireland 1998 with Historic Houses Castles & Gardens	£29.95		
CD ROM – Recommended Hotels & Inns N. America and Recommended Hotels Europe 1998	£19.95		
1998 Privilege Card – 10% discount, room upgrade when available. VIP Service at participating establishments		FREE	
The Independent Traveller – Johansens newsletter including many special offers		FREE	
Postage & Packing UK: £4 – or £2 for single orders and CD-Roms Outside UK: Add £5 – or £3 for single orders and CD-Roms			
	TOTAL £		

CALL THE JOHANSENS CREDIT CARD ORDER SERVICE FREE ☎ 0800 269397

PRICES VALID UNTIL 31/08/98   2J4

Guest Survey Report

Your own Johansens 'inspection' gives reliability to our guides and assists in the selection of Award Nominations

Name/location of hotel: _____ Page No: _____

Date of visit: _____

Name & address of guest: _____

_____ Postcode: _____

Please tick one box in each category below:	Excellent	Good	Disappointing	Poor
Bedrooms				
Public Rooms				
Restaurant/Cuisine				
Service				
Welcome/Friendliness				
Value For Money				

PLEASE return your Guest Survey Report form!

Occasionally we may allow other reputable organisations to write with offers which may be of interest.
If you prefer not to here from them, tick this box ☐

To: Johansens, FREEPOST (CB264), 175-179 St John Street, London EC1B 1JQ

- -

Guest Survey Report

Your own Johansens 'inspection' gives reliability to our guides and assists in the selection of Award Nominations

Name/location of hotel: _____ Page No: _____

Date of visit: _____

Name & address of guest: _____

_____ Postcode: _____

Please tick one box in each category below:	Excellent	Good	Disappointing	Poor
Bedrooms				
Public Rooms				
Restaurant/Cuisine				
Service				
Welcome/Friendliness				
Value For Money				

PLEASE return your Guest Survey Report form!

Occasionally we may allow other reputable organisations to write with offers which may be of interest.
If you prefer not to here from them, tick this box ☐

To: Johansens, FREEPOST (CB264), 175-179 St John Street, London EC1B 1JQ

Order Coupon

To order Johansens guides, simply indicate which publications you require by putting the quantity(ies) in the boxes provided. Choose you preferred method of payment and return this coupon (NO STAMP REQUIRED). You may also place your order using **FREEPHONE 0800 269397** or by fax on **0171 251 6113**.

❏ I enclose a cheque for £_____ payable to Johansens.

❏ I enclose my order on company letterheading, please invoice me. (UK companies only)

❏ Please debit my credit/charge card account (please tick)

❏ MASTERCARD ❏ VISA ❏ DINERS ❏ AMEX ❏ SWITCH

Switch Issue Number ☐

Card No ☐☐☐☐

Signature _____ Expiry Date _____

Name (Mr/Mrs/Miss) _____

Address _____

_____ Postcode _____

(We aim to despatch your order within 10 days, but please allow 28 days for delivery)

Post free to: Johansens, FREEPOST (CB264), 43Millharbour, London E14 9BR

Occasionally we may allow reputable organisations to write to you with offers which may interest you. If you prefer not to hear from them, tick this box ❏

save £10

	PRICE	QTY	TOTAL
The Collection of 4 Johansens Guides + *Recommended Hotels & Inns – North America FREE* £53.80	£43.80		
The Collection in a Presentation Boxed Set £58.80 + *Recommended Hotels & Inns – N. America FREE*	£48.80		
The 2 CD ROMS £49.90	£39.00		
Recommended Hotels – Great Britain & Ireland 1998	£18.95		
Recommended Country Houses and Small Hotels – GB & Ireland 1998	£10.95		
Recommended Inns with Restaurants – GB & Ireland 1998	£9.95		
Recommended Hotels – Europe 1998	£13.95		
Recommended Hotels – North America 1998	£9.95		
Historic Houses Castles & Gardens, Published and mailed to you in March 1998	£6.95		
CD ROM – Hotels, Country Houses & Inns Great Britain & Ireland 1998 with Historic Houses Castles & Gardens	£29.95		
CD ROM – Recommended Hotels & Inns N. America and Recommended Hotels Europe 1998	£19.95		
1998 Privilege Card – *10% discount, room upgrade when available. VIP Service at participating establishments*		FREE	
The Independent Traveller – *Johansens newsletter including many special offers*		FREE	
Postage & Packing *UK: £4 – or £2 for single orders and CD-Roms Outside UK: Add £5 – or £3 for single orders and CD-Roms*			
	TOTAL £		

CALL THE JOHANSENS CREDIT CARD ORDER SERVICE FREE ☎ **0800 269397**

PRICES VALID UNTIL 31/08/98 2J4

✂ ··

Order Coupon

To order Johansens guides, simply indicate which publications you require by putting the quantity(ies) in the boxes provided. Choose you preferred method of payment and return this coupon (NO STAMP REQUIRED). You may also place your order using **FREEPHONE 0800 269397** or by fax on **0171 251 6113**.

❏ I enclose a cheque for £_____ payable to Johansens.

❏ I enclose my order on company letterheading, please invoice me. (UK companies only)

❏ Please debit my credit/charge card account (please tick)

❏ MASTERCARD ❏ VISA ❏ DINERS ❏ AMEX ❏ SWITCH

Switch Issue Number ☐

Card No ☐☐☐☐

Signature _____ Expiry Date _____

Name (Mr/Mrs/Miss) _____

Address _____

_____ Postcode _____

(We aim to despatch your order within 10 days, but please allow 28 days for delivery)

Post free to: Johansens, FREEPOST (CB264), 43Millharbour, London E14 9BR

Occasionally we may allow reputable organisations to write to you with offers which may interest you. If you prefer not to hear from them, tick this box ❏

save £10

	PRICE	QTY	TOTAL
The Collection of 4 Johansens Guides + *Recommended Hotels & Inns – North America FREE* £53.80	£43.80		
The Collection in a Presentation Boxed Set £58.80 + *Recommended Hotels & Inns – N. America FREE*	£48.80		
The 2 CD ROMS £49.90	£39.00		
Recommended Hotels – Great Britain & Ireland 1998	£18.95		
Recommended Country Houses and Small Hotels – GB & Ireland 1998	£10.95		
Recommended Inns with Restaurants – GB & Ireland 1998	£9.95		
Recommended Hotels – Europe 1998	£13.95		
Recommended Hotels – North America 1998	£9.95		
Historic Houses Castles & Gardens, Published and mailed to you in March 1998	£6.95		
CD ROM – Hotels, Country Houses & Inns Great Britain & Ireland 1998 with Historic Houses Castles & Gardens	£29.95		
CD ROM – Recommended Hotels & Inns N. America and Recommended Hotels Europe 1998	£19.95		
1998 Privilege Card – *10% discount, room upgrade when available. VIP Service at participating establishments*		FREE	
The Independent Traveller – *Johansens newsletter including many special offers*		FREE	
Postage & Packing *UK: £4 – or £2 for single orders and CD-Roms Outside UK: Add £5 – or £3 for single orders and CD-Roms*			
	TOTAL £		

CALL THE JOHANSENS CREDIT CARD ORDER SERVICE FREE ☎ **0800 269397**

PRICES VALID UNTIL 31/08/98 2J4

Guest Survey Report

Your own Johansens 'inspection' gives reliability to our guides and assists in the selection of Award Nominations

Name/location of hotel: _____   Page No: _____

Date of visit: _____

Name & address of guest: _____

_____   Postcode: _____

Please tick one box in each category below:	Excellent	Good	Disappointing	Poor
Bedrooms				
Public Rooms				
Restaurant/Cuisine				
Service				
Welcome/Friendliness				
Value For Money				

PLEASE return your Guest Survey Report form!

Occasionally we may allow other reputable organisations to write with offers which may be of interest.
If you prefer not to here from them, tick this box ☐

To: Johansens, FREEPOST (CB264), 175-179 St John Street, London EC1B 1JQ

Guest Survey Report

Your own Johansens 'inspection' gives reliability to our guides and assists in the selection of Award Nominations

Name/location of hotel: _____   Page No: _____

Date of visit: _____

Name & address of guest: _____

_____   Postcode: _____

Please tick one box in each category below:	Excellent	Good	Disappointing	Poor
Bedrooms				
Public Rooms				
Restaurant/Cuisine				
Service				
Welcome/Friendliness				
Value For Money				

PLEASE return your Guest Survey Report form!

Occasionally we may allow other reputable organisations to write with offers which may be of interest.
If you prefer not to here from them, tick this box ☐

To: Johansens, FREEPOST (CB264), 175-179 St John Street, London EC1B 1JQ

Order Coupon

To order Johansens guides, simply indicate which publications you require by putting the quantity(ies) in the boxes provided. Choose you preferred method of payment and return this coupon (NO STAMP REQUIRED). You may also place your order using FREEPHONE 0800 269397 or by fax on 0171 251 6113.

❏ I enclose a cheque for £_____ payable to Johansens.

❏ I enclose my order on company letterheading, please invoice me. (UK companies only)

❏ Please debit my credit/charge card account (please tick)

❏ MASTERCARD ❏ VISA ❏ DINERS ❏ AMEX ❏ SWITCH

Switch Issue Number ☐

Card No ☐☐☐☐

Signature _____ Expiry Date _____

Name (Mr/Mrs/Miss) _____

Address _____

_____ Postcode _____

(We aim to despatch your order within 10 days, but please allow 28 days for delivery)

Post free to: Johansens, FREEPOST (CB264), 43Millharbour, London E14 9BR

Occasionally we may allow reputable organisations to write to you with offers which may interest you. If you prefer not to hear from them, tick this box ❏

save £10

	PRICE	QTY	TOTAL
The Collection of 4 Johansens Guides + *Recommended Hotels & Inns – North America FREE* £53.80	£43.80		
The Collection in a Presentation Boxed Set £58.80 + *Recommended Hotels & Inns – N. America FREE*	£48.80		
The 2 CD ROMS £49.90	£39.00		
Recommended Hotels – Great Britain & Ireland 1998	£18.95		
Recommended Country Houses and Small Hotels – GB & Ireland 1998	£10.95		
Recommended Inns with Restaurants – GB & Ireland 1998	£9.95		
Recommended Hotels – Europe 1998	£13.95		
Recommended Hotels – North America 1998	£9.95		
Historic Houses Castles & Gardens, Published and mailed to you in March 1998	£6.95		
CD ROM – Hotels, Country Houses & Inns Great Britain & Ireland 1998 with Historic Houses Castles & Gardens	£29.95		
CD ROM – Recommended Hotels & Inns N. America and Recommended Hotels Europe 1998	£19.95		
1998 Privilege Card – *10% discount, room upgrade when available. VIP Service at participating establishments*	FREE		
The Independent Traveller – *Johansens newsletter including many special offers*	FREE		
Postage & Packing *UK: £4 – or £2 for single orders and CD-Roms Outside UK: Add £5 – or £3 for single orders and CD-Roms*			
	TOTAL	£	

CALL THE JOHANSENS CREDIT CARD ORDER SERVICE FREE ☎ 0800 269397

PRICES VALID UNTIL 31/08/98 2J4

✂ ···

Order Coupon

To order Johansens guides, simply indicate which publications you require by putting the quantity(ies) in the boxes provided. Choose you preferred method of payment and return this coupon (NO STAMP REQUIRED). You may also place your order using FREEPHONE 0800 269397 or by fax on 0171 251 6113.

❏ I enclose a cheque for £_____ payable to Johansens.

❏ I enclose my order on company letterheading, please invoice me. (UK companies only)

❏ Please debit my credit/charge card account (please tick)

❏ MASTERCARD ❏ VISA ❏ DINERS ❏ AMEX ❏ SWITCH

Switch Issue Number ☐

Card No ☐☐☐☐

Signature _____ Expiry Date _____

Name (Mr/Mrs/Miss) _____

Address _____

_____ Postcode _____

(We aim to despatch your order within 10 days, but please allow 28 days for delivery)

Post free to: Johansens, FREEPOST (CB264), 43Millharbour, London E14 9BR

Occasionally we may allow reputable organisations to write to you with offers which may interest you. If you prefer not to hear from them, tick this box ❏

save £10

	PRICE	QTY	TOTAL
The Collection of 4 Johansens Guides + *Recommended Hotels & Inns – North America FREE* £53.80	£43.80		
The Collection in a Presentation Boxed Set £58.80 + *Recommended Hotels & Inns – N. America FREE*	£48.80		
The 2 CD ROMS £49.90	£39.00		
Recommended Hotels – Great Britain & Ireland 1998	£18.95		
Recommended Country Houses and Small Hotels – GB & Ireland 1998	£10.95		
Recommended Inns with Restaurants – GB & Ireland 1998	£9.95		
Recommended Hotels – Europe 1998	£13.95		
Recommended Hotels – North America 1998	£9.95		
Historic Houses Castles & Gardens, Published and mailed to you in March 1998	£6.95		
CD ROM – Hotels, Country Houses & Inns Great Britain & Ireland 1998 with Historic Houses Castles & Gardens	£29.95		
CD ROM – Recommended Hotels & Inns N. America and Recommended Hotels Europe 1998	£19.95		
1998 Privilege Card – *10% discount, room upgrade when available. VIP Service at participating establishments*	FREE		
The Independent Traveller – *Johansens newsletter including many special offers*	FREE		
Postage & Packing *UK: £4 – or £2 for single orders and CD-Roms Outside UK: Add £5 – or £3 for single orders and CD-Roms*			
	TOTAL	£	

CALL THE JOHANSENS CREDIT CARD ORDER SERVICE FREE ☎ 0800 269397

PRICES VALID UNTIL 31/08/98 2J4